Andrew James Symington, Olafur Pálsson

Pen and Pencil Sketches of Faröe and Iceland

With an appendix containing translations from the Icelandic and 51 illustrations

engraved on wood by W. J. Linton

Andrew James Symington, Olafur Pálsson

Pen and Pencil Sketches of Faröe and Iceland
With an appendix containing translations from the Icelandic and 51 illustrations engraved on wood by W. J. Linton

ISBN/EAN: 9783337316310

Printed in Europe, USA, Canada, Australia, Japan

Cover: Foto ©Thomas Meinert / pixelio.de

More available books at **www.hansebooks.com**

PEN AND PENCIL SKETCHES

OF

FARÖE AND ICELAND

WITH AN APPENDIX
CONTAINING TRANSLATIONS FROM THE ICELANDIC

AND 51 ILLUSTRATIONS ENGRAVED ON WOOD BY W. J. LINTON

BY

ANDREW JAMES SYMINGTON
Author of "Harebell Chimes," "The Beautiful in Nature, Art, and Life," &c.

LONDON
LONGMAN, GREEN, LONGMAN, AND ROBERTS
1862

PREFACE.

The greater part of this volume consists of a diary jotted down in presence of the scenes described, so as to preserve for the reader, as far as possible, the freshness of first impressions, and invest the whole with an atmosphere of human interest.

The route taken may be thus shortly indicated: Thorshavn; Portland Huk; the Westmanna Islands; Reykjavik; the Geysers; then, by sea, round the south coast of the island, with its magnificent Jökul-range of volcanoes; along the east coast, with its picturesque Fiords, as far north as Seydisfiord; and thence home again, by the Faröe Isles.

The aim, throughout, has been both to present pictures and condense information on matters relating to Faröe and Iceland. In obtaining the latter I have had the advantages of frequent intercourse with Icelanders, both personal and by letter, since my visit to the North in the summer of 1859, and would here mention, in particular, the Rev. Olaf Pálsson, Dean and Rector of Reykjavik Cathedral; Mr. Jón Arnason, Secretary to the Bishop, and Librarian; Mr. Gísli Brynjúlfsson, the Icelandic poet and M.P.; Mr. Sigurdur Sivertsen, a retired merchant, and Mr. Jacobson.

And so too with the Faröese.

I acknowledge obligations to Dr. David Mackinlay of Glasgow, Dr. Lauder Lindsay of Perth, and several other friends who have visited Iceland and rendered me assistance of various kinds. Thanks are also due to Mr. P. L. Henderson, for transmitting, by the *Arcturus*, letters, books and newspapers to and from the north.

The APPENDIX comprises thirteen Icelandic stories and fairy tales translated by the Rev. Olaf Pálsson; specimens of old Icelandic poetry; poems on northern subjects in English and Icelandic; information for intending tourists; a glossary; and lastly, a chapter on our Scandinavian ancestors—treating of race, history, characteristics, language and tendencies. This paper, originally intended for an introduction, may be perused either first or last, at the option of the reader. There is also a copious INDEX to the volume.

The illustrations, engraved by Mr. W. J. Linton, are all from original drawings by the writer, with the exception of half a dozen,[1] taken from plates in the large French folio which contains the account of Gaimard's Expedition.

Should these pages induce photographers and other artists to visit this strange trahytic island resting on an ocean of fire in the lone North Sea, or students to become familiar with its stirring history and grand old literature, I shall feel solaced, under a feeling almost akin to regret, that this self-imposed task—which, in spite of sundry vexatious delays and interruptions, has afforded me much true enjoyment—should at length have come to an end.

A. J. S.

MAY 1862.

---

[1] Nos. 19, 20, 21, 23, 24, and 31.

CONTENTS.

LIST OF ILLUSTRATIONS.

LITTLE DIMON—FARÖE.

PEN AND PENCIL SKETCHES

OF

FARÖE AND ICELAND.

LEITH TO THORSHAVN.

Can Iceland—that distant island of the North Sea, that land of Eddas and Sagas, of lava-wastes, snow-jökuls, volcanoes, and boiling geysers—be visited during a summer's holiday? This was the question which for years I had vaguely proposed to myself. Now I wished definitely to ascertain particulars, and, if at all practicable, to accomplish such a journey during the present season.

Three ways presented themselves—the chance of getting north in a private yacht—to charter a sloop from Lerwick—or to take the mail-steamer from Copenhagen. The first way seemed very doubtful; I was dissuaded from the second by the great uncertainty as to when one might get back, and the earnest entreaties of friends, who, with long faces, insinuated that these wild northern seas were not to be trifled with. However, the uncertainty as to time, and the expense, which for one person would have been considerable, weighed more with me than any idea of danger. Of the mail-steamer it was difficult to obtain any information.

One morning, when in this dilemma, my eye fell on an advertisement in the *Times*, headed "Steam to Iceland," informing all whom it might concern that the Danish mail-steamer "Arcturus," would, about the 20th of July, touch at Leith on its way north, affording passengers a week to visit the interior of the island, and would return to Leith within a month. I subsequently ascertained that it was to call at the Farӧe and Westmanna Isles, and that it would also sail from Reykjavik round to Seydisfiord, on the east of Iceland, so that one might obtain a view of the magnificent range of jökuls and numerous glaciers along the south coast.

The day of sailing was a fortnight earlier than I could have desired, but such an opportunity was not to be missed. Providing myself with a long waterproof overcoat, overboots of the same material—both absolutely essential for riding with any degree of comfort in Iceland, to protect from lashing rains, and when splashing through mud-puddles or deep river fordings—getting together a supply of preserved meats, soups, &c. in tin

caus, a mariner's compass, thermometer, one of De La
Rue's solid sketch-books, files of newspapers, a few
articles for presents, and other needful things, my traps
were speedily put up; and, on Wednesday the 20th of
July, I found myself on board the "Arcturus" in Leith
dock.

It was a Clyde-built screw-steamer, of 400 tons burden.
Captain Andriessen, a Dane, received me kindly; the
crew, with the exception of the engineer, a Scotchman,
were all foreigners. In the first cabin were eight fellow-
passengers, strangers to each other; but, as is usual at
sea, acquaintanceships were soon formed; by degrees we
came to know each other, and all got along very
pleasantly together.

There was only one lady passenger, to whom I was
introduced, Miss Löbner, daughter of the late governor
of Faröe, who had been south, visiting friends in
Edinburgh. Afraid of being ill, she speedily disappeared,
and did not leave her cabin till we reached Thorshavn.
Of our number were Professor Chadbourne, of William's
College, Massachusetts, and Bowdoin College, Maine,
U.S.; Capt. Forbes, R.N.; Mr. Haycock, a gentleman
from Norfolk, who had recently visited Norway in his
yacht; Mr. Cleghorn, lately an officer in the Indian
army; Mr. Douglas Murray, an intelligent Scottish
farmer, from the neighbourhood of Haddington, taking
his annual holiday; Dr. Livingston, an American M.D.;
and Capt. B——, a Danish artillery officer, *en route*
from Copenhagen to Reykjavik.

There were also several passengers in the second cabin,
some of whom were students returning home from their
studies in the Danish universities.

There was a large boat to be got on board, for discharging the steamer's cargo at Iceland, which took several hours to get fastened aloft on the right side of the hurricane deck—with the comfortable prospect of its top-heaviness acting like a pendulum, and adding considerably to the roll of the ship, should the weather prove rough.

Shortly after seven P.M. we got fairly clear of the dock. Strange to think, as the last hawser was being cast off, that, till our return, we should hear no postman's ring, receive no letters with either good tidings or annoyances—for we carry the mail,—and see no later newspapers than those we take with us! Friends may be well or ill. The stirring events of the Continent, too, leave us to speculate on changes that may suddenly occur in the aspect of European affairs, with the chances of peace, or declarations of war.

However, allowing such thoughts to disturb me as little as possible, and trusting that, under a kind Providence, all would be well with those dear to me, hopefully, and not without a deep feeling of inward satisfaction that a long cherished dream of boyhood was now about to be realised, I turned my face to the North.

A dense mist having settled on the Frith of Forth, the captain deemed it prudent to anchor in the roads. During the night it cleared off, and at five o'clock on Thursday morning, 21st July, our star was in the ascendant, and the "Arcturus" got fairly under way.

The morning, bright and clear, was truly splendid; the day sunny and warm; many sails in sight, and numerous sea-birds kept following the ship.

Breakfast, dinner, and tea follow each other in regular

succession, making, with their pleasant reunions and friendly intercourse, a threefold division of the day. On shipboard the steward's bell becomes an important institution, a sort of repeating gastronomical chronometer, and is not an unpleasant sound when the fresh sea-air has sharpened one's appetite into expectancy.

The commissariat supplies were liberal, and the department well attended to by a worthy Dane, who spoke no English, and who was only observed to smile once during the voyage. Captain Andriessen's fluent English, and the obliging Danish stewardess' German, enabled us all to get along in a sort of way; although the conversation at times assumed a polyglot aspect, the ludicrous *olla-podrida* nature of which afforded us many a good hearty laugh.

The chief peculiarities in our bill of fare were *lax* or red-smoked salmon; the sweet soups of Denmark, with raisins floating in them; black stale rye-bread; and a substantial dish, generally produced thrice a day, which, in forgetfulness of the technical nomenclature, we shall venture to call beef-steak fried with onions or garlic— that bulb which Don Quixote denounced as pertaining to scullions and low fellows, entreating Sancho to eschew it above all things when he came to his Island. At sea, however, we found it not unpalatable. There must ever be some drawbacks on shipboard. One of these was the water produced at table, of which Captain Forbes funnily remarked, that it "tasted badly of bung cloth—and dirty cloth, too!" But, such as it was, the Professor and I preferred it to wine.

Thus much of culinary matters, for, with the exception of a few surprises, which, according to all our previous ideas, confused the chronology of the dishes—making a literal mess of it—and sundry minor variations in the cycle of desserts proper, the service of one day resembled that of another.

There was only wind enough to fill the mainsail, and in it, on the lea side of the boom, as if in a hammock, sheltered from the broiling sun, I lay resting for hours. Off Peterhead, we saw innumerable fishing boats—counted 205 in one fleet. Off Inverness, far out at sea, we counted as many, ere we gave in and stopped. Their sails were mostly down, and we, passing quite near, could observe the process of the fishermen shooting their nets; the sea to the north-east all thickly dotted with boats, which appeared like black specks. A steamer was sailing among them, probably to receive and convey the fish ashore.

·Perilous is the calling of the fisherman! Calm to-day, squalls may overtake him on the morrow—

"But men must work, and women must weep,
Though storms be sudden, and waters deep,
And the harbour bar be moaning."

As the sun went down, from the forecastle we watched a dense bank of cloud resting on the sea; its dark purple ranges here and there shewing openings, with hopeful silver linings intensely bright—glimpses, as it were, into the land of Beulah. Then the lights and shadows grandly massed themselves, gradually assuming a sombre hue; while starry thoughts of dear ones at home rose, welling up within us, as the daylight ebbed slowly away over the horizon's rim.

Friday morning, July 22.—Rose at seven; weather dull; neither land, sky, nor sail, visible; our position not very accurately known. At four in the morning the engine had been stopped, the look-out having seen breakers a-head—no observation to be had. Our course to the North Sea lay between the Orkney and Shetland Islands. After breakfast it cleared, and on the starboard bow, we saw Fair Isle, so that our course was right, although we had not known in what part of it we were.

There was cause for thankfulness that the Orkneys had been passed in safety. Where the navigation is intricate and requires care at best, our chances of danger during the uncertainty of the night had doubtless been great. The south of the Shetland Isles also appeared to rise from the sea, dim and blue, resting on the horizon, like clouds ethereal and dreamlike.

At 11 o'clock A.M., sailing past Fair Isle, made several sketches of its varied aspects, as seen from different points. Green and fair, this lonely island lies about thirty miles south-west of the Shetland group, and in the very track of vessels going north.

It has no light-house, and is dreaded by sailors; for many are the shipwrecks which it occasions. Before now, we had heard captains, in their anxiety, wish it were at the bottom of the sea. Could not a light be placed upon it by the Admiralty, and a fearful loss of life thus be averted?

The island contains about a hundred inhabitants, who live chiefly by fishing and knitting. They are both skilful and industrious. During the winter months, the men, as well as the women, knit caps, gloves, and waistcoats;

and for dyeing the wool, procure a variety of colours from native herbs and lichens.

True happiness, springing as it ever does from above and from within, may have its peaceful abode here among those lonely islanders quite apart from the noise and bustle of what is called the great world, although the stranger sailing past is apt to think such places "remote, unfriended, melancholy, slow." [1]

Ere long we could distinguish the bold headland of Sumburgh, which is the southern extremity of Shetland; and a little to the north-west of it, by the aid of an opera-glass, Fitful Head,[2] rendered famous by Sir Walter Scott as the dwelling place of Norna, in "The Pirate."

Last summer I visited this the most northern group of British islands, famed alike for skilful seamen, fearless fishermen, and fairy-fingered knitters; for its hardy ponies, and for that soft, warm, fleecy wool which is peculiar to its sheep.

Gazing on the blue outline of the islands, I now involuntarily recalled their many voes, wild caves, and splintered skerries, alive with sea gulls and kittiwakes. The magnificent land-locked sound of Bressay too, where her Majesty's fleet might ride in safety, and where Lerwick—the capital of the islands, and the most northerly town in the British dominions—with its quaint, foreign, gabled aspect, rises, crowning the heights, from the very water's edge, so that sillacks might be fished

---

[1] Reduced to extreme destitution, by the failure of crops, subscriptions are at present (1862) being collected to enable the inhabitants of Fair Isle to emigrate.

[2] The original name is Fitfiel—probably the white mountain—*fit* signifying white, and *fiel*, fell or mountain. In the same way England was called *Albion*, from its white cliffs.

from the windows of those houses next the sea. Boating
excursions and pony scamperings are also recalled; the
Noss Head, with its mural precipice rising sheer from
the sea to a height of 700 feet, vividly reminding one of
Edgar's description of Dover Cliff, in "Lear," or of that
which Horatio pictured to Hamlet—

> "The dreadful summit of the cliff,
> That beetles o'er his base into the sea .   .   .
> The very place puts toys of desperation,
> Without more motive, into every brain
> That looks so many fathoms to the sea,
> And hears it roar beneath."

Nor is the much talked of *cradle* forgotten, slung on
ropes, for crossing the chasm between a lower cliff and
the Holm of Noss;—a detached rocky islet, the top of
which only affords pasture, during the summer months,
for some half dozen sheep.

The curious and singularly-perfect ancient Pictish
or Scandinavian Burgh, in the Island of Moosa, rises
again before me; Scalloway Bay, with its old Castle in
ruins, its fishermen's cots, and fish-drying sheds. A
high, long, out-jutting rocky promontory too, on which
I had stood watching the "yeasty waves" far below, as
they rolled thundering into an irregular cave, which, in
the course of ages, they had scooped out among the
basaltic crags, and, leaping up, scattered drenching
showers of diamond spray. Every succeeding dash of
the billows produced a loud report like the discharge
of artillery, the reverberations echoing along the shore.
In the black creek below, the brine seething like a
caldron was literally churned into white foam-flakes,
which, rising into the air on sudden gusts of wind,

sailed away inland, high overhead, like a flock of sea-birds. These flakes were of all sizes, large masses of froth at times floating down, and alighting at our very feet, from so great a height that they had merely shewed as black specks against the bright sunlight. In lulls one could actually lift them bodily from the ground, upwards of two cubic feet in size; but when the wind rose, such masses of whipped sea-cream were again seized upon, swept aloft, divided into smaller portions, and carried away across the island. These and other pleasing memories presented themselves as we now gazed on the distant, dim-blue Shetland Isles.

Saw a large vessel disabled and being towed south-wards from Shetland, where she appears to have come to grief. Topmasts gone, sides battered and patched with boards. She is high out of the water, so that the cargo must have been discharged. All our opera-glasses and telescopes are in requisition.

FOOLA.

Sat on the boom for hours, the vessel rolling heavily over the great smooth Atlantic billows. In the afternoon passed the island of Foola, which has been called the St.

Kilda of Shetland. It lies about sixteen miles west of Mainland, and is high and precipitous. The cliffs are tenanted by innumerable sea-fowls, which are caught in thousands by the cragsmen, and afford a considerable source of revenue to the inhabitants.

Blue and cloudlike the detached and isolated heights of Mainland, Yell, and Unst—the promontory of Hermanness, on the latter, being the most northerly point of the British islands—are fast sinking beneath the horizon. Ere long Foola, left astern, follows the others. No land in sight, not a sail on the horizon; all round is now one smooth heaving circular plain of blue water—the ever changing level producing a most singular optical effect.

In the evening walked the deck with Mr. Haycock, discoursing of Norwegian scenery, and of yacht excursions thither. The evening clear and pleasant, although the ground-swell continued to increase. Turned in, at half-past ten o'clock. The vessel rolled much during the night. Professor Chadbourne, Mr. Murray, and Mr. Cleghorn's berths were in the same state-room as mine. The quarter-deck being elevated, one of our windows opened towards the deck, and *could* at all times afford good and safe ventilation; but the stewards always *would* shut it, watching their opportunity of doing so when we were asleep. We always opened it again, when on waking we found the deed had been done; and all of us made a point of shouting out ferociously when we caught them stealthily at it. This shutting and opening occurred several times every night, and seemed destined to go on, spite of all our remonstrances; a nuisance only relieved by a slight dash of the ludicrous. Danes don't seem to like fresh air.

Saturday morning, July 23.—No land in sight, open sea from Norway to America; heavy swell on the Atlantic, and wind changing from N.E. to N.W.; numerous whales blowing, quite close to the vessel; gulls and kittiwakes flying about.

At mid-day came in sight of the Faröe Islands rising above the horizon; fixed the first glimpse of them, and continued sketching their outline from time to time, as on nearing them it developed itself—watching with great interest the seeming clouds slowly becoming crags. Little Dimon, a lofty rock-island, somewhat resembling Ailsa, and purple in the distance, was, from the first, the most prominent and singular object on the horizon line.

The waves rolling so heavily that not only the hull, but the mast of a sloop, not very far off, is quite hid by each long swell. The Professor, Dr. Livingston, and Mr. Murray all agree in saying that they never had such heavy seas in crossing the Atlantic.

The Faröe group consists of twenty-two islands, seventeen of which are inhabited. A bird's-eye view of them would exhibit a series of bare, steep, oblong hills, in parallel ranges; with either valleys or narrow arms of the sea between them, and all lying north-west and south-east. The name Faröe is said to be derived from *faar* or *foer*, the old word for a sheep; that animal having probably been introduced by the Norse sea-rovers long before these islands were permanently colonised in in the time of Harold. However, *fier*—the Danish word for feathers—is more likely to be the correct etymology; for these islands are the native habitat of innumerable sea-birds.

They lie 185 miles north-west of the Shetland Isles,

400 west of Norway, and 320 south-east of Iceland; population upwards of 3000, and subject to Denmark.

We are now approaching Suderoe, the most southerly of the islands. On our left lie several curious detached rocks, near one of which, called the Monk, is a whirlpool, dangerous in some states of the tide; although its perils, like those of Corrivreckan between Jura and Scarba in the Hebrides, have been greatly exaggerated. On one occasion I sailed over the latter unharmed by Sirens, Mermaids, or Kelpies; only observing an irregular fresh on the water, where the tide-ways met, and hearing nothing save a dripping, plashing noise in the cross-cut ripple, as if many fish were leaping around the boat.

In storms, however, such places had better receive a wide berth.

The approach to the Faröe group is very fine, presenting to our view a magnificent panorama of fantastically-shaped islands—peaked sharp angular bare precipitous rocks, rising sheer from the sea; the larger-sized islands being regularly terraced in two or more successive grades of columnar trap-rock. Some of these singular hill-islets are sharp along the top, like the ridge of a house, and slope down on either side to the sea, at an angle of fifty degrees. Others of them are isolated stacks.

The hard trap-rock, nearly everywhere alternating with soft tufa, or claystone, sufficiently accounts for the regular, stair-like terraces which form a striking and characteristic feature of these picturesque islands. The whole have evidently, in remote epochs, been subjected to violent physical abrasion, probably glacial, during the period of the ice-drift; and, subsequently, to the disintegrating crumbling influences of moisture, and of the atmosphere itself. Frost converts each particle of moisture into a crystal expanding wedge of ice, which does its work silently but surely and to an extent which few people would imagine.

We now pass that singular rock-island, Little Dimon, which supports a few wild sheep; and Store Dimon, on which only one family resides. The cliffs here, as also on others of the islands, are so steep that boats are lowered with ropes into the sea; and people landing are either pulled up by ropes, or are obliged to clamber up by fixing their toes and fingers in holes cut on the face of the rock. Sea-fowls and eggs are every year collected in thousands from these islets by the bold cragsmen. These men climb from below; or, like the samphire-gatherer—"dreadful trade"—are let down to the nests by means of a rope, and there they pursue their perilous calling while hanging in "midway air" over the sea. They also sometimes approach the cliffs at night, in boats, carrying lighted torches, which lure and dazzle the birds that come flying around them, so that they are easily knocked down with sticks, and the boat is thus speedily filled. As many as five thousand birds have been taken in one year from Store Dimon alone, and in former times they were much more numerous.

We watch clouds like white fleecy wool rolling past, and apparently being raked by the violet-coloured peaks; whilst others lower down are pierced and rest peacefully among them.

Having passed Sandoe, through the Skaapen Fiord, we see Hestoe, Kolter, Vaagoe, and other distant blue island heights in the direction of Myggenaes, the most western island of the group. We now sail between

Stromoe on the west, and Naalsöe on the east. Stromoe is the central and largest island of the group, being twenty-seven miles long and seven broad. It contains Thorshavn, the capital of Faröe. Naalsöe, the needle island, is so called from a curious cave at the south end which penetrates the island from side to side like the eye of a needle—larger, by a long way, than Cleopatra's.

NAALSÖE.

Daylight shews through it, and, in calm weather, boats can sail from the one side to the other. We observe a succession of sea-caves in the rocks as we sail along, the action of the waves having evidently scooped out the softer strata, and left the columnar trap-rock hanging like a pent-house over each entrance. These caves are tenanted by innumerable sea-birds. On the brink of the water stand restless glossy cormorants; along the horizontal rock-ledges above them, sit skua-gulls, kitti-wakes, auks, guillemots, and puffins, in rows; and generally ranged in the order we have indicated, beginning with the cormorant on the lower stones or rocks next the sea, and ending with the puffin, which takes the highest station in this bird congress.

If disturbed, they raise a harsh, confused, deafening noise; screaming and fluttering about in myriads. Their numbers are so frequently thinned, and in such a variety of ways, that old birds may, on these occasions, be excused for exhibiting signs of alarm.

The Faröese eat every kind of sea-fowl, with the exception of gulls, skuas, and cormorants; but are partial to auks, guillemots, and puffins. They use them either fresh, salted or dried. The rancid fishy taste of sea-birds resides, for the most part, in the skin only—that removed, the rest is generally palatable. In the month of May the inhabitants of many of the islands subsist chiefly on eggs. Feathers form an important article of export.

We watched several gulls confidingly following the steamer; one in particular, now flying over the deck as far as the funnel, now falling astern to pick up bits of biscuit that were thrown overboard to it. Long I stood admiring its beautiful soft downy plumage, its easy graceful motions, the great distance to which a few strokes of its powerful pinions urged it forward, or, spread bow-like and motionless, allowed it simply to float and at times remain poised in the air right over the deck, now peering down with its keen yet mild eyes, and leaving us to surmise what embryo ideas of wonder might now be passing through its little bird-brain.

The Danish officer raised, levelled his piece, and fired; the poor thing screamed like a child, threw up its wings, turned round, and fell upon the sea like a stone; its companions came flying confusedly in crowds to see what was wrong with it, and received another shower of lead for their pains.

Holding no peace-society, vegetarian, homeopathic &c.

views, I do not object to the *bona fide* clearing of a country from dangerous animals; or to shooting, when rendered necessary for supplying our wants; but—from the higher, healthier platform of Christian manliness, reason and common sense—would most emphatically protest against thoughtless or wanton cruelty. Such barbarism could not be indulged in, much less be regarded as sport, but from sheer thoughtlessness in the best; while, under almost any circumstances, the destruction of animal life will, by the true gentleman, be regarded as a painful necessity.

Those who love sport for its own sake may be divided into three classes—the majority of sportsmen it is to be hoped belonging to the first of these divisions;—viz., the thoughtless, who have never considered the subject at all, or looked at any of its bearings; those whose blunted feelings are, in one direction, estranged from the beauty and joy of existence; and the third and last class, where civilization makes so near an approach to the depravity of savage natures, that a tiger-like eagerness to destroy life takes possession of a man and becomes a passion. He then only reckons the number of braces bagged, and considers not desolate nests, broken-winged pining birds, and the many dire tragedies wrought on the moor by his murderous gun.

A study of the habits of birds, taking cognizance of all the interesting on-goings of their daily lives, of their wonderful instincts and labours of love, would, we should think, make a man of rightly-constituted mind feel the necessity of destroying them to be painful; and he certainly would not choose to engage in it as sport. The fable of the boys and the frogs is in point, and the term "sport," thus applied, is surely a cruel, and certainly a one-sided word. In low natures, sympathy becomes totally eclipsed and obscured by selfishness; and all selfishness is sin.

Although shocked at witnessing the needless destruction of the poor gull, for the sake of the officer, who was of a gentle kindly nature, doubtless belonging to the "first division," we tried hard to palliate the deed; but that pitiful cry of agony haunts us yet!

> "Farewell, farewell! but this I tell
> To thee, thou Wedding guest!
> He prayeth well, who loveth well
> Both man, and bird, and beast.
>
> "He prayeth best, who loveth best
> All things both great and small;
> For the dear God who loveth us,
> He made and loveth all."

Whales rising to the surface and spouting around the vessel; also shoals of porpoises tumbling and gambolling about; sometimes swimming in line so as closely to resemble the coils of a snake moving along; such an appearance has probably originated the mythic sea-serpent.

There are still many caves in the rocks close on the sea; innumerable birds flying out of them and settling on the surface of the heaving water close under the cliffs.

We now approach a little bay, surrounded by an amphitheatre of bare hills; the hollow, for a wonder, slopes down to the shore; we observe patches of green among the rocks, and a flag flying. Several fishing sloops lie at anchor, but there is no appearance of a town. Here we are told is Thorshavn, the capital of Faröe—

the haven of Thor. As we approach, we discover that it is a town, the chief part of it built upon a rocky promontory which divides the bay; we can also distinguish the church and fort. The green tint we had observed is grassy turf—but it happens to be growing on the roofs of the wooden houses; and the houses are scattered irregularly among the brown rocks. On the promontory, house rises above house from the water's edge; and the black, wooden church tower rising behind appears to crown them all. On an eminence, to the right of the town, is the battery or fort, with a flagstaff in front. All glasses in requisition, we curiously examine the place and discover several wooden jetties—landing places for fishing boats. Beneath the fort and all round, split fish are spread on the rocks to dry; many square fish-heaps also are being pressed under boards, with heavy stones placed above them.

The scenery around is not unlike that of Loch Long in Scotland, while the general aspect of Thorshavn itself resembles the pictures of old towns given in the corners of maps of the fifteenth century.

As we enter the bay with colours flying, the Danish flag is run up at the fort, displayed by the sloops, and flutters from the flagstaff at Mr. Müller's house. This gentleman is one of the local authorities and also agent for the steamer. A cold wind blows down the ravine, boats are coming off, the steam-whistle rejoices on hearing itself echoed among the hills, and the anchor is let go. Now, that we are near it, the town appears really picturesque and carries one several hundred years back, with its veritable old-world, higgledy-piggledy quaintness.

THORSHAVN.

Saturday night, 6 P.M.—Went on shore in the captain's boat, called at Mr. Müller's office—a comfortable new erection—and then separated into parties to explore the place. Crowds of men, women, and children, standing at every door, stare at us with undisguised child-like wonder; the men—middle-sized stalwart fellows with light hair and weathered faces—taking off their caps to us as we pass along returning their salutes.

"An ancient fishy smell," together with a strong flavour of turf-smoke, decidedly predominate over sundry other nondescript odours in this strange out-landish town. The results of our exploration are embodied in the following jottings, which, at all events, participate so far in the spirit of the place as to resemble its ground-plan.

Houses, stone for a few feet next the ground, then wood, tarred or painted black, and generally two stories in height; small windows, the sashes of which are painted white; green turf on the roofs. The interiors of the poorer sort of houses are very dark; an utter absence of *voluntary* ventilation; one fire, and that in the kitchen, the chimney often only a hole in the roof. Yet even in these hovels there is generally a guest-room, comfortably boarded and furnished. In such apartments we observed chairs, tables, chests of drawers, feather-beds, down coverlets, a few books, engravings on the walls, specimens of ingenious native handiwork, curiosities, &c. This juxtaposition under the same roof was new to us, and struck every one as something quite peculiar and contrary to all our previous experiences. The streets of Thorshavn are only narrow dirty irregular passages, often not more than two or three feet wide; one walks upon bare rock or mud. These passages wind up steep places, and run in all manner of zigzag directions, so that the most direct line from one point to another generally leads "straight down crooked lane and all round the square." Observed a man on the top of a house cutting grass with a sickle. Here the approach of spring is first indicated by the turf roofs of the houses becoming green. Being invited, we entered several fishermen's houses; they seemed dark, smoky, and dirty; and, in all, the air was close and stifling. In one, observed a savoury pot of puffin broth, suspended from the ceiling and boiling on a turf fire built open like a smith's forge, the smoke finding only a very partial egress by the hole overhead; on the wall hung a number of plucked puffins and guillemots; several hens seen through the smoke sitting contentedly perched on a spar evidently intended for their accommodation in the corner of the apartment; a stone hand-mill for grinding barley, such as Sarah may have used, lay on the floor; reminding one of the East, from whence the Scandinavians came in the days of Odin.

In passing along the street we saw strips of whale-flesh, black and reddish-coloured, hanging outside the gable of almost every house to dry, just as we have seen herrings in fishing-villages on our own coasts. When a shoal of whales is driven ashore by the boatmen, there are great rejoicings among the islanders, whose faces, we were told, actually shine for weeks after this their season of feasting. What cannot be eaten at the time is dried for future use. Boiled or roasted it is nutritious, and not very unpalatable. The dried flesh which I tasted resembled tough beef, with a flavour of venison. Being "blood-meat," I would not have known it to be from the sea; and have been told that, when fresh and properly cooked, tender steaks from a young whale can scarcely be distinguished from beef-steak.

The costume of the men is curious, and somewhat like that of the Neapolitans;—a woollen cap, like the Phrygian, generally dark-blue or reddish; a long jacket and knee-breeches, both of coarse home-made cloth, blue or brown; long stockings; and thin, soft, buff-coloured lamb-skin shoes, made of one piece of leather, and without hard soles, so that they can find sure footing with them on the rocks, or use their toes when climbing crags almost as well as if they had their bare feet. There is less peculiarity in the female costume. The men and women generally have light hair and blue eyes. Honest and industrious, crime is scarcely known amongst them.

Visited the Fort, which is very primitive; simply a little space on a hill-side, enclosed with a low rough stone wall; four small useless cannon lying on the grass, enjoying a sinecure—literally lying in clover; a wooden sentry-box in the corner; a flag-staff in front of it, and two little cottages behind, to accommodate several of the garrison, who prefer living there to lodging in the town, as their comrades do. There are only some eight or ten soldiers altogether; and these, with the commander, constitute the sole military establishment in

FORT.

Faröe. They appear to occupy themselves with fishing, &c., very much like the other inhabitants of the place.

Visited the library, which was established by a former Amptman or Governor. It occupies two rooms, which are shelved all round and comfortably heated with a stove. We observed many standard Danish, German, French and English books, several valuable folio works of reference, and many trashy modern novels. The

Faröese are inquisitive and intelligent, show a taste for reading, but possess no native literature like the Icelanders.

Visited the church, which is built of wood. The service performed in it is the Lutheran, as in Denmark. It contains an altar-piece intended to represent "Joseph of Arimathea with the dead body of Christ," two large candles, and a silver and ebony crucifix. The galleries, of plain unvarnished wood, are arranged like opera stalls, one above the other from the floor, and with green curtains to each. At the right side of the pulpit were three large sand-glasses, an old custom once common in all our churches; fronting the altar was the organ-loft. Everything about the church was neat, clean, and primitive. Flower-beds were planted so as to form wreaths or crosses on the graves in the church-yard; and all appeared to be carefully tended and kept in order by loving hands.

Went by invitation of Fraulein Löbner to drink tea at her mother's, the Danish· officer with me. We were ushered into a charming old-fashioned room with low panelled roof; everything in it was neat, scrupulously clean, and primitive. A valance of white Nottingham lace-curtain ran along the top of the diamond-paned lattice windows; while a row of flower-pots, with blooming roses and geraniums, stood in the window-sill. There were cabinets with rich old china-ware; several paintings on the wall, two of which were really excellent—one, a portrait in oil of her late father who had been Governor of Faröe; the other a portrait of her brother, also deceased. Her father was a Dane of German extraction; and her mother—a kindly old lady to whom we were now introduced—a native of Faröe.

At tea we had preserves, made from rhubarb grown in their own garden; a silver ewer of delicious cream highly creditable to Faröese dairyship; and buns, tarts, almond-cakes, &c., baked by the one baker of Thorshavn, and quite as good as could be had in London.

While the officer was sketching from the window, our kind hostess wound up a musical box, at the same time expressing her regret that the piano-forte, which I had observed standing in the room, was under repair. She also showed us a folio of her own drawings, and many engravings. Here a lady of cultivated mind, and who has mingled in good society, is happy and content to dwell in this remote isle; for to her it posseses the magic of that endearing word—home !

She tells us that wool, fish, feathers, and skins form the chief articles of export; that barley is the only grain raised in Faröe, but the summer is so short that it has not time to ripen. The ears are plucked by the hand and dried in a kiln. The rye, of which their black bread is made, is imported chiefly from Denmark. The hay-harvest is of great importance to the inhabitants. There are numerous sheep in the islands—some individuals possessing flocks of from four to five hundred, besides a few ponies and cows. Dried, the mutton is serviceable for food during winter, when frequent storms interfere with fishing operations.

As in Shetland, the wool is collected from the sheep by the hand, at the season of the year when they are casting their fleeces; for shearing, besides being a more painful process, would deprive them of the long hair so necessary for their protection in an uncertain climate, and leave them to shiver exposed to the untempered fury of the northern blast. The sheep thus enables the islanders to supply their own home wants, and also annually to export many thousand pairs of knitted stockings and gloves, together with the overplus raw material.

Miss L. informs us that Thorshavn contains about eight hundred inhabitants. Of these, most of the men are fishers when the weather will admit of their going off. The people are very ingenious, and make knives of all sizes, with curiously inlaid wooden handles and sheaths. The wood for such purposes is obtained from logs of mahogany, which are frequently found as driftwood among these islands. We were shewn a home-made fancy work-table, neatly put together in a very ingenious and workman-like manner.

Each man here is a sort of Jack-of-all-trades, from the mending of boats or nets, to the killing of sheep and drying them in sheds for the winter store of provisions; from the making of lambskin shoes to the building of houses, or the manufacture of implements.

Miss Löbner has kindly and obligingly undertaken to procure some specimens of these manufactures and local curiosities against my return from Iceland.

Gazing round, as we take leave of our kind entertainers, I fix in my mind's eye the lady-like air and quaint point-devise costume of the elder lady, who, with silvery hair combed back from her brow, had moved about most assiduously performing all the sacred rites of hospitality to her guests; the mediæval aspect of everything in the room,—from the stove to the timepiece, from the polished wooden floor to the panelled ceiling; the diamond-paned lattice windows, with their old-world outlook on the town and the flat wooden bridge, close by, which crosses a brawling stream rushing impetuously over rocks from the gully behind; the absolute cleanness and polish of everything; and the monthly roses blooming freshly as of old;—all so vividly impress themselves upon my mind that the whole becomes a waking dream of other days; and it would not seem much out of keeping, or at all surprising, were the Emperor Charles V. himself to open the door and walk into the quaint old apartment we are now about to leave.

Nine P.M.—Wandered alone by the shore, and sketched the view, looking north, from beneath the fort; also made a drawing of the bay from the wooden jetty; while engaged on the latter, crowds of fishermen gathered

FROM THORSHAVN—SHOWING FARÖESE BOATS.

around me making odd remarks of wonder, the general scope of which I could gather, as they recognised the steamer, boats, hills, &c., coming up on the paper;

sketched one of the onlookers, an intelligent looking fellow, and here he is.

FARÖESE BOATMAN.

The fishing boats or skiffs, have all the high bow and stern of the Norwegian yawl; square lug-sails very broad and carried low are the most common. The weather is so very uncertain, the gusts so sudden and violent, that, preceded by a lull during which a lighted candle may be carried in the open air, they come roaring down the valleys or between the islands, bellowing with a noise like thunder, and sometimes strip the turf from the hill side, roll it up like a sheet of lead and carry it away into the sea, while the air is darkened by clouds of dust and stones.

Felt comfortably warm when sketching in the open air between ten and eleven P.M., for, though the climate is moist, the mean temperature is warmer than that of Denmark, and, on account of the gulf stream, not much below our own. Forchhammer states that at Thorshavn in mild years, it is 49·2°; in cold years, 42·3°; the average temperature being 45·4°. The greatest height of the thermometer during his observations was 72·5°, and the lowest 18·5°.

Shortly before eleven o'clock the soldiers of the fort manned their boat, and rowed us off to the steamer.

After narrating our various experiences on shore, had a pleasant quiet home-talk with Professor Chadbourne, read a few verses of the New Testament, and as the week was drawing to a close we retired to our berths, wishing each other a good night's rest after all the novel excitement, wonder, and fatigues of the day.

Sabbath, July 24.—Wind high, and the lashing rain pouring down in torrents. Went ashore at ten o'clock to attend church; heard the pleasing sound of psalm-singing in various of the fishermen's dwellings as we passed along. Called for Mr Müller, who had invited me to his pew. The service was Lutheran, and began at eleven o'clock. The pastor was absent, but the assistant, M. Lützen, who is also schoolmaster and organist, officiated. All the people, singing lowly, joined in several fine old German chorales, led by the organist, who also played some of Sebastian Bach's music with much taste and feeling—although little indebted to the instrument, which was old and infirm, piping feebly and tremulously in its second childhood.

The area of the church was entirely occupied by women, many of them with their bare heads, but most of them with a quaint little covering on the back part of the head for hair and comb; only saw two bonnets in the whole congregation. One old lady—with her hair combed back, a black silk covering on the back part of her head, and, from where it terminated behind her ears, a stiff white frill sticking right out—looked as if she had just stepped out from one of Holbein's pictures; others resembled Gerard Dow's old women. The men "were drest, in their Sunday's best;"—long jackets and knee-breeches of coarse blue or brown cloth, frequently ornamented with rows of metal buttons; stockings of the same colours; and the never-varying buff-coloured lamb-skin shoes.

It was pleasing to see these stalwart descendants of the brave old Vikings "the heathen of the Northern sea,"—these men whose daily avocations exposed them to constant perils by sea and land, here, in the very haven of Thor, walking reverently into a Christian church, with their caps and Bibles in their hands, and quietly entering their pews to worship God.

Although the day was very wet, and the regular minister absent, there was present a congregation of about two hundred; and all seemed truly devotional during the service.

From the roof, between two old-fashioned brass chandeliers, was suspended a brig, probably the gift of some sailor preserved from shipwreck. The service began at eleven o'clock, and ended at half-past twelve. When it was over, I spoke with Skolare Lützen, who had officiated. He is a native of Copenhagen, speaks little English, but good German. He took me over the building, and into the pulpit. Altogether, the quaint appearance of the church, the organ, the singing of the people, the devout reading and simplicity of the service, and the curious old costumes carried one back to the time of the Reformation, and to me all was singularly interesting. One could fancy that here, if anywhere, the European world had stood still, and that Luther himself would not have detected the lapse of centuries, if permitted once more to gaze on such a scene as was here presented.

Two of us accompanied Mr Müller to his house before going on board the steamer. His wife and daughter were hospitable and kind; and, as usual on a visit here, tarts, cakes, and wine were produced. His home resembles a museum, containing many stuffed birds, eggs, geological specimens and other natural curiosities collected in these islands. His little son's name is Erasmus.

Captain Andriessen had wished to sail to-day, but could not get men to work on Sabbath discharging the cargo; at which I was well pleased, both for the right feeling it indicated on the part of the Faröese, and for our own sakes. Here we lie peacefully anchored in the bay, enjoying the Sabbath quiet, while the tempest is now howling wildly outside the islands, and the lashing pelting rain is pouring down on the deck overhead like a shower-bath.

> "Such groans of roaring wind and rain I never
> Remember to have heard."

The rain having abated, ere retiring for the night, walked the deck for half an hour. Thorshavn, as seen in the strong light and shade of evening from the steamer's deck, has truly a most quaint old-world look—all the more so now that we know it from exploration—so very primitive that one can scarcely imagine anything like it. It is unique.

Monday morning, July 25.—From an early hour, all hands busily occupied discharging the cargo, heavily-laden boats following each other to the shore. At half-past one o'clock, the last boat pushes off, the steam-whistle is blown, and we sail away round the south point of Stromoe, shaping our course north-west through

BASALT CAVES—SOUTH POINT OF STROMOE.

Hestoe Fiord. The coast of the islands is abrupt, mostly rising sheer from the sea; many basaltic columns, and a succession of wave-worn caves, in front of which countless sea-birds are flying, swimming and diving. The trap hills are regularly terraced like stairs. Clouds drifting among the hills, and from every gully cataracts leaping down in white foam to the sea. The general colour of the rocks is gray and brown, slightly touched here and there with green. These islands might be characterized as several groups or chains of hills, lying nearly parallel to each other and separated by narrow arms of the sea, which run in straight lines north-west and south-east. The summits of the larger islands reach an elevation of from one to two thousand feet; while the highest hill—Slattaretind, near Eide in Oesteroe—is two thousand nine hundred feet high.

The hills around still exhibit a succession of grassy declivities, alternating with naked walls of black or brown rock. The flat heights of these islands, we are told, are either bare rock or marshy hollows. There are also several small lakes, the largest of which, in Vaagoe, is only two miles in circumference, and lies surrounded by wild rugged mountain masses.

We count a dozen foaming cataracts, all in sight at once, and falling down over precipitous rocks around us into the sea. The wind perceptibly sways them hither and thither, and then dispersing the lower portion of the water raises it in silvery clouds of vapour on which rainbows play. They resemble the Staubach in Switzerland; and remind us of the wild mist-veil apparition of Kühleborn, in the charming story of Undine.

The tidal currents, in the long narrow straits which divide the northern islands from each other, are strong but regular; running six hours the one way and six hours the other. Boatmen must calculate and wait for the stream, as the oar is powerless against it.

The atmospheric effects are beautiful;—a bold headland, ten miles to the south, appears in the bright sunshine to be of the deepest violet colour; no magic of the pencil could approach such a tint. It is heightened too by the white gleaming sail of a fishing smack relieved against it.

When we got clear of the islands, the ground-swell

became much heavier; for the storm of the preceding day had been terrific. Great heavy waves of smooth unbroken water, worse than Spanish rollers; boat tumbling and plunging about, with sail set to steady her; walked the deck for an hour and found use for my sea-legs.

Several gulls follow the ship; I never tire of watching their graceful motions, as, with white downy plumage and wings tipt with black, they fly forward round the mast, remain poised over the deck, or fall astern keeping in the steamer's wake. Two of our companions have discovered a capital sheltered nook and sit smoking, perched up inside the large inverted boat which we are taking north with us.

An Icelander and a Dane are among the second-class passengers; got them to read aloud to me Icelandic and Danish, also Greek and Latin. In pronouncing the latter two, they follow the classic mode and give the broad vowel sounds, as taught in the German and Scottish universities but not at Oxford or Cambridge.

The dim Faröes are fast falling astern—

"Far-off mountains turnéd into clouds."

The vessel by the log makes eight knots—course, N. by W. and sails set.

The day lengthens as we go north, and at midnight I can now see to read large print, although the sky is very cloudy.

No land—no sail in sight; we heave over the billows of the lonely Northern Sea, and now all is clear before us for Iceland!

PORTLAND HUK.

THE WESTMANNA ISLANDS — REYKJAVIK.

Tuesday morning, July 26. Open sea and not a sail visible, although we carefully scan "the round ocean."

Tremendous rolling all night; everything turning topsy-turvy and being knocked about—my portmanteau, which was standing on the cabin floor, capsized. Only by dint of careful adjustment and jambing in the form of the letter z could we prevent ourselves from being shot out of our berths.

To-day we have the heaviest rolling I ever experienced. It is impossible even to sit on the hurricane deck without holding on by a rope, and not easy even with such assistance. Deck at an angle of 40 to 45°. The boat fastened aloft aggravates matters. A very little more, or the slightest shifting of the cargo, would throw us on our beam ends. The boat getting loose from its fastenings when we are on the larboard roll would break off the funnel. The Captain has hatchets ready, at once to send it overboard or break it up if requisite for our safety.

The bell tolling with the roll of the ship, first on the one side, and then on the other; generally four or five times in succession. A series of large rollers alternate with lesser waves; the bell indicates the former. Waves without wind roll in from the N. and N.W., both on the starboard and port bow.

In the afternoon saw a piece of wreck—mast and cordage—floating past, most likely a record of woe; involving waiting weary hearts that will not die.

Not a speck on the whole horizon line; a feeling of intense loneliness would at times momentarily creep over us. Birds overhead flying south brought to mind Bryant's beautiful poem addressed to "The Waterfowl," which he describes as floating along darkly painted on the crimson sky:

> "There is a Power whose care
> Teaches thy way along that pathless coast,—
> The desert and illimitable air
> Lone wandering but not lost.
>
> Thou'rt gone, the abyss of heaven
> Hath swallowed up thy form; yet, on my heart,
> Deeply hath sunk the lesson thou hast given,
> And shall not soon depart.
>
> He, who from zone to zone
> Guides through the boundless sky thy certain flight,
> In the long way that I must tread alone
> Will lead my steps aright."

The heavy rolling still continues. Hope the cargo will keep right, or we shall come to grief. Thought of the virtues of my friends. However, maugre a dash of danger, a group of us on the hurricane deck really enjoyed the scene as if we had been veritable Mother Carey's chickens. One sang Barry Cornwall's song

"The Sea;" another by way of contrast gave us "Annie Laurie" and "Scots wha hae wi' Wallace bled;" and towards evening we all joined in singing "York;" that grand old psalm tune harmonizing well with the place and time—

"The setting sun, and music at the close!"

The gulf-stream and the rollers meeting make a wild jumble. Barometer very low—28$\frac{10}{}$; low enough for a hurricane in the tropics. Stormy rocking in our sea-cradle all day and all night.

Wednesday, July 27.—Vessel still rolling as much as ever. Saw a skua—a black active rapacious bird, a sort of winged pirate—chasing a gull which tried hard to evade it by flying, wavering backwards and forwards, zigzagging, doubling, now rising and now falling, till at last, wearied out and finding escape impossible, it disgorged and dropt a fish which the skua pounced upon, picking it up before it could reach the surface of the sea. The fish alone had been the object of the skua's pursuit. The skua is at best but a poor fisher and takes this method of supplying its wants at second hand. Subsequently we often observed skuas following this their nefarious calling; unrelentingly chasing and attacking the gulls until they gave up their newly caught fish, when they were at once left unmolested and allowed to go in peace; but whether the sense of wrong or joy at escape predominated, or with what sort of feelings and in what light the poor gulls viewed the transaction, a man would require to be a bird in order to form an adequate idea.

We cannot now be far from Iceland, but clouds above and low thick mists around preclude the possibility of taking observations or seeing far before us. In clear weather we are told that the high mountains are visible from a distance of 100 or 150 miles at sea.

At half-past Three o'clock P.M., peering hard through the mist, we discover, less than a mile ahead, a white fringe of surf breaking on a low sandy shore for which we are running right stem on. It is the south of Iceland; dim heights loom through the haze; the vessel's head is turned more to the west and we make for sailing, in a westerly direction with a little north in it, along the shore up the western side of the island which in shape somewhat resembles a heart.

The mist partially clears off and on our right we sight Portland Huk, the most southern point of Iceland. Here rocks of a reddish brown colour run out into the sea rising in singular isolated forms like castellated buildings; one mass from a particular point of view exactly resembles the ruins of Iona, even to the square tower; other peaks are

NEEDLE ROCKSOFF— PORTLAND HUK.

like spires. Strange fantastic needle-like rocks or drongs shoot up into the air—the Witches' fingers (Trollkonefinger) of the Northmen. The headland exhibits a great arched opening through which, we were told, at certain states of the tide, the steamer could sail if her masts

were lowered. It is called Dyrhólaey—the hill door—
and from it the farm or village close by is named
Dyrhólar. Behind these curious rocks appeared a range
of greenish hills mottled with snow-patches, their white
summits hid in the rolling clouds.

There are numerous waterfalls; glaciers—the ice of a
pale whity-green colour—fill the ravines and creep down
the valleys from the Jökuls to the very edge of the water.
Their progressive motion here is the same as in
Switzerland, and large blocks of lava are brought down
imbedded in their moraine. I perceived what I thought
to be curved lines on the surface like the markings on
mother-of-pearl, indicating that the downward motion of
a glacier is greater in the centre than where impeded by
friction at the sides.

On the shoulders of the range of heights along the
coast, snow, brown-coloured patches and green-spots
were all intermingled; while the upper mountain regions
of perpetual snow were meanwhile for the most part hid
in clouds which turban-like swathed their brows in
fleecy "folds voluminous and vast."

The steamer is running, at nine knots, straight for the
Westmanna Islands, where a mail is to be landed.
They lie off the coast nearly half way between Portland
Huk, the south point, and Cape Reykjanes the south-
west point of Iceland.

How gracefully the sea-birds skim the brine, taking
the long wave-valleys, disappearing and reappearing
amongst the great heaving billows. We note many
waterfalls leaping from the mountain sides to the shore,
and at times right into the sea itself, from heights
apparently varying from two to four hundred feet.

We now approach the Westmanna Islands, so called
from ten Irish slaves—westmen—who in the year A.D. 875
took refuge here after killing Thorleif their master. They
are a group of strange fantastically shaped islets of
brown lava-rock ; only three or four however have any
appearance of grass upon them, and but one island,
Heimaey—the home isle, is inhabited. The precipitous
rock-cliffs are honeycombed with holes and caves which
are haunted by millions of birds. These thickly dot the
crevices with masses of living white; hover like clouds
in the air, and swarm the waters around like a fringe—
resting, fluttering, or diving, by turns.

Westmannshavn, the harbour of the islands, is a bay
on the north-west of Heimaey where a green vale slopes
down to the sea. It is sheltered by the islands of
Heimaklettur on the North, and Bjarnarey on the East.
We observed a flag flying, and a few huts scattered
irregularly and sparsely on the slope. This place is
called Kaupstadr—or head town—but there is no other
town in the group. The roofs of the huts were covered
with green sod and scarcely to be distinguished from the
grass of the slope on which they stood save by the light
blue smoke which rose curling above them from turf
fires.

A row-boat came off for the mail, which, we were told,
had never before been landed here from a steamer; the
usual mode is to get it from Reykjavik in a sailing
vessel. For those accustomed to at least half a dozen
deliveries of letters every day, it was strange to think
that here there were fewer posts in a whole year. These
Islands have, on account of their excellent fisheries, from
very remote periods been much frequented by foreign

vessels. Before the discovery of Newfoundland, British merchants resorted hither, and also to ports on the west coast of Iceland, to exchange commodities and procure dried stock-fish. Icelandic ships also visited English ports. This intercommunication can be distinctly traced back to the time of Henry III.; but by the beginning of the fifteenth century it had become regular and had risen to importance. It was matter of treaty between Norway and England; but, with or without special licenses, or in spite of prohibitions—sometimes with the connivance and permission of the local authorities, and at other times notwithstanding the active opposition of one or both governments—the trade being mutually profitable to those engaged in it continued to be prosecuted. English tapestry and linen are mentioned in old Icelandic writings, and subsequently we learn that English strong ale was held in high estimation by the Northmen.

Edward III. granted certain privileges and exemptions to the fishermen of Blacknie and Lyne in Norfolk on account of their Icelandic commerce. In favourable weather the distance could be run in about a fortnight.

From Icelandic records we learn that in the year A.D. 1412, "30 ships engaged in fishing were seen off the coast at one time." "In A.D. 1415 there were no fewer than 6 English merchant ships in the harbour of Hafna Fiord alone."

Notwithstanding the proclamations and prohibitions both of Eric and Henry V. the traffic still continued to increase; and we incidentally learn that in the year A.D. 1419 "Twenty-five English ships were wrecked on this coast in a dreadful snow-storm." Goods supplied to the natives then, as in later times, were both cheaper and

better than could be obtained from the Danish mono-
polists.   It will be remembered by the reader that when
Columbus visited Iceland he sailed in a bark from the
port of Bristol.

Gazing on this singular group of rocky Islands, on the
coast of Iceland, so lone and quiet, and reverting to the
early part of the thirteenth century, it was strange to
realize that into this very bay had then sailed and cast
anchor the ships of our enterprising countrymen—quaint
old-fashioned ships, such as we may still see represented
in illuminated MSS. of the period; and that their latest
news to such English merchants or fishermen as had
wintered or perhaps been stationed for some time at
Westmannshavn—supposing modern facilities for the
transmission of news—would not have been the peace of
Villafranca but the confirmation of Magna Charta;—
instead of the formation of volunteer corps, nobles
hastening to join the fifth Crusade;—not the treading
out of a Sepoy revolt, but Mongolian hordes overrunning
the Steppes of Russia;—and instead of some important
law-decision, celebrated trial, or case in Chancery,
they might hear of an acquaintance who had perished in
single combat, or who had indignantly and satisfactorily
proved his or her innocence by submitting to trial by
ordeal.   These were the old times of Friar Bacon—the
days of alchemy and witchcraft.   Haco had not yet been
crowned King of Norway; Snorre Sturleson was yet a
young man meditating the "Heimskringla."   The chisel
of Nicolo Pisano and the pencil of Cimabue were at
work in Italy.   Neither Dante nor Beatrice as yet
existed; nor had the factions of Guelph and Ghibeline
sprung into being.   Chaucer was not born till the

following century. Aladin reigned; Alphonzo the Wise, King of Leon and Castile, had not promulgated his code of laws. Not a single Lombard moneylender had arrived to settle in London; and the present structure of Westminster Abbey had not then been reared.

BJARNAREY.

On leaving Westmannshavn, sailing north between the islands of Heimaklettur and Bjarnarey, we saw two men rowing a boat deeply laden to the gunwale with sea-fowls, probably the result of their day's work. The cliffs everywhere alive with birds, and the smooth sea beneath them, in the glorious light of the evening sun, dotted black as if peppered with puffins and eider-ducks.

Nine P.M. Sketched various aspects of the islands and several of the strange outlying skerries.

WESTMANNA SKERRIES.

When the Westmanna Islands are reckoned at fourteen, that number does not include innumerable little rocky stacks and islets of all fantastic shapes alone or in groups; some like Druidical stones or old ruins, others of them far out and·exactly like ships in full sail, producing a strange effect on the horizon.

The island nearest the coast of Iceland on the east of Heimaey is called Erlendsey; that furthest north-west is Drángr; and the furthest west Einarsdrángr. On the south-west is an islet called Alsey; we have also an Ailsa in the frith of Clyde: both names probably signifying fire-isle. The islet furthest south is called Geirfuglasker. These names are necessarily altogether omitted on common small maps.

We witness a glorious sunset on the sea,—the horizon streaked with burning gold :

"Now 'gan the golden Phœbus for to steepe
His fiery face in billows of the west,
And his faint steedes watered in ocean deepe
Whiles from his journall labours he did rest."

Although the surface of the sea is quite smooth, a heavy ground swell keeps rolling along. A bank of violet cloud lies to the left of the sun, while dense masses of leaden and purple-coloured clouds are piled above it. An opening glows like a furnace seven times heated, darting rays from its central fire athwart the sky, and opening up a burning cone-shaped pathway of light on the smooth heaving billows, the apex of which reaches our prow.

Such the scene, as we sail north-west between the northernmost out-lying skerries of the Westmanna group and the south-west coast of Iceland and silently watch the gorgeous hues of sunset. Strangely at such times "hope and memory sweep the chords by turns," till the past, fused down into the present, becomes a magic mirror for the future.

The air is mild and warm; time by Greenwich twenty-minutes to eleven. The sun is not yet quite down, and—by the ship's compass, without making any allowance for deviation—is setting due north. At a quarter-past 12 A.M. when we leave the deck, it is still quite light.

Thursday Morning, July 28. Rose early—we are sailing along the Krisuvik coast in the direction of Cape

CAPE REYKJANES LOOKING SOUTH.

Reykjanes—smoky cape—which runs out from the south-west of Iceland. The low lying coast is of black

COAST NEAR REYKJAVIK.

lava; behind it rise serrated hill-ranges, and isolated conical mountains; some of a deep violet colour, others covered with snow and ice, the dazzling whiteness of which is heightened by contrast with the low dark fire-scathed foreground. White fleecy clouds are rolling among the peaks, now dense and clearly defined against the bright blue sunny sky—now hazy, ethereal, and evanescent. We observe steam rising from a hot sulphur spring on the coast. These are numerous in this neighbourhood, which contains the principal sulphur mines of the island. Here, where we sail, volcanic islands have at different times arisen and disappeared; flames too have sometimes been seen to issue from submarine craters; this latter phenomenon the natives describe as "the sea" being "on fire."

ELDEY.

On our left we pass Eldey—or the Fire Isle—a curious isolated basaltic rock resembling the Bass, but much smaller. It rose from the deep in historic times. The top slopes somewhat, and is white; this latter appearance has originated its Danish name "Maelsek," which is pronounced precisely in the same way as "meal-sack" would be in the Scottish dialect;—in fact the words are the same. Many solan geese flying about; whales gamboling and spouting close to the vessel.

Nine A.M., Greenwich time. Got first glimpse of Snæfells Jökul—the fifth highest mountain in Iceland—height 4577 feet—lying nearly in a north-west direction, far away across the blue waters of the Faxa Fiord. A pyramid covered with perpetual snow and ice, gleaming in the sun, its outline is now traced against a sky of deeper blue than any of us ever beheld in Switzerland or Italy.

The Faxa Fiord, situated on the south-west, is the largest in the island, and might be described as a magnificent bay, forming a semicircle which extends fifty-six miles from horn to horn; while its shores are deeply and irregularly indented by arms of the sea, or Fiords proper, which have names of their own, such as Hafnafiord, Hvalfiord, or Borgarfiord. Snæfell, on the north side of it, rises from the extremity of the long narrow strip of steep mountain promontory that runs out into the sea, separating the Faxa from the Breida Fiord—another large bay;—while on the south the Guldbringe Syssel, terminating with Cape Reykjanes, is a bare low-lying black contorted lava field.

The Faxa Fiord, then, sweeping in a semicircle from Snæfell to Reykjanes, contains several minor Fiords, and is crowded with lofty mountain-peaks, sharp, steep, and bare. The intense clearness of the northern atmosphere through which these appear, together with the fine contrast of their colours—reds, purples, golden hues, and pale lilacs; rosy-tinted snow or silvery-glittering ice—all sharply relieved against the blue sky, as if by magic confound southern ideas of distance, so that a mountain which at first glance appears to be only ten or fifteen miles distant, may in reality be forty or fifty, and perhaps considerably more.

The capital of Iceland lies in the south-east of this great bay. We have been sailing due north from Cape Reykjanes to the point of Skagi, and, rounding it, we sail east by north right into the Faxa Fiord, cutting off the southern segment of the bay, and are making straight for Reykjavik.

Several low-lying islands shelter the port and make the anchorage secure; one of these is Videy on which some of the government offices formerly stood, but it is now noted as a favourite resort of eider ducks which are here protected by law in order to obtain the down with which their nests are lined

Solitary fishermen are making for the shore in their skiff-like boats. A French frigate and brig, a Danish war schooner and several merchant sloops are seen lying at anchor, shut in by the islands and a low lava promontory. All are gaily decked with colours. On rounding the point, Reykjavik the capital of Iceland lies fairly before us. It is situated on a gentle greenish slope rising from the black volcanic sand of that "Plutonian shore." There are grassy heights at either side of the town and a fresh water lake like a large pond behind it. The cathedral in the centre, built of brick plastered brown stone colour, and the windmill on the height to the left, are the two most prominent objects. The front street consists of a single row of dark-coloured Danish looking wooden houses facing the sea. These we are told are mostly merchants' stores. Several of them have flag-staffs from which the Danish colours now flutter. All our glasses are in requisition. Numerous wooden jetties lead from the sea up to the road in front of the warehouses, and, on these, females like the fish-women of Calais, "withered, grotesque, wrinkled," and seeming "immeasurably old," with others younger and better looking, are busily engaged in carrying dried fish between the boats and the stores. Young and old alike wear the graceful Icelandic female head-dress—viz. a little black cloth scull-cap, jauntily fastened with a hair pin on the back part of the head. From the crown of this cap hangs a silver tube ornament, out of which flows a long thick black silk tassel falling on the shoulder.

Two streets run inland from the front street, and at right angles to it. That on the left contains the Governor's house, and the residences of several officials. It leads to the house where the Althing or Icelandic Parliament now assembles, and where, in another part of the same building, Rector Jonson teaches in the one academy of the island. The other street on the right contains several shops, merchants' dwelling houses, the residence of Jón Gudmundson, president of the Althing, advocate, and editor of a newspaper. It leads to the hotel, and to the residence of Dr. Hjaltelin, a distinguished anti-quarian and the chief physician of the island. In the same direction, a little higher up, is the lonely church-yard.

Between these two streets, houses stand at irregular intervals, and nearly all have little garden-plots attached to them.

On the outskirts, flanking the town, which in appear-ance is more Danish than Icelandic, are a few fishermen's huts, roofed over with green sod; and these, we afterwards found, were more like the style of build-ings commonly to be met with throughout the island.

As we cast anchor, the morning sunshine is gloriously

D

bright and clear, sea and sky intensely blue, and the atmosphere more transparent than that of Switzerland or Italy. Beyond Reykjavik, wild bare heights rise all round the bay; here—mountains of a ruddy brown colour, deeply scarred and distinctly showing every crevice; there—snow-patches gleaming on dark purple hills; here—lofty pyramids of glittering ice; there—cones of black volcanic rock; while white fleecy clouds in horizontal layers streak the distant peaks, and keep rolling down the shoulders of the nearer Essian range.

The arrival of the steamer is quite an event to the Icelanders. A boat came off from the shore, and another from the French brig, to get the mail-bags. We brought tidings of the peace of Villafranca, and heard the cheering of the French sailors when the news was announced to them. Dr. Mackinlay, who had remained, exploring various parts of the island, since the previous voyage of the Arcturus, and for whom we had letters and papers, kindly volunteered to give us information about the Geyser expedition. From his habits of keen observation, patient research, and kind-heartedness, he was well qualified to do so.

He recommended Geir Zöga, who had accompanied him on board, as a good trustworthy guide. We wished to start at once, so as to make the most of our time, but the undertaking was a more serious affair than we had anticipated. Ultimately, before landing, we arranged to start next morning at eight o'clock, as the very best we could do.

The distance to be got over is 72 miles, literally without roads or shelter; and mostly over wild rough stony wastes, in comparison with which the bed of a mountain water-course would be a good macadamized road. Provisions, traps, and everything we require have to be taken along with us.

We are a party of six; the guide has two assistants; nine riders in all, each requires a relay horse, so that eighteen ponies for the riders, and six for the baggage are requisite for our expedition. These have to be bargained for and collected together by Zöga from the farms· around Reykjavik; and as the ponies now run almost wild over the wastes in pursuit of scant herbage, and neither receive grooming, stabling, nor feeding, this is a work of time, and will occupy, Dr. Mackinlay tells us, not only the whole afternoon but the greater part of the night.

No one had brought provisions north but myself, so arrangements are made with the steward of the steamer for supplying them, and mine thrown in with the rest pro bono publico. Having fixed that Zöga should call in the evening at the hotel and report progress, at half-past 11 o'clock A.M. we got into the Captain's boat to land, where, long ago, Ingolf the first colonist had drawn his ship on shore. As the remainder of the day is at our disposal, curiosity is on edge to explore Reykjavik, the general plan and appearance of which has already been described—partly by anticipation.

The sun-glare is oppressively hot. As we approach the jetty we observe groups of men and women standing on the beach to see the passengers land. Some of the younger women are good-looking, and become the picturesque costume of the country;—those curious little black caps with silver ornaments and long black silk tassels already described; jackets faced with silver lace or rows of metal buttons; belts similarly ornamented; long flowing dark wadmal skirts of home manufacture; and primitive shoes made of one bit of cow-skin or any kind of hide, prepared so as in colour to resemble parchment or the skin one sometimes sees stretched like a drum-head over the mouth of a jar of honey.

A few other ladies are in morning dress, with shawls or handkerchiefs thrown gracefully over their heads, and nothing peculiar or different in their costume from what we are accustomed to see at home.

Mr. Haycock had received a letter of introduction to Mr. Simson, and I had one to Mr. Sievertsen; the latter is a retired merchant, and the former carries on a large business of a very miscellaneous kind—such being the character of all the stores or factories here. As the houses of these gentlemen both lay in the same direction, we set out together in order to obtain advice as to what was to be seen in Reykjavik and its neighbourhood. In passing along the front street, the stores—mostly belonging to Danish merchants—presented quite a bustling business aspect; while the dwelling houses, with lattice windows, white curtains and flower-pots of blooming roses and geraniums, exhibited an air of cleanliness comfort and refinement. From the absence of roads, carts are useless; one wheel barrow which we saw, belonging to an enterprising storekeeper, we were told, was the only wheeled vehicle in the island.

Mr. Sigurdur Sievertsen received us most cordially. This intelligent old gentleman conducted Sir George Mackenzie, who was his father's guest, to the Geysers; and he is alluded to by Sir George, in his travels, as "young Mr. Sievertsen." Time works changes! or, as

Archbishop Whately would more accurately put it, changes are wrought, not by, but "*in* time." However, Mr. Sievertsen is hale and hearty, and many summers may he yet see! On the wall we saw the portrait of his gifted and much lamented son, who several years ago died in Paris. He had been taken there by Louis Philip to receive a free education, as a graceful acknowledgment to the Icelanders for kindness shewn to the crew of a French vessel wrecked on their coast.

Our host has visited Britain, and both speaks and writes English fluently. Neither he nor his amiable wife spared any pains in trying to be of service to us. They gave us all manner of information, and kindly assisted us in procuring specimens of native manufacture,

L Men's shoes. G Girls' shoes. S Snuffbox made of walrus tusk. H Female-headdress with flowing silk tassel (see p. 49). D Distaff. M Two-thumbed mits.

such as—silver trinkets of beautiful workmanship; fine knitted gloves soft as Angola wool; fishermen's mits with no divisions for the fingers but each made with two thumbs, so that when the fishing line wears through one side the other can be turned; caps; men and women's shoes; quaint snuff boxes made of walrus tusk, or horn; and sundry other souvenirs which we wished to take south with us.

In Mr. Simson's store we saw everything from a needle to an anchor; from the coarsest packsheet to French ribbons. At Mr. Smith's, whose son had come north with us on his way from Copenhagen, we invested in seal-skins and eider-down—the latter for pillows and coverlets. This down, the eider-duck plucks from its breast to line its nest; it and the eggs are taken away. Again the nest is lined, and again robbed. The third time, the drake repairs it, supplying the down; and if this be also taken away the nest is altogether deserted by the ill-used pair. One nest yields about two and a half ounces of the finest clean down, or about half a pound in all if removed three times. What is plucked from the dead bird, it is said, possesses none of that wonderful elasticity which constitutes the value of the other. We should think, however, that this would depend on the state of the plumage at the time. Many thousand pounds weight of it are annually exported for quilts, pillows, cushions, &c. It sells in Iceland at from 10/6 to 17/6 per ℔. From three to four ℔s. are sufficient for a coverlet, which, to be enjoyed in perfection, ought to be used unquilted and loose like a feather bed. Quilting is only useful where a small quantity of down is required to go a long way; but, with three or four pounds at command, there is no comparison in point of comfort between loose and quilted—we have tried both. The

eider coverlet combines lightness and warmth in a degree
which cannot be otherwise obtained. With a single
sheet and blanket, it is sufficient for the coldest wintry
night. Its elasticity is proverbial; hence the Icelandic
conundrum we had propounded to us by our good friend
Mr. Jacobson, "What is it that is higher when the head
is taken off it?" *Answer*—"An eider-down pillow!"

In walking along we saw some young ladies, in elegant
Parisian costume, out sunning themselves like butterflies.
The thermometer stood at 72°, so, light coloured fancy
parasols were in requisition and enjoyed no sinecure
to-day, even in Iceland. Single days here are sometimes
very bright and warm, though rarely without showers;
for the weather is very changeable, and summer short at
best. Less rain falls in the northern part of the island
than in the southern; because the mountains in the
south first catch and empty the rain clouds floating from
the south-west over the course of the gulf-stream. For
this reason there is more sunshine in the north, crops too
are heavier and earlier; for, notwithstanding the 3°
higher latitude, the summer temperature is nearly the
same as that of the south. In winter, however, it is
colder, from the presence of Spitzbergen icebergs and
Greenland ice-floes stranded on the shore, while the sea
to the north and east is filled with them. Last winter
was very severe: the south and west were also filled.
My friend Dr. Mackinlay has treated this subject—the
the climate of Iceland—so admirably, that I cannot
refrain from quoting his MS. notes:

"The number and size of the rivers" says he, "cannot
fail to strike the attention of every visitor who sees much
of the country especially along the coasts. The main

cause of this is, of course, the abundant rain-fall which is out of all proportion to the latitude of Iceland.

"This excess is owing to two causes—The mountainous nature of the country; and its geographical position. Iceland lies in the direct course of one of the branches of the gulf-stream. No land intervenes between it and the Bermudas. The rain-charged clouds from the south-west are therefore ready to part with their moisture as soon as they touch the shores of Iceland. As they move northwards, to the back-bone of the island, their temperature diminishes so rapidly that the whole of their moisture becomes precipitated. Winds from the S.W., S., and S.E., drench the southern part of the Island, but bring fair weather to the north.

"As the southernly winds are the most frequent, the north side enjoys the greatest number of sunny days in summer; and hence vegetation is more luxuriant there, even though the latitude is 3° higher, and the southernly winds are chilled in passing over the great mountain chain. The mean summer temperature of the north is almost as high as that of the south; but the mean temperature of the year is 14° lower. In the south this is 47°, but in the north it is 33°. The climate of the south is insular in its character, while that of the north is continental. Severe continuous frosts are rare about Reykjavik; while along the north coast the winters are very severe. The severity of the winters is mainly caused by the presence of ice in the adjoining seas. The cold Arctic current from Spitzbergen, which impinges on the north coast, comes freighted in winter with an occasional iceberg; while the westerly winds and the west Icelandic branch of the gulf-stream combine to fill the seas to the north and east of the island with ice floes from Greenland. In ordinary winters, the seas to the south and east are open; but in extraordinary winters they also are filled. Such a winter was that of 1858-9. The corresponding winter in Britain was very mild, and owed its mildness to the same cause which produced the hard winter of Iceland—the unusual prevalence of westerly winds.

"In the first months of 1859, the sea between Greenland and Iceland—200 miles wide—was packed with ice floes; and upon these several bears made their way across to Iceland. Floating ice surrounded the island; but along the north coast the sea itself was frozen so far out that the people of Grimsey, twenty miles or so from the nearest point of Iceland, actually rode across to the mainland. At Akur Eyri in the beginning of April, Réaumur's thermometer registered 26° of cold—a temperature equal to $26\frac{1}{2}°$ of Fahrenheit. So late as June, seven French fishing boats were lost in the ice on the north coast, and a French ship of war nearly met with the same fate. Speaking of northern ice, Captain Launay, of the French man-of-war referred to, told me that its approach could be foreseen at the distance of twenty-five to thirty miles by a peculiar reflection of the sky. As the distance diminishes, the sky gets overcast, the temperature falls rapidly, and fish and sea-fowl disappear. The Greenland ice is much more dangerous than the Spitzbergen. The latter is 120 to 150 feet high, massive and wall-sided, but of no great extent. The former is in immense floes, often forming bays in which ships are caught as in a snare. It seldom exceeds 40 feet in height; but is jagged and peaked. Sometimes drift-timber gets nipped between the floes, and is set fire to by the violent friction it sustains. The sound of the crushing ice was described by Captain Launay as most horrible."

Thus much of the climate.

Dr. Mackinlay took Mr. Haycock and me to call for the Governor, the Count Von Trampe, who is a Dane, and well known for his urbanity to strangers. He kindly introduced us to his family. The house itself resembles, and at once suggests pictures we have seen of missionaries' houses in Madagascar. Within doors, however, all is tasteful and elegant. One peculiarity is worth noting, viz.: that the walls of his suite of apartments are covered with *French* portraits, paintings, engravings, and lithographs, nearly all presentations. In the public room, I only observed one that was not French. Judging from the walls, we might have been in the residence of a French Consul. French frigates are put on this station, year after year, ostensibly to look after the fisheries. Great court is paid to the leading islanders, and France would fain be in the ascendant here as elsewhere. Iceland, meanwhile, costs Denmark an outlay of several thousands a year; because, say some of the Icelanders, more is not invested in improvements of various kinds in order to make it pay. This state of matters would render negotiations easy on the part of Denmark, were the acquisition of the island an object to France. It would be an easy method of paying for assistance rendered in any Holstein difficulty or other cunningly laid European mine that may yet explode; when the cause of justice and right, as it ever is, being declared all on the side of France, she will disinterestedly go forward with her eagles for freedom and glory.

Such contingencies may arise, although the Danes are
our natural allies and our Scandinavian brethren. It may
be asked, what would the French do with the island?
It would be chiefly useful to them for forming and
training hardy seamen for the navy, as they already do
to some extent both here and on the Newfoundland
coast where the fisheries are maintained and subsidized
for that very purpose. It would furnish a station in the
North Sea, from which to descend and menace our
North American traffic; and it contains extensive
sulphur mines, which, in the event of Sicily being shut
against us, are available for munitions of war in our
gunpowder manufactories; in another point of view, it
is invaluable, as the great salmon-preserve of Europe.

Intelligent Icelanders who cherish the memory of
their ancient freedom, to my certain knowledge, regard
all such French tendencies and contingencies with
decided aversion. But in the event of a transfer being
mooted, would the Icelanders be consulted in the matter?
I fear not, and that it would only be announced to them
in the French fashion, as *fait accompli*: may such
however, never be the fate of this interesting island!

These remarks, although suggested here by the
pictures in the Governor's drawing-room, have no
reference, it is right to state, to the Count Von Trampe's
views on this subject, which I do not happen to know;
nor on the other hand, to the officers' of the vessels
stationed here, who all seem to be gentlemanly kind-
hearted fellows. A variety of facts and observations,
however, all tended to confirm me in this impression;
besides, it is the policy which the French are pursuing
elsewhere.

From the Governor's, we proceed to call for Mr. Randröp, the states apothecary, and receive a most hospitable, true, northern welcome. We meet several French officers and see the usual quantum of French prints on the walls. But he is the French consul or agent. Coffee, cakes, and wine, are handed round to us *by the ladies*, this being the custom of the country, and in drinking to us, the form is always, "Welcome to Iceland." Mr. Randröp speaks a little English, and the two young ladies, his step-daughters, are acquiring it. Here, as in Germany, the class book in common use is "The Vicar of Wakefield." Madame Randröp, who speaks French and German and plays on the piano-forte, shewed us several beautiful silver trinkets, bracelets, pins, &c., of Icelandic manufacture; the style an open mediaeval looking fretwork, that might satisfy the most fastideous artistic taste.

The Governor's house and Mr. Randröp's are the two centres of Reykjavik society, and at one or other of them, of an evening, any stranger visiting these parts is almost certain to be found. One is expected to make quite a round of visits if he be authenticated, or have any sort of introduction to any one of the circle; an omission would even be regarded as a slight. Hence Dr. Mackinlay took us to call for a considerable number of people, all of whom were cordial and glad to see us.

Our next visit was to the Rev. Olaf Pálsson, Dean and Rector of the Cathedral. Learned, intelligent, communicative and obliging, he at once, in the kindest manner possible, placed himself at our service and offered us every assistance in his power. In his library I observed many standard works of reference in various languages, and opened several volumes that seemed to recognize me as a friend whom they had met before: "Lord Dufferin's Letters from High Latitudes"—a presentation copy—"Caird's Sermons;" "Life of the Rev. Ebenezer Henderson"—the Icelandic traveller; "Stanley's Sinai and Palestine," &c. The worthy pastor both speaks and writes English fluently, and has translated a number of Icelandic stories and fairy tales.[1]

The Pastor's honest ruddy face, light flaxen hair, and unassuming manner; his rosy cheeked children, the monthly roses in the window-sill, and the library—all go to form a pleasing picture in the Walhalla of memory. He afterwards accompanied us to call for Rector Jonson. The Rector is a good specimen of the genus homo; tall and burly, while his active mind is vigorous, inquisitive, and accomplished. He showed us over various rooms, where the different branches are taught, some of them containing cabinets of geological and zoological specimens. The school is supported by government; and about sixty select young men intended for the church and other learned professions here receive a free education; a few of them only go to Copenhagen yet further to complete their studies.

Although the island contains 64,603 inhabitants, this, as we have said, is the only Academy or College; and there is not a single juvenile school.

The population is so widely scattered that schools would be quite impracticable; for the six thousand farms which the island contains, on the habitable coast belt which surrounds the central deserts, are often separated

---

[1] For a selection of these, see Appendix.

from each other by many dreary miles of lava wastes and rapid rivers dangerous to ford.

Parents, however, all teach their children to read and write by the fire-side on the long winter evenings, as they themselves were taught; and the people are thus home educated from generation to generation, and trained to habits of intellectual activity from their youth. Thus, as a mass, the Icelanders are without doubt the best educated people in the world.

For six centuries the Icelanders have evidenced their love of literature by writing and preserving old Sagas and Eddas;—by producing original works on mythology, law, topography, archaeology, &c.—several of these at once the earliest and best of their kind in Europe; and by executing many admirable translations from the classics.

Such literary labours have often been carried on by priests in remote districts, who subsist on a miserable pittance, and dwell in what we would consider mere hovels,—men who are obliged to work, at outdoor manual labour, the same as any of their neighbour peasants and parishoners, in order to keep the wolf from the door. Henderson found Thorláksson, the translator of "Paradise Lost," busy making hay. His living only yielded him £7 per annum, and the one room in which he slept and wrote was only eight feet long by six broad. This translation was not printed till after his death. Verily good work lovingly done is its own reward. These men had little else to cheer them on.

We next visited the Cathedral, which stands in the back part of the town, with an open square space in front of it, and a little fresh water lake—inland—to the left. It is a modern edifice, built of brick, plastered. At the entrance we were joined by our friend Professor Chadbourne. The interior is very neatly fitted up with pews, has galleries, organ, &c.; and can accommodate three or four hundred people.

An oil painting above the communion table represents the resurrection; but the only object of artistic interest is a white marble baptismal font, carved and presented to the Cathedral by Thorwaldsen, whose father was an Icelander. It is a low square obelisk. The basin on the top is surrounded with a symbolical wreath of passion-flowers and roses, delicately carved in high relief out of the white marble. On the front is represented, also in relief, the baptism of our Saviour by St. John; on the left side, the Madonna and Child, with John the Baptist as an infant standing at her knee; on the right, Christ blessing little children; while at the back, next the altar, are three cherubs, and underneath them is inscribed the following legend: "Opus haec Romae fecit, et Islandiae, terrae sibi gentiliacae, pietatis causâ, donavit Albertus Thorvaldsen, anno MDCCCXXVII." It is a chaste and beautiful work of art.

In the vestry the Rev. Olaf Pálsson opened several large chests, and shewed us numerous vestments belonging to the bishop and priests; one of these with gorgeous embroideries had been sent here to the bishop by Pope Julius II. in the beginning of the sixteenth century. The cloth was purple velvet, embroidered and stiff with brocade of gold.

Above the church, immediately under the sloping roof, an apartment runs the whole length of the building. In it is deposited the free public library of Reykjavik, which consists of more than 6000 volumes in Icelandic, Danish,

Latin, French, English, German, and various other languages. A copy of every book published at Copenhagen is sent here by government, and from time to time it receives numerous presentations from foreigners. The ancient original Icelandic MSS. have all been removed to Denmark, so that here there is now nothing very old to be seen, except what has been reprinted. With great interest we turned over the leaves of a copy of Snorre Sturleson's "Heimskringla," and the "Landnáma Bok," shewn us by the librarian and learned scholar Mr. Jón Arnason.

The hotel at Reykjavik is merely a kind of tavern, with a billiard room for the French sailors to play, lounge, and smoke in; a large adjoining room, seated round, for the Reykjavik fashionable assemblies; a smaller room up stairs, and some two or three bedrooms. On reaching it we were received by the landlord and shewn up stairs, where we found Mr. Bushby, who gave us a most courteous English welcome, notwithstanding our unintentional intrusion. He had, that morning, when the steamer came in sight, set out and ridden along the coast from the sulphur mines at Krisuvik—perhaps one of the wildest continuous rides in the world—to meet Captain Forbes.

Knowing the scant accommodation at the landlord's disposal, he at once placed the suite of rooms he had engaged at our service, to dress and dine in, thus proving himself a friend in need. A good substanial dinner was soon under weigh, and rendered quite a success by the many good things with which Mr. Bushby kindly supplimented it, contributing them from his own private stores.

Mr. Gísli Brynjúlfsson, the young Icelandic poet—employed in antiquarian researches by the Danish Government chiefly at Copenhagen, but at present here because he is a member of the Althing or Parliament now sitting—joined us at table, having been invited by Dr. Mackinlay. He speaks English fluently, and gave us much interesting information. He kindly presented me with a volume "Nordurfari," edited by himself and a friend, and containing amongst other articles in prose and verse, "Bruce's Address at Bannockburn," translated into Icelandic, in the metre of the original. This northern version of Burns' poem may interest the reader.[1]

BANNOCK-BURN
'AVARP ROBERT BRUCE TIL HERLITHS SINS.
EPTIR BURNS.

Skotar, er Wallace vördust med
Vig med Bruce opt hafid sjed ;
Velkomnir ad blódgum bod,
    Bjartri eda sigurfraegd !

Stund og dagur dýr nú er ;
Daudinn ógnar hvar sem sjer ;
Jatvards ad oss aedir her—
    Ok og hlekkja naegd !

Hverr vill bera nidings nafn ?
Ná hver bleydu sedja hrafu ?
Falla thrael órfjálsum jafn ?
    Flýti hann burtu sjer !

Hverr vill hlinur Hildar báls
Hjör nu draga hins góda mála,
Standa baedi og falla frjáls ?
    Fari hann eptir mjer !

[1] Where the two Icelandic letters occur which are wanting in the English alphabet, they are here represented, respectively, by d and th.

E

Ánaudar vid eymd og grönd!
Ydar sona thrældóms bönd!
Vjer viljum láta lif og önd,
    Eu leysa úr hlekkjum thá!

Fellid grimma fjendur thví!
Frelsi er hverju höggí í!
Sjái oss hrósa sgiri ný
    Sól, eda ordna ad ná!

After finally arranging with Zöga to start for the
Geysers at 8 o'clock next morning, Dr. Mackinlay, Mr.
Haycock, Professor Chadbourne and I took a walk through
the town, called for Dr. Hjaltelin, who unfortunately was
not at home, and strolled along to the church-yard.   It is
surrounded by a low stone and turf wall.   We gathered
forget-me-nots, catch-flies, saxifrage and buttercups
among the grass; observed artificial flowers, rudely made
of muslin and worsted, stuck upon a grave, but do not
know if this is an Icelandic custom or the work of the
stranger over the last resting place of a comrade.

Looking down upon Reykjavik from the elevation on
which we stand all is bright in the mellow glare of
evening; the windows of the houses gleam in the sun
like the great jewel of Ghiamsheed; the near Essian
mountains have a ruddy glow, and the bay, intensely
blue, is gay with vessels and flags.

Gazing inland all is one wild dreary black lava waste—
miles upon miles of bog, stones and blocks of rock.
Botanized for an hour with the Professor.

On returning saw several heaps of large cod-fish heads,
piled up near the sod-roofed houses of the fishermen in
the outskirts of the town.   On enquiry we were told that
the heads of fish dried for exportation are thus retained;

the people here eat them, and one head is said to be a good breakfast for a man.

Most of the houses in and around Reykjavik have little plots of garden-ground surrounded with low turf walls. In these we generally observed common vegetables such as parsley, turnips, potatoes, cresses, a few plants for salads, &c.; here and there a currant bush, and sometimes a few annuals or other flowers. These, however, seldom come to any great degree of perfection, and are often altogether destroyed; for the climate is severe and very changeable, especially in the southern portion of the island.

REYKJAVIK.

The Governor called at the hotel for Mr. Haycock and me, insisted on us taking the loan of his tent, and kindly invited us to come along and spend the evening with him. As we had to start in the morning for the Geysers for the present we declined the proferred hospitality, but promised to call on our return.

As there was not accommodation for us at the hotel, we were rowed off to the "Arcturus" by the indefatigable Zöga at half-past 10 o'clock at night, and slept on board.

ICELANDIC LADY IN FULL DRESS.

ROUTE TO THINGVALLA.

RIDE TO THE GEYSERS.

Friday morning, July 29. Landed from the
steamer between 7 and 8 o'clock, and found the baggage
and riding horses with the relays, twenty-four in all,
assembled at the hotel court; Zöga the guide, with his
brother and a boy who were also to accompany us, busy
adjusting saddles, stirrup straps, &c. For four days we
shall be thrown entirely upon our own resources, so that
provisions, tent, plaids and everything we are likely to
need during a wilderness journey, must be taken with
us. Our traps had been sent on shore late on the
previous evening. The mode of loading the sumpter
ponies is peculiar; a square piece of dried sod is placed
on the horses back, then a wooden saddle with several
projecting pins is girded on with rough woollen ropes; to

either side of the saddle, is hooked on, a strong oblong
wooden box generally painted red; while on the pins are
hung bags, bundles, and all sorts of gipsy looking gear.
These need frequent re-adjustment from time to time;
as the ponies trot along, one side will weigh up the
other, or the animals get jammed together and knock
their loads out of equilibrium, the saddles then perhaps
turn round and articles fall rattling to the ground. The
strong little boxes are constructed and other arrangements made with a view to such contingencies, and
however primitive, rude, or outlandish they may at first
seem to the stranger, he will soon come to see the why
and the wherefore, and confess their singular adaptation
to the strange and unique exigences of Icelandic travel.

The baggage train at length moved off, accompanied
by the relief ponies, which were tied together in a row,
the head of the one to the tail of the other before it.

Dr. Mackinlay, Mr. Bushby, Mr. Sievertsen, and
other acquaintances came to see us start. Equipped
with waterproofs and wearing caps or wide-awakes, no
two of us alike, at half-past eight o'clock, a long straggling line of non-descript banditti-looking cavaliers, all
in excellent spirits and laughing at each others odd
appearance, we rode at a good pace out of Reykjavik.

"Rarely it occurs that any of us makes this journey
on which I go,"[1] words spoken to Dante by his guide,
in the ninth Canto of the *Inferno*, forcibly suggested
themselves to me as I "entered on the arduous and
savage way," and gazed around on the "desert strand."

[1] "Di rado
Incontra, me rispose, che di nui
Faccia il cammino alcun per quale io vado." L 19-21.

The road terminated when we reached the outskirts of the town, and the track lay over a wild black stony waste with little or no vegetation; everything seemed scorched. The relay ponies were now loosed from each other, and, perfectly free, driven before us like

"A wild and wanton herd,
Or race of youthful and unhandled colts,
Fetching mad bounds, bellowing and neighing loud,
Which is the hot condition of their blood."

They were apt to scatter in quest of herbage, but Zöga, when his call was not enough or the dogs negligent, quickly out-flanked the stragglers, upon which, they, possessed by a salutary fear of his whip, speedily rejoined their fellows.

We soon lost sight of the sea, and in a short time came to the Lax-elv—or salmon river—which we forded.

Enormous quantities of fish are taken at the wears a little higher up where there are two channels and an arrangement for running the water off, first from the one and then from the other, leaving the throng of fishes nearly dry in a little pool from which they are readily taken by the hand. The fishermen wear rough woollen mittens to prevent the smooth lithe fish from slipping through their fingers when seizing them by head and tail, to throw them on shore. From five hundred to a thousand fishes are sometimes taken in a day. The fishery is managed by an intelligent Scotchman sent here by a merchant in Peterhead who leases the stream and has an establishment of some. fifteen tin-smiths constantly at work making cans for "preserved salmon." The fish are cut into pieces, slightly boiled—then soldered and hermetically sealed up in these tin cases containing

say 2 or 4 ℔s. each, and sent south packed in large
hogsheads to be distributed thence over the whole world.

The few grass-farms we saw were like hovels;
many separate erections, stone next the ground, the gable
wood, and the roof covered with green sod. The rafters
are generally made of drift wood or whale's ribs. Turf
is used as fuel; but in common Icelandic houses there is
only one fire—that in the kitchen—all the year round.
The beds are often mere boxes ranged around the
room, or, where there is such accommodation, underneath
the roof round the upper apartment, which is approached
by a trap-stair. They are filled with sea-weed or feathers
and a cloth spread over them. In the farm houses we
entered there was a sad want of light and fresh air; in
fact, these sleeping rooms were so close and stifling that
we were glad to descend and rush out to the open air
for breath.

The little bit of pet pasture land, round each farm,
enclosed by a low turf wall, is called "tun," a word still
used in rural districts of Scotland—spelt toon, or town—
with the same sound and similar signification.

Rode many miles through wild black desolate dreary
volcanic wastes—no near sounds but the metallic bicker
of our ponies' hoofs over the dry rocks and stones, or
fearless splashing through mud puddles—and no distant
sounds save the *eerie* cries, tremulous whistlings and
plaintive wails of the curlew, plover, and snipe. Observed
the abrasions of the ice-drift very distinctly traced on
the rocks, these all running nearly south-west. The
slightly elevated rock-surface was frequently polished
quite smooth, scratches here and there showing the
direction of the friction by which this appearance had

been produced. In some instances the rock was left bare, in others detached stone blocks of a different formation rested on the surface.

Wild geranium, saxifrage, sedum, and tufts of sea-pink are very common, when we come to anything green. The wild geranium, from the almost nightless summer of the north, is six times larger than in Britain, and about the size of a half-penny.

RAVINE.

Came to a deep ravine, wild, horrid, and frightful; rode along the edge of it, and then through dreadfully rough places, with nothing to mark the track; amidst great and little blocks of stone—trap, basalt, and lava—mud-puddles—up-hill, down-hill, fording rivers, and through seemingly impassible places; yet the Icelandic horse goes unflinchingly at it. Mr. Haycock says it would be sheer madness to attempt such break-neck places in England; there, no horse would look at it; steeple-chasing nothing to it. His horse was repeatedly up to the girths in clayey mud, and recovered itself notwithstanding its load as if it were nothing to pause about. Truly these are wonderful animals, they know their work and do it well.

Came to a grassy plot, in a hollow by a river's side, where we halted, changed the saddles and bridles to the relief ponies, and, clad in mackintosh, thankfully sat down on the wet grass to rest, while we ate a biscuit and drank of the stream. In the course of the day, we had come to several green spots, like oasis in the black desert, where the horses rested for a short time to have a feed of grass.

After starting, ascended for about an hour through a ravine, where we saw some lovely little glades full of *blae-berries*—sloe,—low brushwood, chiefly of willows and birch, and a profusion of flowers, such as wild geranium, thyme, dog-daisy, saxifrage, sea-pink, catch-fly, butter-cup, a little white starry flower, and *diapensia;* the latter is found, here and there, in round detached patches of fresh green like a pincushion, gaily patterned with little pink flowers. I am indebted to Professor Chadbourne for the name of it. Obtained a root of this plant for home, and gathered flowers of the others to preserve.

We now came to an elevated plateau which stretched away—a dreary stony moor—bounded in one direction by the horizon-line and in another by hills of a dark brown colour. Here there was not a patch of verdure to be seen; all one black desert lava-waste strewn with large boulders and angular slabs, lying about in all conceivable positions. In riding, one required to keep the feet in constant motion, to avoid contact with projecting stones, as the ponies picked their way among them. Our feet consequently were as often out of the stirrups as in them. Shakspere says "Wisely and slow, they stumble that run fast;" not so, however, with the sure footed Icelandic ponies; for, even over such ground, they trotted at a good pace and no accident befell us. ·

I generally rode first with Zöga the guide, or last with Professor Chadbourne. The driving of the relief horses before us, like a stampedo, and the keeping of them together afforded some of us much amusement as we rode along. Here no sheep or cattle could live. It was literally "a waste and howling wilderness." We saw several snow-birds and terns flying about, and often heard the *eerie* plaintive whistle of the golden plover. These birds were very tame and examined us with evident curiosity. They would perch on a large lava block before us, quite close to our track, and sit till we came up and passed—then fly on before, to another block, and sit there gazing in wonder; and so on for miles. They had evidently never been fired at. Mr. Murray humanely remarked that it would be murder to shoot them! In this black stony plateau there was often not the least vestige of a track discernible; but we were kept in the right direction by cairns of black stones placed here and there on slight elevations. These guiding marks— "varder" as they are called—are yet more needed when all the surface is covered with snow; then, "vexed with tempest loud," Iceland must resemble Milton's description of Chaos.

> "Far off,
> Dark, waste and wild under the frown of night,
> Starless exposed and ever threatening storms
> Of Chaos blustering round."

We saw one rude house of refuge, without any roof, built of lava blocks, in the midst of this black desert where everything seemed blasted. Came now on spots where a few tufts of sea pinks, and many bright coloured wild-flowers were springing up among the stones. Saw flat rock-surfaces shrivelled up and wrinkled like pitch, an effect which had evidently been produced when the lava was cooling; others were ground down and polished smooth in grooves by the ice-drift. As near as I can calculate, some fourteen or fifteen miles of our journey lay over this one long long dreary stony waste, henceforth, ever to be associated in memory with the plover's wild lone plaintive tremulous whistle.

At 3 P.M. we came in sight of the blue lake of Thingvalla,[1] lying peacefully in the valley before us; while the range of the hills beyond it, bare, bold and striking in their outline, was mostly of a deep violet colour.

During the day, arrowy showers of drenching rain "cold and heavy," like that described by Dante in the third circle of the *Inferno*, or wet drizzling mists had alternated with gleams of bright clear sunshine. Towards the afternoon the weather had become more settled and the effect of the prospect now before us, although truly lovely in itself, was heightened by our previous monotonous though rough ride over the dreary stony plateau. The lake far below us, with its two little volcanic islands Sandey and Nesey, lay gleaming in the sun like a silver mirror; while the wild scenery around forcibly reminded us of Switzerland or Italy.

Thingvalla was to be our resting place for the night, and seeing our destination so near at hand in the valley

---

[1] Pronounced Tingvatla.

below us, some one purposed a rapid scamper, that we might the sooner rest, eat, and afterwards have more leisure to explore the wondrous features of the place. Forthwith we set off at a good pace, but the Professor was too tired to keep up with us, so I at once fell behind to bear him company. The others were speedily out of sight. Knowing that dinner preparations would occupy Zöga for some time after his arrival, we rode leisurely along, admiring the green level plain far below us. When wondering how we were to get down to it, we suddenly and unexpectedly came to a yawning chasm or rent running down through the edge of the plateau. It seemed about 100 feet deep, 100 feet wide, and was partially filled with enormous blocks of basalt which had toppled down from either side; where more, cracked and dissevered, still impended, as if they might fall with a crash at the slightest noise or touch. This was the celebrated Almanna Gjá or Chasm, of which we had read so much but of which we had been able to form no adequate idea from descriptions.

Of a scene so extraordinary, indeed unique, I can only attempt faithfully to convey my own impressions, without hoping to succeed better than others who have gone before me.

Let the reader imagine himself, standing on the stony plateau; below him stretches a beautiful verdant valley, say about five miles broad, and about 100 feet below the level on which he is standing; to the right before him also lies the lake which we have been skirting for some miles in riding along. It is in size about ten miles each way, and is bounded by picturesque ranges of bare volcanic hills. This whole valley has evidently sunk down in one mass to its present level, leaving exposed a section of the rent rocks on either side of the vale. These exposed edges of the stony plateau running in irregular basaltic strata, and with fantastic shapes on the top like chimneys and ruined towers, stretch away like black ramparts for miles, nearly parallel to each other, with the whole valley between them, and are precipitous as walls, especially that on the left.

The top of the mural precipice, overlooking the gorge at our feet, is the original uniform level of the ground before the sinking of the valley. It forms the edge of the plateau which stretches away behind and also before us to the left of the precipice; for we look down the chasm lengthways, along the front of the rock-wall, and not at right angles from it. A mere slice of the rock has been severed and is piled up on our right, like a Cyclopian wall. It runs parallel with the face of the rent rock to which it formerly belonged, for, say, about the eighth of a mile N.E. from where we stand, and then terminates abruptly there in irregular crumbling blocks like a heap of ruins; while the trench or gjá itself also runs back in a straight line S.W. for about two miles, and terminates at the brink of the lake.

The N.E. side of the valley is the highest, and the S.W. the lowest—shelving beneath the blue water, and forming the bottom of the lake. The river Oxerâ, which thunders over the rock-wall on the right, forms a magnificent waterfall, and then flows peacefully across the south-west corner of the valley to the lake.

Between these two rock-walls—the left forming the real boundary of the valley on that side, but the right wall being only a slice severed from the left, and not the other boundary of the valley, which is situated about five miles distant—a long narrow passage descends, leading to the plain below. The flat bottom of this passage 100 feet deep is strewn with debris, but otherwise covered with tender green sward. The bottom is reached from the elevated waste where we stand by a very rough irregular winding incline plane—for although the descent is full of great blocks of stones, dreadfully steep, and liker a deranged staircase than anything else, we still call it a steep incline plane from the level of the plateau to the passage beneath which leads into the valley—high rock-walls rising on either' side as we descend. Entering the defile and moving along on level ground, the wall on the right, evidently rent from the other side as if sliced down with some giant's sword from the edge of the plateau, soon terminates in the valley; but that on the left runs on for many miles like a fire-scathed rampart. The stony plateau stretches back from the edge or level of the summit of this rock-wall, and the lovely green valley of Thingvalla extends from its base to the Hrafna Gjá or Raven's Chasm—the corresponding wall and fissure, like rampart and fosse—which bounds the other side of the valley.

I am thus particular, because certain descriptions led me to suppose that here we would encounter a precipice at right angles to our path, and have to descend the face of it, instead of descending an incline *parallel to its face*, from where the *stair* begins on the old level. As it is, however, it seemed quite steep enough, with the rock-walled incline reaching from the valley to our feet. This wild chasm is called the Almanna Gjá—all men's or ' main chasm; while the one on the other side of the

vale of Thingvalla is called the Hrafna Gjá or Raven's
Chasm. The whole character of the scene, whether
viewed by the mere tourist, or dwelt upon by the man
of science, is intensely interesting, and in several
respects quite unique; hence I have tried to describe it
so minutely.

When Professor Chadbourne and I came up to it, we
gazed down in awe and wonder. We knew that our
companions must have descended somehow, for there
was no other way: but how, we could not tell. Were we
to dismount and let the horses go first, they might
'escape and leave us; if we attempted to lead them down
they might fall on the top of us; to descend on foot
would be extremely difficult at any time, and dismount-
ing and mounting again at this stage of our proceedings,
was rather a formidable undertaking. "How shall we
set about it?" I asked my friend. "You may do as you
please," said he, "but I must keep my seat if I can."
"So shall I, for the horse is surer footed than I can
hope to be to-day." "Lead on then" said the Professor,
"and I'll follow!"

So leaving my pony to choose its steps, it slowly
picked its way down the steep gorge; zig-zagging from
point to point and crag to crag, or stepping from one
great block of stone to another. I was repeatedly
compelled to lean back, touching the pony's tail with
the back of my head, in order to maintain the perpen-
dicular, and avoid being shot forward, feet first, over its
head, among the rocks. Sometimes at steep places it
drew up its hind legs and slid down on its hams, many
loose stones rattling down along with us as the pony
kicked out right and left to keep its balance, and

made the sparks fly from its heels. Descending in silence, at last we reached the bottom in safety, thinking it rather a wild adventure in the way of riding, and one not to be attempted elsewhere.

DESCENT INTO THE ALMANNAGJA.

Looking back with awe and increasing wonder at the gorge we had descended, for it certainly was terrifically steep, we both remarked the cool indifference and utter absence of fear with which we had ridden down such a break-neck place. The fresh air and excitement prevent one from thinking anything about such adventures till they are over.

The high rock-walls, now hemming us in on either side, bore a considerable resemblance to the pictures of Petra —Wady Mousa—in Arabia, and here we could fancy mounted Bedouins riding up with their long matchlocks. All was silent as the grave. The ground was green with

F

tender herbage; great blocks of stone lay about, and others seemed ready to topple over and fall down upon us. Riding along, the rocks on the right soon terminated

ALMANNAGJA.

like a gigantic heap of burned ruins, and allowed us to gaze across the vale of Thingvalla, with the river Oxerâ in the foreground. Here we overtook our friends who told us that they had all dismounted and led their horses down the chasm, and would scarcely believe that we had ridden down. All of us were lost in wonder and struck with awe at the scenes we had witnessed. We forded the river in a row, following Zöga's guidance; and at 5 o'clock in the afternoon rode up to the priest's house on the other side. It was simply a farm, like others we had seen, consisting of a group of separate erections with wooden gables, green sod on the roof and the whole surrounded with a low stone wall coped with turf. Beside it was the silent churchyard with its simple grassy graves of all sizes. Immediately behind the house were piles of sawn timber, and several carpenters at work rebuilding the little church, which having become old and frail had been taken down. Its site was only about 25 feet by 10.

FORDING THE OXERA.

Zöga went in to tell the pastor of our arrival, leaving us to dismount in a deep miry lane between two rough stone walls leading to the house. He had been busy with his hay, but speedily appeared and hospitably offered us what shelter he could afford.

Zöga arranged for the grazing of the ponies; we were to dine in the largest room of the house, and he was to have the use of the kitchen fire to cook our dinner—the preserved meats, soups, &c.—which of course we had brought with us. The pastor provided a splendid trout from the river, to the great delectation of half a dozen travellers all as hungry as hawks.

Now commenced the unstrapping and unpacking, presided over by the indefatigable Zöga; boxes, bags, and packages, bespattered with mud, lay about singly and in piles. Everybody seemed to want something or other which was stowed away somewhere, and forthwith the patient obliging Zöga, in a most miraculous manner, never failed to produce the desiderated articles. Taking a rough towel and soap, I performed my ablutions in the river close by, while dinner was getting ready and felt quite refreshed. "Time and the hour runs through the roughest day," and this was certainly one to be marked in our calender. Shortly after 6 o'clock we dined and attempted some conversation in Latin with the priest, Mr. S. D. Beck. He is a pastor literally and metaphorically,

PRIEST'S HOUSE AT THINGVALLA.

farming and fishing as well as preaching. Hay, however, is the only crop which is raised here; and the Icelanders are consequently very dependent upon the hay-harvest. With their short summer they might not inappropriately quote Shakspeare's lines,

"The sun shines hot; and if we use delay
Cold biting winter mars our hoped for hay."

The scythe used by the Icelanders is quite straight and not half the length of ours. The numerous little hummocks, with which pasture land is covered, necessitate the use of a short implement, so that it may mow between and around them; the hillocks are from one to two feet high, and from one to four feet across. In some places the ground presents quite the appearance of a churchyard or an old battle-field. These elevations are occasioned by the winter's frost acting on the wet subsoil. If levelled they would rise again to the same height in about 7 or 8 years; but the farmers let them alone, because they fancy they get a larger crop from the greater superficial area of the field, and this old let-alone custom certainly saves them much labour. The primitive state of their agriculture, as well as the peculiar nature of the Icelandic soil, may be inferred from the fact, that there are only two ploughs in the whole island and no carts. A spade, a scythe two feet long, a small rake with teeth about an inch and a half deep, and ropes made of grass or hair to bind the hay, which is carried on men's backs or conveyed by horses to be stacked, are all that the farmer requires for his simple operations. The hay, especially that which grows in the tuns, is of fine quality, tender and nutritive; and, with even any ordinary attention to drainage, many a fertile vale could be made to yield much more than is now obtained from it. Latin was our only mode of communicating directly with the priest; but having had little colloquial practice of that kind, we blundered on, feeling that, in appropriating the stately language of Cicero and Virgil to creature comforts and the vulgar ongoings of daily life, we were almost committing a species of desecration: yet the ludicrous combinations and circumlocutions, grasped at in desperation to express modern things in a dead language, afforded us no little amusement. Professor Chadbourne, Mr. Murray, and myself got most of the work to do, and were often greeted with the pastor's goodnatured "Ita," or "Intelligo," when our propositions could not have been particularly remarkable for perspicacity. Amongst foreigners, charity covers a multitude of sins of this kind. We cannot however apply the same remark to our own countrymen, who are often more inclined to laugh at a foreigner's mistakes than to help him.

The fragrant tedded hay and the green vale of Thingvalla stretching before us were peculiarly refreshing to the eye, after the dreary rugged lava-wastes through which we had passed—where tracks of flat rocks were corrugated and shrivelled up like pitch, having been left so when the lava set; and where other rock-surfaces appeared ground and polished in grooves by the ice-drift; or where all was covered with a pack of lava blocks and slabs, of all sizes and lying in every conceivable direction,

After tea I walked out alone a little way north-west of the church to examine the Althing, on the upper part of which stands the Lögberg or sacred law hill, where, when the Parliament or Althing was assembled, the judges sat; and where justice was administered to the Icelanders for nearly 900 years; thus rendering Thing-valla, with its numerous associations and stirring memories, to speak historically, by far the most interesting spot in the island.

The Althing is a long sloping ridge of lava, about 200

feet long and from 30 to 50 broad, covered on the top
with the most tender herbage and flowers. At the end
next the church it is low and approachable, by climbing
over a few stones among and below which one can see
water, but it is entirely separated from the surrounding
plain by two deep perpendicular rocky fissures or chasms
running parallel on either side and joining at the further
end. Only at one place is the chasm so narrow—16 feet—
that, once on a time, Flosi, leader of the burners of
Njal's house, made his escape from justice by taking a
desperate leap. These chasms contain clear water, so
that the Althing is in fact a narrow peninsula, which
with the entrance guarded was as secure as a fortress.

ALTHING AND LÖGBERG FROM BEHIND THE CHURCH.

One looks sheer down, say 20 or 30 feet, to the surface
of the water in the chasms; while the water itself is from
80 to 90 feet deep, and in some places said to be un-
fathomable. These fissures run S.W. to the lake which

is about a mile distant. Through the water, one sees huge blocks of lava of a whitish blue colour and dark masses of basalt gleaming from the green depths. Beautiful tender fairy-like ferns grow on the edges and in the sheltered crevices of the rocks; and I gathered specimens of grasses, mosses, violets, butter-cups and for-get-me-nots, from the soft verdant carpet which covered the surface. Here, the Icelandic Parliament, such as it was, continued to meet, down to the year 1800, when the seat of government was finally removed to Reykjavik.

In the old palmy days, prior to A.D. 1261 when the island became subject to Norway, the Althing was the scene of many a spirited debate; affairs of the greatest import were here freely discussed, and finally disposed of, in open assembly. Thus, in the year A.D. 1000, after a stormy debate, it was determined that Christianity should be introduced as the religion of the island. Here, measures of general interest were proposed, taxes levied, law-suits conducted, the judgments of inferior courts revised, subordinate magistrates impeached for dereliction of duty and dismissed from their office; while criminals were tried, and if found guilty of capital offences were summarily executed. Criminals were beheaded on the little Island of Thorlevsholm in the Oxerâ; in a pool of the same river, female offenders, sewed in a sack, were drowned; and those condemned for witchcraft were precipitated from the top of a high rock on the east side of the Almannagjá.

The Althing commonly met in the middle of May and sat for 14 days. Every freeholder had a right to attend and express his opinion on measures under consideration: thus, at Thingvalla, friends and acquaintances from distant parts of the island—members and friends of both sexes—annually availed themselves of this opportunity of meeting each other. The people pitched their tents on the banks of the Oxerâ and in the plain around the Althing; so that a wild lone scene usually silent as the grave, for the time became quite a busy one, enlivened by the presence of nearly all the elite of the island.

Gazing from the Althing, so as to take in the general aspect of the wondrous scene around us, the whole valley seems obviously to have sunk down en masse to its present level. The tops of the two extreme wall-like boundaries, with chasms at their base, on either side of the vale, respectively called the Almannagjá and the Hrafnagjá, show the original height of the whole, and

LAKE OF THINGVALLA FROM THE LÖGBERG.

also exhibit a section of the rock. This view of the matter is proved by the fact, that the numerous cracks, rents, or fissures, such as those around the Althing, with which the valley is intersected, when examined are found exactly to correspond in their sections—trahytic trap capped by lava—with the edges left standing as they were before the subsidence of the valley and now bounding it like a black rampart. The pastor's dwelling, from where I stand, presents the appearance of a few grass hillocks or potato-pits. The site of each erection is partly excavated from the side of a little slope, to pro- tect it from the storm. Grass-turf covers the roofs, and the whole group of buildings is surrounded by a three- foot turf-wall; consequently, like many other Icelandic farms we have seen, little more than the roofs appear above ground. At midnight I made several sketches of the lake of Thingvalla; the river Oxerâ as it fell

WATERFALL OF THE OXERA, AS SEEN FROM THE LÖGBERG.

thundering over the dark rock-wall in a sheet of white foam; and the bare heights to the north-east, purple in the evening glow and mottled with snow patches.

On returning to the pastor's, I found my companions

fast asleep on the floor. The canvas tent which had been left by the French expedition served them for a bed, portmanteaus or packages were appropriated for pillows, and plaids and wrappers spread over them for blankets. They lay packed like herrings in a barrel. I stepped over them as quietly as I could, found an unoccupied space near the open window, speedily ensconced myself for the night, and in a few minutes sank into a well-earned and blessed state of obliviousness.

Saturday Morning, July 30.—Breakfasted and left Thingvalla at 9 A.M. The first five miles or so of our journey across the valley lay through low green brushwood, where the vegetation was fresh and luxuriant. This in Iceland is called a forest; but the trees, chiefly birches and willows, are all dwarfs. The birches were about 3 feet high, very few of them attaining to the height of 4 or 5 feet; the willows were of three kinds; one with a leaf resembling bog myrtle; the leaves of another white, green, and flossy—both these varieties only 10 to 12 inches high; while the third, although Professor Chadbourne assured me it was a genuine willow, was only about one and a half inches; we observed catkins on them all. Wild geraniums, forget-me-nots, butter-cups, the beautiful rose-coloured sedum so common in Iceland, clover, sea-pinks, &c., grew in profusion, and imparted to the whole the appearance of a rich fresh green coppice. When the ponies could snatch at a stray bite of grass as they passed along, in doing so, they would often at the same time take up a tree by the roots and carry it off in their mouths.

We came upon yawning chasms, every little way, where the rocks had been rent asunder; the cracks or fissures about 100 feet deep, 10 or 20 wide, dry, and all running in the same direction from the lake. These we either avoided, or crossed at places where blocks of stone had fallen in, so as to fill up part with debris, or form natural bridges which afforded as good footing as the most of the track we had ridden over. The lake of Thingvalla lay peacefully behind us on our right, fair as a silver mirror. Ascending a green bosky hill, where numerous hillocks around were clothed with low brushwood to the very top, we came to the Hrafnagjá, or Raven's chasm, which forms the eastern boundary of Thingvalla. It is a deep broad irregular abyss, several miles in length, and on the further side, high like a rampart. We got across it, and up to the level of the plateau, by picking our way over the ridge of an avalanche of rock and stones, which had fallen in, leaving gaps, rude arches, and frightful openings into the darkness beneath us; while, right and left, the chasm itself stretched away like the dry fosse of a giant's castle which, through successive ages, had withstood the assaults of all the rock-jötuns. Up this perilous way, steeper than a stair, winding, zig-zagging, doubling, leaping like cats from block to block, or standing for a second like goats with four feet on one stone to consider their next move, our patient ponies toiled upwards and took us safely across. Looking back, we bade adieu for a time to the lovely green vale of Thingvalla beneath us, and were lost in wonder, both at the wild savage grandeur of the chasm we had just crossed and at the surefootedness and pluck of our trusty little steeds.

The plateau now attained was of the same level as that over which we had passed before descending into

Thingvalla, but here, it did not extend very far, being bounded by irregular heights and bare hills.

Vegetation disappeared, everything seemed blasted. Plovers again sat quite close to us, or flitted past, uttering their shrill plaintive whistle; passing so near that we could distinctly observe the tremulous motion of their mandibles. The ponies stepped aside from holes in our very track, opening into hollow darkness, where stones thrown in were long heard striking against the sides. At one place, we came to a black cave 20 or 30 feet in size, arched right into and under great blocks of stone. It appeared to be a huge lava-blister which had taken its present shape in cooling. The bottom of the cave, protected from the warm rays of the sun, was covered with snow; and, for the same reason, white patches of snow lay in crevices of the bare rocky hills around us. The path now ascended flanking the sides of the hills on the left, while the whole region seemed fire-scathed and blasted. The hills and slopes were covered with dark volcanic sand, pulverized ashes, and slag, out of which abruptly rose irregular masses of rock. Here, leaving our horses, we turned aside to examine a small extinct crater or vent, called Tintron, crowning a little eminence to the right. In ascending it, we were up to the ancles in fine black sand or slag, which, yielding beneath the feet at every step, made walking extremely awkward, if not difficult. The crater itself was composed of great blocks of red and black vitrified lava, over which we looked down into the darkness as into Pluto's chimney. We threw in some large stones, but could not from their sound form an estimate of the depth. Perhaps this vent may be only a lava-blister which has burst on the top, instead of forming a cave like the other we lately saw. However, though small, it presented the appearance of a regular crater. From it, we saw, on the one side, the beautiful Lake of Thingvalla; and, on the other, the near hills opposite, with the slope between them and us all covered with black scoriæ.

After pocketing a few specimens of the lava, I made a rough sketch of the crater and gathered a sprig of wild

VENT OF TINTRON.

thyme, and a little white flower (*parnassia*), which was blooming all alone on its very brink. Mounting our ponies and descending for about an hour, on clearing the hillside we came in sight of a level plain of green meadow land, lying below us, shaped like a horse shoe, and occupying an area of 3 or 4 miles. It appeared to have been submerged at no very distant period, and, like other Icelandic valleys, was sadly in want of drainage.

The rocky hill-range, which at the same time came into view on the left and formed the boundary of the plain, was one of the most singular I ever beheld. It was composed of black, yellow, and red volcanic rock; rising in fantastic cones, or receding into savage gorges, steep, abrupt, and angular. The surface was absolutely without vegetation of any kind, and every cleavage, rent or crevice, so fresh, bare, and unweathered, one could fancy that the rocks had only during the last hour been smitten, shattered, and splintered by Thor's hammer; while the rich effect of their vari-coloured tints was heightened by the pure white clouds which incense-like were now muffling and rolling about their summits, and by the verdure which extended to their base like a carpet. Our track lay along the foot of them, and wonder only increased as we obtained a nearer view of their Tartarian wildness.

Here we halted, and I made a slight sketch of a por-

VARI-COLOURED HILLS.

tion of the range. As a mere study of light and shade, to say nothing of other striking features, the scene would have made a magnificent photograph.

Starting, we rode on, till we reached the end of the cinder range, doubled the outmost spur, and, after ascending for sometime, came in sight of gently sloping hills. Their flowing outlines were covered with verdure to the very top, and, from our path, opened up here and there into little green bosky valleys "where the blae-berries grow." Before us, in a vast level plain which stretched away from the roots of the hills near to the horizon, lay the Lauger-vatn; and further to the south, linked by a river, the Apa-vatn, a lake much larger; while several other rivers meandered in gleaming serpen-tine courses over the vast green prairie-like meadow.

On the brink of the Lauger-vatn are several hot springs from which it takes its name. We observed columns of white steam rising from them on the brink next us, just below the farm of Laugervalla; and also across on the other side of the lake. Approaching the farm, we halted, outside the tun, to lunch, rest for an hour and let the horses graze. It presented the usual appearance of Icelandic farms; not unlike an irregular group of potato-pits or tumuli. The roofs were of the same colour as the plain, and the whole shut in from the surrounding pasture land by a rude four-foot wall, also covered on the top with green turf. The tun, or few acres thus enclosed, receives a top-dressing of manure and bears a luxuriant crop of hay; the rest is left in a state of nature, and reaped without sowing. The hay, when stacked, is protected from the rain by thin slices or strips of turf from 6 to 10 feet long. Nearly all Ice-landic farming has reference to the rearing of stock— the summer being too short for grain to reach maturity.

A few words, here, while we rest, as to Icelandic Farms in general.

Most farms have a weaving room, a smithy, a milk room, a sitting room—used also for eating and sleeping in —called stofa; a guest-chamber, cattle-houses, which are sometimes placed immediately under the sleeping-room but more frequently detached, and a kitchen; which last my friend Dr. Mackinlay neatly describes as often "a dingy dark place, with a peat fire on a lava block, and a hole in the roof to let in light and let out smoke." The turf is inferior; wood is too scarce and valuable to be much used for fuel. Coal costs £5 per ton, is retailed in small packages at about 2d. per pound, and is only used in smithies. When turf is not available, the Icelanders, like the Arabs, burn dried cows' dung; and on the coast, where even that is scarce, they use the dried carcases of sea-fowl. Why do they not burn dried sea-weed, which is extensively used for fuel in the Channel Islands?

Their daily food is taken cold, and consists chiefly of raw dried stockfish and skier. The latter dish is simply milk allowed to become acid and coagulate, and then hung up in a bag till the whey runs off. In this form it is both nutritive and wholesome, being more easily digested than sweet milk; while, to those who take to it, it is light, palatable and delightfully cooling. Milk is prepared in this way by the Shetlanders, who in the first stage call it "run milk," and when made into skier "hung milk." The same preparation is made use of by the Arabs, and it is also the chief diet of the Kaffirs and Bechuanas at the Cape. Our idea that milk is useless or hurtful when soured is merely an ignorant prejudice. Those who depend for their subsistence

G

chiefly on milk diet, and have the largest experience, prefer to use it sour, and medical authority endorses their choice. In Icelandic farms hard black rye bread is at times produced as a luxury; butter is always cured without salt, and used rancid, however, after it reaches a certain mild stage it gets no worse; meat is dried at certain seasons of the year for occasional use, and the rivers abound in excellent fish. The chief use to which the kitchen fire is put, is to prepare a cup of warm coffee. Snaps, sugar candy, coffee, grain, and other foreign commodities, they obtain at the factories.

The scarcity of fuel tempts people to crowd together for heat; sometimes 15 or 16 people in one small sleeping apartment, and that often placed over another where cattle are kept. The state of such an atmosphere may be imagined, while many dirty habits and the frequent recourse to stimulants are thus accounted for. Nor will any one wonder much, although there were no other causes, that, in one district of the south, 75 per cent of all the children born die before they complete their twelfth month.

As for indoor occupations, the farmers, as in colonial outposts, of necessity are Jacks-of-all-trades. They forge scythes, make saddles and bridles, make their simple household furniture, horse-shoe nails, and even build or repair their own houses. Females do the tailoring, but men make their own shoes and take their turn at the spinning wheel, the knitting needles, and the loom. All work together by lamplight, while some one reads aloud some old-world story. The out-door occupations are both fishing and farming. The ver-tima, or fishing season, lasts from February till May, and is chiefly carried on, on the south-west coast, which, from thus becoming a source of wealth, is called Guld-bringu—or the gold bringing—Sysla. At the beginning of the season, men move down to the fishing stations. The boats have each from 4 to 10 oars, and crews of from 10 to 20 men.

Lines only are used, and the fish caught are chiefly cod and ling. Part are salted and dried for exportation, part dried for home use without salt and left at the stations to be fetched at midsummer, when many people resort to the annual fair for the sale of produce, or rather the exchange of commodities. The deep sea fishing is not prosecuted by the Icelanders, but is chiefly carried on by the Norwegians, French, and Dutch. All journeys are performed on horseback.

These statements will enable the reader to form an idea of the ongoings of daily life in the numerous farms, which are scatteued over the habitable belt of pasture-
-land which nearly surrounds the island.

Through Zöga, we had an interview with the farmer, and arranged for the grazing of the ponies on the farm of Laugervalla. A girl brought out a large basin of skier, together with a plentiful supply of milk and cream to us.

We looked wistfully to the south-east in the direction of Hekla which lay about 35 miles distant, but at this time it was quite hid by an impenetrable veil of clouds resting on the horizon line. As we were about half-way from Thingvalla to the Geysers, we mounted the relay horses, and now it was the turn of those that brought us thither to be driven before us.

In Iceland, at whatever pace the ponies run, they are supposed to be resting, when they carry no load.

Our course lay over some wet marshy land—from which we gathered heather, moss, cotton-grass, and buck-bean—across a shallow river brawling over white and slaty coloured stones on its way to the lake; and then higher up, along the sides of the green hill-range which trends in the direction of the Geysers. Here dwarf-birches and willows grew in profusion; while the broken cakes of black lava, which projected from among them, served by contrast to add freshness to the greenth of the foliage, and yet more brilliance to the vari-coloured flowers which bloomed in beauty on every side. We saw innumerable coveys of ptarmigan on the hill-sides, many plovers, snipe, and a few snow-birds. All were very tame, flitted quite near and seemed to wonder at our intruding on their amenities. We did not abuse their confidence, but admiringly allowed them to go, as they came, in peace.

Coming to a part where the soil was of soft earth and turf, we found it, for miles, worn by the ponies into very narrow tracks, averaging two feet in depth. There were from six to twelve of these tracks, with thin grassy ledges between them, lying close together nearly parallel and every little way running into each other; where the ground sloped, they were dry; and, where it was level or low, they were full of mud or water. Riding along at a hard trot, we required to be ever on the alert, and to maintain an incessant motion of the feet, in order to avoid collision with the irregular surface and the projecting stones on either side of us. Tempted by a wild flower of unusual beauty, I dismounted, but was astonished to find that the deep tracks were so narrow that I could not walk in them, there not being width for my one foot to pass the other: yet a horse finds no difficulty in trotting along; actually, however paradoxical it may seem, requiring less space for its feet than a man.

We saw numerous farms as we passed along, each consisting of a group of irregular hillocks, with the windows hid deep in the grassy turf like port-holes, and generally all turned inwards so as to be sheltered from the roaring blasts of winter. We met ponies trudging along conveying lambs from one farm to another. It was curious to see the little animals looking out of square crate-like boxes, made of spars of wood, slung in the manner of panniers on a donkey, and to hear them bleat: reminding one of the old nursery rhyme "young lambs to sell!"

They could not be otherwise transported over lava tracks and across the rivers which separate one valley from another. We saw several small caravans or companies of Icelanders on the way. They had the same sort of boxes as our baggage ponies, and the same quaint horse gear, down to the rough hair cords tied and fastened by passing a sheep's knee-bone through a loop to prevent knots from slipping. They had tents and provisions; one of the ponies carried a leather bottle probably filled with skier. It was a calf's skin sewed up, with the head and legs left on it, so that it presented a quaint old world look ; and recalled pictures in the catacombs of Egypt. Notwithstanding the difference of climate, when in contact with the people, one is here, at every point, reminded of the East and carried back to patriarchal times. We touched our hats in returning

the salutations of those we met, although we did not
know the exact import of what was said to us on such
occasions till afterwards, when Dr. Mackinlay told me
that an Icelander when he meets a stranger invariably
doffs his bonnet and accosts him with the phrase "Saellar
verith thèr!"—"Happy may you be!" or occasionally
with one still more expressive, "Guts fride!"—"God's
peace be with you!"   On saying good-bye, he uncovers
again, and repeats the first phrase with a slight inversion,
"Verith thèr saellar!"—"Be ye happy!"

After the customary salutations, he accosts everybody
on the road with a series of questions, like a master
hailing a ship.   The first question put, is "What is your
name?" the second "Whose son are you?"—for the
general absence of surnames renders this necessary—
the third "Where do you come from?"   Then follows
"Whither are you going?" and "What are you going to do
there?"   These questions are not regarded as impert-
inent, but as exhibiting a kindly interest.   Henderson
says, "When you visit a family in Iceland, you must
salute them according to their age and rank, beginning
with the highest and descending according to your best
judgment to the lowest, not even excepting the servants;
but, on taking leave, this order is completely reversed;
the salutation is first tendered to the servants, then to
the children, and last of all to the mistress and master
of the family."   Old friends meeting, salute each other, in
the old Icelandic way, with the kiss of peace.   Clergy-
men are a privileged body, for, in salutation, even
strangers male or female give them the kiss of peace
and address them as "Sira," Father.   Hence our words
sire and sir.   Out of Reykjavik, and away from the

factories, there is much of the oriental type about the manners and customs of the Icelanders; the same simplicity, the same native politeness, the same disregard of cleanliness, and the same dislike of change.

We now rode over uneven rocky ground, enriched with brushwood, till we reached the banks of the Bruarâ. This broad, deep, rapid river drains the valley of Laugervalla, receiving the waters of two lakes, Laugervatn and Apavatn; which in turn are fed by rivers and streams from the snow mountains beyond. A few miles south of us, near Skálholt, it receives the joint waters of the Túngufljot from Haukadal with the overflow of the Geysers, the magnificent river Hvitá which flows from a lake of the same name at the foot of Lang Jökul, and the Laxá, from Grœnavatn; further down to the southwest it also receives the Sog flowing from the lake of Thingvalla; and after draining several hundred miles of country, these waters, united in a little gulf called Olfusá, flow into the sea on the west coast.

Properly speaking, the Bruarâ terminates when it joins the longest and principal river of those named—the Hvitá or White-river—and below the junction, the whole waters united in one river are simply called the Hvitá; while the gulph, formed on the coast where it debouches into the sea, is called Olfusá.

The place selected for fording the Bruarâ is immediately above a singular waterfall shaped like a horseshoe—the concave looks downwards—with a volcanic fissure or rent from two to three hundred feet long in the middle of it. This wedge-shaped gap in the bed of the river runs back to a point, and the water rushes down into it, from either side, falling into the chasm with a noise

like thunder. Over this chasm, near the point or part of
it highest up the river, are placed some planks with a
slight hand-rail on either side, forming a rude bridge
about twenty feet long and seven or eight broad. The

CROSSING THE BRUARA.

river was swollen by recent rains, so that at least a
foot of water lay upon or rather rushed over the bridge
itself. Some thirty feet of the river had to be waded
through ere the bridge in the middle could be reached;
and—guessing its whole width here, say at 70 feet—
again other 20 feet had to be forded after the bridge was
passed, ere the steep rough bank, up which we had to
scramble on the other side, could be attained. The water
was deep, turbulent and rapid; while we could hear large
stones grating on each other as they were borne along
in the current. The eye took in all these bearings at a
glance; there was no pause, Zöga led on and we followed.
Our horses were up to the girths, and seemed walking
over large movable boulders. They leant up the river so

as to withstand the current. The arrowy swiftness of the flowing water produced a strange illusory feeling, akin to giddiness; one could not tell whether the motion pertained to one's self, or to the river. A little to our right was the roaring cataract, so we kept the horses' heads well up the river, to avoid missing the bridge; in that case we should inevitably have been swept over. The view, from the bridge, of the foaming mass of water through which we moved, and of the yawning gulph into which it was tumbling and furiously rushing along, far below our very feet, impressed the situation on our minds as something unique.

All having got over in safety, we paused for a few minutes on the top of the high bank to gaze back on the strange spectacle; while, before us, the river rushing along into the chasm, although on a smaller scale and different in kind, suggested Dr. Livingstone's description of the great Victoria Falls on the Zambesi. The bridge has been renewed here from of old. On this account, the river is named Bruará or Bridge-river; a sufficient reason, when we mention that there is only one other bridge in the whole island.[1]

In the neighbourhood of the river we saw many small butterflies—blue and white—both fluttering and flying kinds; and were much annoyed with mosquitoes like gnats, that bit our faces severely and would get in about our necks, persecuting us most pertinaciously.

The Iceland ponies are truly wonderful animals. They carry one over smooth bare rocks, over great blocks of lava, up places steeper than a stair but with footing not

[1] In the same way a river in Perthshire is called Bruar; evidently from the natural rock-bridge by which it is spanned.

half so good; through mud-puddles, water or bogs; over tracks of volcanic sand; through coppices; up hill, down hill; or across rivers. Patient and sure-footed, they stick at nothing. They are guided by the feet as much as by the bridle; a gentle touch with the heel being the Icelandic they are trained to understand. Some riders, we saw, kept up a constant drumming on the poor beasts' sides. After their day's work is done, they receive no manner of grooming or stabling; saddle and bridle taken off, they are then left to shift for themselves.

To our intense satisfaction, Zöga pointed out a hill about ten miles off, on the other side of which lay the Geysers. It was detached from the range of hills we had to skirt, rising with a gentle slope at right angles to them, and falling abruptly on the other side; forming a sort of bluff head-land resting on a marshy plain. Part of our track lay through a plashy bog; then we had long level tracks of beautiful velvet turf at the foot of the hills, which both riders and horses seemed to think were made expressly for running races upon. When the ponies could be got into their peculiar amble, we progressed very pleasantly, and almost as fast as at a gallop. The hills on our left were mostly green, covered with dwarf birches, willows and blae-berries. On their slopes we saw farms, here and there, as we passed along. The plain immediately on our right, bounded by distant mountains and jökuls, was marshy. When it became very spongy and impassible, generally, we had only to move a little way higher up along the hill side, in order to obtain firmer footing. Approaching the hill which separated us from the Geysers, we crossed the morass, forded a river, rode up a miry lane past a farm house, turned the flank of the hill, and beheld clouds of white steam rising from the slope. The wished for goal now lay before us. Pushing on rapidly, my trusty little pony soon reached and picked its way over a gritty slope, among numerous plopping pits, steaming holes, boiling springs and fountains, up to the side of the Great Geyser, where I dismounted at 9 o'clock at night, having been ten and a half hours in the saddle.

The Geysers are boiling springs, situated seventy-two miles north-east of Reykjavik, on a gritty slope, at the foot of a trap-hill three hundred feet high; and on the upper border of a green-marshy plain, sloping down towards a small river which runs meandering through it in a southern direction. They are about a hundred in number, and all located in an area of about a quarter of a mile. Three of them are erupting—the Great Geyser, Strokr, and the Little Geyser. These, with Blesi, the most beautiful of the non-erupting springs, and situated a little way above the great Geyser, are the principal attractions to a traveller; although all the others, with everything pertaining to such phenomena, are intensely interesting.

Geyser means gusher or rager; Strokr is derived from the verb to agitate, and signifies a churn. Instead of an abstract summary, I shall endeavour as far as possible to give a detailed account of what we saw, and in the order of its occurrence. This will enable the reader, as it were, to accompany us, and gather the distinctive and varied features of this marvellous scene from the same points of view.

We stand at the side of the great Geyser, on the upper or north-west corner of a slope; a low trap-hill above us, the green valley of Haukadal below, and columns, jets,

and clouds of white steam rising, curling and waving
from the numerous springs on this upper arid slope on
which we stand. The surface immediately around us—
flinty and paved in thin scaly layers—is of a gritty
reddish irony colour, with streamlets of hot steaming
water trickling along from the overflow of the Geysers,
on their way to join the river below. A long continuous
strip of verdant turf runs up into this slaggy region, between the great Geyser and Strokr; and elsewhere
various little round green islet-patches about a foot in
diameter occur in it; blooming like oases, and covered
with parnassia, sea-pink, wild-thyme and butter-cups, all
thriving and seeming to enjoy the thermal heat. Here
we found many bits of stick, turf, moss, and flowers, in-
crusted over with the silicious deposit of the water and
converted into beautiful petrifactions.

The great Geyser basin is situated on the top of a
cone shaped mound, which, on account of the uneven
nature of the surrounding ground, seems, from every
different point of view, to vary in height. As we
approached, it appeared seven feet; moving downwards
from the plain, it seemed more than twice as high; while,
from the bottom of a deep gully running immediately
behind and separating it in one direction from the hill,
it seemed to attain an elevation of thirty feet.

The basin—perfectly smooth, of a whitish colour,
saucer-shaped, slightly oval instead of round, seventy-
two feet at its greatest breadth, seventy feet mean
diameter, and about four feet deep—is full of water to
the brim. In the bottom or centre of this gigantic
saucer, through the clear hot fluid, is seen a round hole
ten feet in diameter. This is the top of a stony funnel

or pipe which goes down perpendicularly to a depth of eighty-three feet.

The Geyser-water,[1] like many hot springs in India and other parts of the world, holds in solution a large proportion of silica or flint. It is well known that this substance, when fused with potash or soda, under certain circumstances readily dissolves in boiling water; and, under various other conditions, it diffuses itself throughout the arcana of nature; finding its way to varnish the stalk of corn in our fields, or the bamboo in Indian jungles, both preserving them from damp and adding strength to their extreme lightness. Fused masses of silica have at times been found among the ashes of a haycock which has been accidentally burned; and the same substance, arrested and deposited in crystalline lumps, is at times met with, though rarely, in joints of cane, and when so found is by the natives called Tabasheer.

This flint-depositing property, resident in the water, has enabled the Geyser to raise its own pipe, basin and mound. The original basin or orifice, when the spring began, must have been at the bottom of the tube; the overflow, spreading, would then continue to go on and form thin laminated cakes of silicious deposit around it; eruptions would keep the hole open and smooth at the edge, ever adding layer to layer till it became a tube.

[1] Dr. Black's analysis of the Geyser water is—

Soda, - - -	0.95
Dry Sulphate of Soda,	1.46
Muriate of Soda, -	2.46
Silica, - - -	5.40
Alumina, - -	0.48
	10.75

Thus through the lapse of time—probably about a thousand years—tube, basin and cone have, without doubt, been built up to their present elevation; and will continue to rise till the weight of the super-encumbent column of water becomes so great as to exceed the eruptive forces, or these latter from any other cause cease to operate, when the Geyser will probably remain tranquil for a time, and then slowly continue to deposit flint on the surface edges, till at length they meet and finally altogether seal up the cone.

This supposition is not altogether hypothetical, but is deduced from our having observed, both here and elsewhere, mounds, plainly of Geyserine formation, thus covered over, extinct and silent; little rocky elevations left like warts on the surface of the ground; and even the tracks or dry-beds of the meandering rivulets, which once carried away their overflow, still left, distinctly traceable, down the sintery slope.

Strokr is situated about four-hundred feet south from the great Geyser. It has not a regularly formed basin like the other, but is surrounded to a considerable distance by a slight elevation, of light flinty grit and laminae, with sundry depressions in it; all being deposited after the manner already described. In the centre, through brown coloured sinter, is a deep hole, like a well, six feet in diameter at the surface, contracting as it descends and attaining a depth of nearly fifty feet. On looking down, the water is seen, ten or twelve feet from the surface—boiling hard, plop-plopping, roaring, choking, and rumbling continually; in fact, as its name indicates, agitated and seething like a churn. The edge, however, must be approached with great caution, as eruptions occur without any warning; when jets of boiling water shoot up to the height of sixty feet, or, when choked with turf to provoke an eruption, to the height of 150 feet.

The Little Geyser, situated upwards of 300 feet south of Strokr, presents a similar appearance, only it is on a smaller scale; the tube is less than forty feet deep. The eruptions, occurring every half-hour or so, were like playing fountains; but they only attained a height of 10 to 15 feet, and lasted about five minutes.

The chief non-erupting spring, Blesi—so called from its fancied resemblance to white marks on a horse's face—is situated say about 250 feet to the west of the Great Geyser, and a little higher up the hill. It is a large irregular oval opening into a cavern full of clear hot water, up to the same level as the ground. It is about 40 or 50 feet long, 10 to 20 broad, and spanned across the centre, so as apparently to form two separate oval pools, by a natural rock bridge. The top of this bridge is only about a foot broad, and raised an inch or so above the surface of the water, while the arch is quite under it. One can thus see through the clear water from the one pool to the other, the same as if this curious division were not there.

Standing with our backs to the hill, we observed that the south edge of the spring was only a shelving ledge of silicious sinter, covering in or roofing the water; and that, 3 or 4 feet further in, the side of the cavern, dipping abruptly and continuing to cave into fathomless darkness, with its whitish crags, precipices, and projecting ledges, could be distinctly followed for 40 or 50 feet far down through the clear pure scalding water which was perfectly still. It never boils; but its gentle overflow winds southward along the slope, steaming all the way. The blue tint of the transparent water near the side was exquisitely delicate, and appeared to be caused by light, modified and reflected somehow from the craggy sides, although they were whitish in colour, while the crystalline water near the sides was actually as bright as lapis-lazuli, shading magically into the most tender sea-green. Gazing down on the subaqueous jags, the yawning fissure, spite of its stillness and heat, suggested Schiller's poem of the Diver, and then again Hans Christian Andersen's brilliant word picture of the Blue grotto of Capri; combining, as it does, elements both of terror and beauty. We were strangely fascinated by this spring, which although now so tranquil only ceased to be an active erupting Geyser in A.D. 1784, the year after the terrific eruption of Skaptar, when earthquakes disturbed and wrought sundry changes on the Geyser ground, and, according to Henderson, opened up thirty-five new springs.

The rest of the springs are situated chiefly on the lower or south-west corner of the slope, and also at the foot of the hill, in the deep gully at the back of the great Geyser. They are of various kinds and close together; little pools of hot water level with the surface; others, boiling hard, below it; dark holes with steam rising from them; others where, though no water could be seen, it was heard seething below, and felt to be boiling by the vibratory motion it communicated to the ground on which we stood; others seemed caldrons of seething clay; while, in many places around, when a stick was thrust 12 or 18 inches into the ground and withdrawn, steam issued from the hole so made.

Nearly all these springs have an alkaline reaction, and give out more or less sulphurated hydrogen. My thermometer, dipt in at the edge of the great Geyser when at rest but full to the brim, indicated 178°, and the temperature was pretty equal all round its basin. Blesi was hotter, and on repeated trials stood at 196°.

While Zöga was busy pitching the tent, lent us by the Count Von Trampe, on the narrow turf plat, about 30 or 40 yards south-west of the great Geyser, we observed, besides the white vapour which always hovers over it, bubbles rising from the surface of the water over the hole in the centre of the saucer-shaped basin; then the water became troubled; a stream of hissing steam rushed up with a noise resembling the whiz of a rocket; we heard subterranean sounds like the rumbling of distant thunder, broken in upon at intervals by the booming of artillery; a dome of water, like a gigantic glass shade eight or ten feet high, then rose and burst with a loud explosion, as if a submarine blast had just been fired. We expected a grand eruption, but this time were disappointed; for only one other bell, smaller than the first, rose and fell, enveloped in dense clouds of steam slightly impregnated with sulphur; the troubling of the water speedily subsided, low muffled sounds died away, losing themselves in distant mutterings, and the Geyser pot boiled over; but very quietly, as there was no fire outside to be put out by the little rills of scalding water. These ran trickling down the sides all round, but chiefly on the south-west where there are several slight indentations in the lip of the basin, and where at the foot of the mound the bed of a shallow streamlet has been formed which winds through the gritty slope,

H

conveying the Geyser's overflow, steaming as it runs, down to the river. This little rivulet spreads out broad and shallow, as it flows over the gritty surface, being only, excepting after eruptions, one or two inches deep, with many little islet-patches of verdure in it.

These islets are sometimes formed by a single tuft of butter-cups, sea-pinks, wild-thyme, or parnassia; quietly blooming in freshness and beauty in this strange habitat, cared for and cherished by the same beneficent hand that controls the under-lying and central fires, with all their marvellous and terrific phenomena.

Our attention was now called to the Little Geyser, which exhibited great activity, shooting up several jets of water at the same time like a fountain, while great volumes of steam rolled away from it to the leeward. Its eruptions did not attain, as already stated, more than a height of from ten to fifteen feet, and lasted only for about five minutes; but they occurred every little while during our stay.

We sketched this singular region from various points of view; wonder ever increasing, as we wandered about and discovered one marvel after another. For, be it confessed, that on approaching the Geysers, utterly fagged and weary, I felt all curiosity so blunted, that, for the first fifteen minutes, I believe I would scarcely have risen from the turf on which I sat to walk a mile, though it had been to see the earth split open to its very centre; and, for the moment, serious thoughts of how I was ever to undergo the ride back occupied my mind. Such however are the recuperative powers of nature, that, after a rest of twenty minutes, I again felt equal to anything, and wandered about seeing what was to be seen till 11 o'clock P.M., when Zöga announced that dinner was ready.

Tea was made with hot water from the great Geyser, because it afforded the nearest supply; but our provisions were cooked in Blesi, because it was of a higher temperature. The water had no unpleasant taste and was quite fit for our temporary use.

Zöga's mode of cooking was simple, a fine large trout, with head and tail tied together, was fastened to one end of a string, and a big stone to the other; the fish was plumped into the water and the stone left outside near the edge to moor it; so with tins of preserved meats, soups, &c. They required to be immersed for about twenty minutes. With these, a plentiful supply of bread, biscuit and cheese, and the addition of a pailful of milk from the farm, we fared sumptuously; dining al-fresco, in broad day-light and the thermometer indicating 58°, although it was near midnight.

Several loud reports, rumblings, noises, and minor troublings of the water, again brought us to the side of the great Geyser, in expectation of a grand eruption, but these came to nothing, and again we were disappointed.

The tent was small; three of our companions crept in and lay down, leaving a place for me to follow. Professor Chadbourne, fearing he might miss an eruption, would not leave the ground, although he had been offered quarters at the farm; but, selecting a warm ledge of rock immediately under the Geyser, on the north side, lay down to sleep, wrapt up in my storm-coat.

All had now retired but Mr. Murray who accompanied me to the hill behind, from which we obtained a bird's-eye view of the plain, with the river meandering through it, and of the numerous springs in the corner immediately below us.

The sun in the north did little more than dip and skim along a little way below the horizon; so that between twelve and one o'clock A.M. it was lighter than on a southern cloudy day at noon; while the whole atmosphere, in the light "dim," exhibited a northern depth, transparency, and calm spiritual purity, surpassing the loveliest of our summer twilights. Those who love Dante will perhaps realize the impression it produced on our minds, when we say, that, although it was too light for any stars to be visible, the ethereal beauty of the sky suggested Beatrice. Returning to the tent before one o'clock, Mr. Murray ensconced himself comfortably outside, in the lee of it; and I crept in, spread my plaid and lay down without disturbing any one, although the four of us inside were packed together as closely as sardines.

After Mr. Murray had bade me good night through the canvas, hearing the harsh croak of the raven, and the eerie whistle of the plover, I, too, quickly fell asleep, and dreamt a queer disjointed jumble of Scandinavian myths new and old, of which I only remembered, Odin's Raven flapping its wings and leading me to Rabna Floki; seeing that worthy thrash Thor, after having eaten his hammer; and Loki kindling Midgard with fire from the Serpent's eyes; the winds, all the while, sighing a requiem for Baldur, through Igdrasill the ash tree of existence. The rocks were being hurled about by the Jötuns, who in the midst of their conflict opened a space and respectfully stood aside, to allow Professor Chadbourne to approach me. Hearing myself called upon by name, I suddenly woke up, and saw my friend, in front of the tent, beckoning to me in a state of great excitement.

Subterranean noises like thunder were waxing louder and louder; each earth-shock accompanied by a tremor of the ground, more or less violent, but quite unmistakeable. Bells of water in quick succession were rising from the basin and falling again, ever increasing in size, till a large one burst; and then jets of water, in successive spurts, rushed up in sheafs from the tube; at first about 10 feet, then the height was 15, 20, 30, 50 feet and so on, each effort surpassing the preceding, till it attained the height of 200 feet. The fountain did not fall down between each jet, but, nearly holding the elevation once gained, the whole grew up bodily by a series of jerks each higher than the last. Dense clouds of steam enveloped the whole, and only afforded occasional glimpses of the columns of water from the leeward side. White vapour also spread out above the fountain, rolling away in vast curling volumes, which, condensing in the air, came down like heavy dew. Tremendous sounds were continuously heard, like the roaring of an angry sea, broken in upon by the near discharge of minute guns. It is at last, what we longed to behold, a grand eruption of the great Geyser.

Professor Chadbourne, who came running to the tent to rouse me, had been sleeping for warmth on a ledge immediately under the basin; and, when wakened by the loud noises, two streams of boiling water were running down the mound in minature cascades on either side of him.

The vast body of water from the central pipe continued jetting up, till, as I have said, it attained the height of 200 feet, falling down again into the basin which was brimful to overflowing.   The subterranean rumbling sounds and reports, accompanied with vibration of the ground, were fearful.   Jets of water rushed up, in sheaf, with a continuous noise, such as would be produced by 500 rockets discharged into the air at the same instant.

Even the beautiful clouds of steam which robed the Geyser were regarded by us with an indescribable feeling of mysterious awe and wonder, as if we had actually discovered the fabled magic vapour, from which the eastern Ufret, or any other vision, might arise; while the sharp tinkling plash of the descending water could, at times, be heard amidst the loud hissing, roaring, booming and confused Babel of all unearthly sounds. The eruptive forces having now expended themselves for the time, the fountain gradually subsided in the same manner, though more speedily than it had risen.   The whole terrific spectacle lasted about twenty minutes. We were singularly fortunate, as, from what we were told, few eruptions of late have lasted more than four or five minutes, or attained half the height of this which we had just witnessed.

When over, the water subsided and left the basin empty, so that one could walk in it to the edge of the central tube-hole, and look down.   As the water thus sank, so great was the heat in the stone that the cup was instantaneously, though bit by bit, left as dry as an oven. Smooth and of a whitish colour, it resembled the chalice of a gigantic water-lily.   At the edges however, where silex has been deposited from the spray and condensed steam, the surface, although of the same colour, is rough like coral, or rather granulated like the head of a cauliflower. I broke off specimens of this singular formation from the lip, and also obtained bits of shingly laminæ from the mound, the latter not unlike the outside of an oyster-shell; on several of the fragments was a deposit of sulphur.

I now retired to the tent, but the Professor made to sleep, sitting on the edge with his feet in the dry basin, determined to miss nothing. In an hour or so he was warned back by the water gradually rising and again filling the cup. There was not much hazard in his so doing, as the premonitory symptoms are generally "loud enough," as my friend Dr. Mackinlay quaintly remarked, "to disturb the repose of Rip Van Winkle himself." However, danger may arise from these symptoms being disregarded, as they also precede abortive attempts, in a very deceptive and tantalizing way; getting louder and louder up to a certain point, and then, instead of coming to a head, gradually subsiding again into perfect stillness. The deafening detonations and rumblings are most frequent fast and furious, immediately before, and during eruptions.

The Geyser made another grand display, early in the morning between four and five o'clock; but it fell far short of the first in magnitude. Tired with the fatigues of the preceding days, with broken rest and excitement, I only mechanically sat up, thrust aside the canvas of the tent and gazed out on the strange scene, scarcely able to keep my eyes half open the while. My recollections of it are consequently somewhat vague and nebulous; having reference to loud discordant noises muffled up in white clouds, both strangely rising from the earth. In fact, to me scarcely half awake and perfectly passive, all seemed an evanescent dream, and I speedily sank back again to enjoy "the honey heavy dew of slumber;" for to the way-worn and weary, nature's soft nurse proffers that which is best for them, viz., repose; and as the laureate sings,

> "Why should a man desire in any way
> To differ from the kindly race of men?"

July 31.—Had the luxury of a hot bath at the great Geyser; dipping a rough towel into its basin, and tempering down the heat in one of the cooler little pools formed on its ledge by the overflow. When bathing my feet and half dressed, the Geyser exhibited premonitory symptoms of an eruption, the water bubbling violently over the pipe, streams of hissing steam, noises like thunder, then like artillery, a tremor of the ground, then a transparent dome of water heaved up about four feet and burst. Gathering up my clothes, bare-footed, I scampered off as fast as possible; fortunately without cutting myself on the flinty scale-like laminæ, which on the edges are as hard and sharp as knives. It was only a little disturbance which subsided in a few minutes, but shallow streams of boiling water flowed down over the very part of the basin where I had been standing. Afterwards returning with Professor Chadbourne, we completed our toilet, giving a keen edge to our razors by dipping them into the hot water of the great Geyser, at the same time making use of a little pool at the side as a mirror. The matter-of-fact oddness of the situation recalled sundry adventures of Don Quixote, when in quest of another basin—that of the barber, which he mistook for the enchanted golden helmet of Mambrino. The Geyser also did efficient duty as pot and tea-kettle for breakfast.

About ten o'clock A.M. we witnessed an eruption of Strokr. All of a sudden, we heard as it were the whiz of a rocket, and saw a jet of water spouting up in a single column, to the height of fifty or sixty feet, straight as the trunk of a palm tree, but spreading out at the top, bending gracefully down all round, and falling in clouds of spray. It lasted for about ten minutes, subsided, and began again. Some of us, looking down, narrowly escaped being scalded by its sudden vehement and un-expected spurts. The ascending water shewed beauti-fully clear and transparent against the sky; and gleam-ing rainbows came and went—now bright as the tint of flowers, now dim and evanescent—lending opaline lustres to the falling showers of diamond spray.

After all was over, Zöga collected several heaps of turf at the side, and then at once plumped them all in, to provoke an eruption. We expected the dose would take effect in twenty minutes or half-an-hour; but a whole hour having elapsed without any sign, we began to fear it would exhibit no resentment at being made to eat dirt. Five minutes more, however, and up it came, rushing with tremendous force, in several jets, and attaining a height of from a hundred to a hundred and fifty feet. The water falling back, nearly in a perpen-dicular line, was met by up-rushing steam, and thus formed a glassy dome, from which jets of water sprang up. This disturbance lasted twenty-one minutes; was followed by a lull; then it commenced again, subsided and ended by one or two explosions and spurts, after which the water sunk down into the pipe, rumbling, seething, boiling hard, and plop-plopping as before. The water this time was black and dirty with the particles of sand and turf which had been administered to it; so that, although higher, it lacked the fairy-like beauty of the last eruption. I had thrown in a white cambric pocket handkerchief with some turf tied in it; but, instead of its being washed and thrown up, suppose it must have been cooked, and reduced to "shreds and patches" or pulp, as I saw no more of it.

Several cows were wandering near the Geysers quite unconcerned. Many sheep and lambs browse in the valley beneath, occasionally approaching the springs. Accidents, however, seldom occur; although we were told of an unlucky ox having once stumbled into Blesi, where it was boiled alive. Sea-swallows were flying overhead; and at our feet, among the stony grit, grew isolated patches of wild-thyme, sea-pinks, dandelions, butter-cups, sorrel and parnassia—all of them old friends, and quite home-like. The thermometer stood at 60° in the shade. At noon, being Sabbath, we sat down in the lee of the tent, which was fluttering in the breeze, and Mr. Haycock read the service for the day—Professor Chadbourne and I taking the lessons; gave an English Testament, and some of the Religious Tract Society's illustrated publications to Zöga, who could both read and translate them to his brother guides.

After dinner walked down to the river. On either side of its course lies a strip of meadow, where the herbage is rich, green, tender and luxuriant like a velvet carpet; the valley around, though also green, is in many places wet and spongy; covered with heather and moss-hags.

The overflow of the Geysers comes down, steaming, to the river, through the brown shingle which is variegated here and there with little strips and patches of verdure. After great eruptions there is some body of water; at other times it merely trickles, spread over a wide bed.

Wandering about, I visited every one of the springs alone. In the south corner of the Geyser ground, steam-ing pits occur every little bit: the crust there is very thin, so that one requires to tread with caution. Some of them are merely holes in this thin crust, showing steaming pools of hot water, flush with the surface and extending under it; others are holes in rocks, deep, dark and craggy, with the water far down boiling furiously and seething in white foam; such is Strokr. Some are as if one looked down the kitchen chimney of a castle in the olden time when good cheer was preparing: you hear boiling going on but see nothing, for all is dark. Others throw up jets of steam. At many places you hear internal cauldrons boiling violently, at others you can also see puffs of steam escaping at intervals from small clay holes. The Little Geyser enlivens the scene by throwing up many jets of steaming water, at different angles, playing like a fountain several times in the course of an hour or so; nor does the great Geyser allow itself to be long forgotten: loud noises, rising bells of water, and other premonitory symptoms frequently calling us up to its side in expectation of grand erup-tions; for, more perfect in its formation and larger than any of the other springs, it is justly regarded as the chief attraction of the place.

Sir George Mackenzie attempted to explain the mechanism of the Geyser eruptions, by supposing that the tube was fed from hot water confined in a neighbouring subterranean cavern. This water was forced into and up the tube by the pressure of steam, accumulated between the surface of the water and the roof of the hypothetical cavern, when it had attained power sufficient to overcome the resistance of the column of water contained in the tube.

For several reasons, this explanation is unsatisfactory; and the more likely theory is the chemical one, propounded by Bunsen who spent eleven days here. In few words it is as follows. The water in the lower part of the tube gets heated far above the boiling point by the surrounding strata; water, thus super-heated for a length of time, is known to undergo certain changes which materially modify its composition; particles of air are expelled, the component molecules consequently adhere more closely together, so that it requires a much higher temperature to make it boil. When, however, under these conditions, it does boil, the production of steam is so great and instantaneous as sufficiently to account for all the phenomena of a Geyser eruption.

This theory is supported by various facts. The temperature, both in the Geyser tube and in Strokr, gradually rises towards the bottom, and increases before eruptions. It has actually been found as high as 261° Fahrenheit, which is 39° above the boiling point. In ordinary circumstances it would be found equal throughout, or, if a difference were appreciable, the hottest water, being the lightest, would rise to the top. Stones have been suspended at the bottom and remained undisturbed by eruptions, showing that the super-heating process went on above them in the tube itself; and lastly, M. Donny, of Ghent, has produced precisely the same effects in miniature; using for the experiment a brass tube stopped with a cork, and heating it all round with charcoal fires; one, if we remember rightly, at the bottom of the pipe, and another half-way up.

This theory would also explain the terrific and destructive water eruptions of Kötlugjá, provided the water actually does come from the crater, as is said, and not rather from the great deposits of surface snow and ice melted by the internal heat of the mountain. One of these eruptions in 1755—the year of the earthquake at Lisbon—destroyed 50 farms in the low country, with many men and cattle. Of the two Geyser-theories, Bunsen's is the more likely to prove the correct one.

After exploring the plain and gazing on the farm of Haukadal, which is situated on a height about three quarters of a mile to the north of the Geyser and celebrated as the birth-place of Ari Frodi the earliest historian of the north and the first compiler of the Land-námabok, accompanied by Mr. Murray, I ascended the hill behind so as to get a complete bird's-eye view of the Geyser ground, and the whole valley of Haukadal or Hawk-dale. The view of this singular region from thence, is peculiar, and I shall try to convey an idea of it, even at the risk of repetition.

Below, a green marshy plain runs nearly north and south; the river, winding through it, shows here and there little serpentine reaches of water like bits of mirror; the horizon, on the south and south-east, is bounded by a low sloping range of purple hills, and several low detached heights shaped like the Nineveh mounds. On the north and north-east rise several distant mountains. One of them is a Jökul, with perpetual snow and ice on its summit, and ribbed with white streaks down its sides. On the west is the hill-range on which we now stand. It is considerably higher, rougher, and wilder in character than the heights on the other side of the valley. Near the foot of the hills, at our feet, are bluff banks covered with reddish irony mould, not unlike old red sandstone; these deposits however we afterwards found to be fine clay, containing iron oxidized by exposure to the air, and very slippery to walk upon. From these red banks there stretches a gentle slope, mostly covered with a brown and white silicious stuff like slag, such as is seen on many garden walks. On this little slope are the Geysers; and all the springs occur within the small space of about fifty acres.

The great Geyser is the most northern, and lies on our extreme left. From where we stand, it resembles an artificial mill pond with an embankment rising all round it and slanting—to compare great things with small—like the sides of a limpet-shell from which the top or cone has been struck off. Clouds of white vapour hovered over it, as it lay gleaming like a silver shield. Near it, is our tent, and a heap of boxes, saddles, and other gear lying piled on the ground.

A little higher up and nearer us, on the right, lies the tranquil and beautiful spring of Blesi. More to the right, but lower down, that dark hole like a well is Strokr. Yet further, in the same direction, the little Geyser is in full play, sending up numerous jets of

water like a fountain; while volumes of steam are
rising from it, and rolling away to the south. To the
right of the little Geyser, and on the slope which runs
down eastward below it, are numerous little round pools,
close together, which reflect the sky, and look as if
they were blue eyes gazing from earth to heaven. Little
jets and puffs of white vapour rise from among them.
Several farms are in sight; cattle are grazing on the
plain; tern and snipe are flying athwart the sky; wind-
clouds are gathering in the north; but the hazy veil in
the south-east, which conceals Hekla and other mountains in that direction, has not been lifted. Instead of
being sated with the scene before us, wonder increases
every time we survey it, or dwell on the striking features
of its marvellous phenomena.

It was now between ten and eleven o'clock P.M. We
descended leisurely to the brink of the Geyser, were
joined by several of our party, and there sang several fine
old psalm-tunes, such as "York" and the "Old Hundred,"
in full harmony.

These, associated as they ever are in our minds with
the language of Scripture, lost none of their impressive
grandeur, thus heard by waters that are not always still,
in the land of destroying mountains, burnt mountains,
earthquakes, and storms. Where we have Geysers—
gushers or pourers forth—as in the valley of Siddim;
indeed, there is a valley with the very same name, rendered
in Icelandic instead of Hebrew, viz. Geysadal, a little to
the north-west of Krabla. Places with parched ground,
waste and desolate; a wilderness wherein there is no
man. A land where red-hot pumice or ashes, fire and
brimstone, shot up into the air by volcanoes, have oft-times

been rained from heaven; and, on every side the once
molten lava flood—which is graphically described by Job
as overtaking and arresting mortals, carrying their
substance away and devouring their riches by fire—
may be observed crossing the ancient track.

Where, excepting for a few months in the year, hoar-
frost is scattered like ashes, and the treasures of the snow
or of the hail are not hid; and the face of the deep itself
is often frozen.   Again, He causeth His wind to blow
and the waters flow.

Where spring comes with the small rain on the tender
herb; valleys are watered by springs; grass grows for
the cattle, and the pastures are clothed with flocks.
Where we encounter nomades pitching their tents, and
many old eastern customs that remind us of the dwellers
in Mesopotamia.   Where we behold the eagle mounting
on high and spreading abroad her wings, and hear the
young ravens which cry.   The swan too, and other
migratory birds may be seen stretching their wings
towards the south.   Around its shores leviathans
play in the deep; and there too go the ships.

Here in an especial manner we are reminded, at every
step, of the wondrous works of Him who looketh on the
earth and it trembleth; He toucheth the hills and they
smoke: the mountains quake at Him and the hills melt,
and the earth is burnt at His presence.   His fury is
poured out like fire, and the rocks are thrown down
by Him.   The earth shook and trembled, the foundations of the hills moved and were shaken.   Truly
wonderful are His works, who maketh His angels spirits,
His ministers a flaming fire!

Such were some of our thoughts as we stood, at midnight, singing these grand old psalm tunes, by the side of the Geyser; reminded, in a peculiar manner, that the whole surface of the globe is after all but a thin crust, cooled down and caked over the great molten central mass of liquid fire which constitutes our planet; and how easily, were latent forces called forth, or even were those powers which are already developed only roused into more energetic action, the whole might explode[1] like a shell filled with molten iron—the myriad scattered fragments then "spinning down the ringing grooves of change" as a shower of asteriods—nor could the orphaned moon survive the dire catastrophe!

THE GREAT GEYSER.

Although midnight is spoken of, it was quite light, and I sketched for nearly an hour and a half, beginning at a

---

[1] From the specific gravity of the globe, taken in connection with the increasing ratio of heat as we descend from the surface, it is calculated that all metals and rocks are melted at a depth of thirty miles below the sea level, and that the fluid mass is chiefly *melted iron;* while the temperature would indicate somewhere about 4000° Fahrenheit.

I

quarter-past 12 o'clock. Before Professor Chadbourne left for the night-quarters which Zöga had secured for him at the neighbouring farm, we two stood together on the brink of the Great Geyser, filled our glasses with its hot water—pure, and, as soon as it cooled down below the scalding point, drank to absent friends on both sides of the Atlantic; this toast having special reference to our own distant homes. Then four separate Geyser-bumpers were devoted respectively to Longfellow, William and Mary Howitt, Dr. Laurence Edmondston of Shetland, and Gísli Brynjúlfsson the Icelandic poet.

Properly speaking there was no night at all; only a slight dim towards two o'clock in the morning, which I took as a hint to get quietly under the canvas of our tent. The wind rose, increasing to a gale; our tent-lining came down and the sides flapped up, fluttering in the wind with a noise like platoon firing. For me, sleep was impossible; but as I was very tired and things could not well be much worse, I patiently lay still till five o'clock in the morning, when we all rose, and Zöga struck the tent. The wind blowing from the north-coast, on which many icebergs were at present stranded, was piercingly cold, and reminded us of the Duke's allusion, in the forest of Arden, to

> " The icy fang
> And churlish chiding of the winter's wind;
> Which when it bites and blows upon my body
> Even till I shrink with cold, I smite and say,
> This is no flattery."

As breakfast would not be ready for a couple of hours, I took some brandy and hot water at the Geyser, literally to stop my teeth from chattering, and descended into the

gully behind to examine the banks of coloured clay.
These lie, just under the Geyser, on the north-west side.
Steam may be observed escaping from many little clay
holes, and the sound of boiling may be heard inside at
places where there are no holes. This hot clay is deposited
in horizontal layers, red, purple, violet, white, light blue,
and pale green. These colours occur by themselves,
and are also occasionally found mixed together, mottled
and variegated like a cake of fancy soap or a sheet of
marble paper. Judging by the taste, the clay seems
impregnated with sulphuric acid; and, to the touch, it is
of a very fine consistency, having no grit whatever. I
secured specimens of the finest colours, cutting them like
butter with a table knife, and filled several empty pre-
served-meat cans to take home for analysis. The colours
are most beautiful, but, apparently caused by oxydized
iron, would, I fear, be useless as pigments. If this fine
clay could be put to any use in the potteries, thousands
of tons might be obtained here and also at Krisuvik.

What leads me to suppose that the colouring matter
of the alumina chiefly consists of iron, is the fact that,
excepting where the layers were evidently freshly laid
bare to view by water or by some other mechanical
means, the banks, however beautifully variegated beneath, invariably exhibited no colour but red on the surface; or, in other words, the iron was uniformly oxydized
by exposure to the air.[1]

Further down the gully, we came upon large rough
slabs of whitish stone, beautifully variegated with tints

[1] The specimens nearly all became red before they got home, and Dr.
R. Angus Smith, F.R.S. &c., has since fully confirmed my surmise as
to the origin of the colours.

of violet, red, and yellow, dashed with blue. These were in compact laminae, and each colour about the fourth of an inch in thickness. In several instances however the colours, as in the clays, were mixed. I broke up several masses, and secured a number of the most characteristic and beautiful specimens. We also obtained chalcedony and agate, at times approaching to opal; these and cornelian being only varieties of silex, colour making the chief difference.

Before filling some bottles with Geyser water, as the wind was fresh, I set one of them afloat to be carried across the basin before it. When the half of its venturous voyage was accomplished and it had reached the tube in the centre, a little eruption came on, by which the bottle was thrown up, and floated over the outer edge of the basin. I succeeded in getting hold of it uninjured, arrested in a little pool amid the boiling water which was flowing down the sides, and afterwards filled it, marking it specially for Dr. R. Angus Smith;—"one whose name," in a different sense however from that in which Keats used the expression, "is writ in water," and let me add, in *air* too; for, in connection with sanatory matters and the supply or purification of these two health-giving elements to towns, no man in Europe has analyzed more water; nor was there any known index of local atmospheric insalubrity but the mortality bills, till he made his great discovery—the Air-test. On all such subjects there is no higher scientific authority.

Wandering, once more to bid farewell to the other springs, we could not but remark that the whole slope is a thin crust, with innumerable caldrons below; these each preserve their individuality, although the central heat be common to all, for the various eruptions seem to be quite independent of each other. Blesi was quite tranquil during the eruption of its neighbour the great Geyser; and the other springs take as little notice of the Little Geyser's activity as it does of Strokr. Wonder ever increases, although the ground has been gone over so often as to be already quite familiar to us.

Breakfast waits and is soon despatched with keen relish. Packing done, horses ready, and a guide left to find three that have strayed, we start on our return journey to Thingvalla and Reykjavik at a quarter to eight A.M. Truly, as Shakspere hath it,

"Nature oftentimes breaks forth
In strange eruptions!"

The wind was still from the north and bitterly chill. On rounding the shoulder of the hill, we picked up the Professor, at the farm house. The room he slept in had been all carefully washed out on purpose to receive him, the earthen floor as well, so that it was very damp. He was assisted to undress by the hostess, till he called a halt, and insisted on retaining some portion of his underclothing. Then, after he lay down, a basin of milk was brought and placed at his bed-side. Had he looked under the pillow, he would probably have discovered a bottle of brandy deposited there for his own especial use; but, as the worthy Professor would have left it precisely as he found it, no "sense of loss" dawned upon him when the probability was hinted at.

Rector Jonson subsequently explained to me the rationale of the hostess, or her daughter, attending to guests. Among the Icelanders, wet feet and thorough drenchings are incident to locomotion. It is the universally acknowledged duty of the female department to render the way-worn traveller such assistance as he may require, taking away his wet stockings and mud-soaked garments at night, and returning them to him, dry and comfortable, in the morning. This simple old custom, which is also to be met with in various parts of Norway and Sweden, will give the key to many funny exaggerations on the subject, where the art of putting things has been employed chiefly in the direction of the ludicrous.

We see on the way many lovely wild flowers, which confirm our previous observation that they are larger in the petals, but smaller in the leaves and stems than the same kinds at home; the aroma is also less. This is caused by their receiving more light and less heat, in the short Icelandic summer, than in more southern climes.

Graceful white sea-swallows are darting about; curlews are very tame, flying within a few yards of us or sitting unconcerned on stones till we ride past them, noting their beautifully speckled breasts, long bent bills, and plaintive tremulous whistle.

SKAPTAR JÖKUL.

The atmosphere was now much clearer, and many distant snow-covered mountains were visible on our left.

Zöga pointed out one of a peculiar shape, which he informed us was Skaptar Jökul, the most destructive volcano in the island. Of this, however, again.

A bird, with a red breast, perched on a block of lava near us; this, the Professor told me, was the American robin. It seemed as large as our blackbird.

Retracing our steps, we crossed the Bruará, ascended the heights, and at length got into the green level plain, halting at the same spot where we had rested in coming along. Here we obtained a magnificent view of Hekla, and made a number of sketches. The prospect varies but little, as we ride along skirting the hills and at length ascend them on the other side of the plain. From

MOUNT HEKLA.

this point, Hekla still appears dome-shaped; the three peaks being scarcely perceptible from the distance—about thirty miles—at which we stand, and only indicated by very slight dints in its rounded outline. The mountain, covered with snow and mottled here and there with black patches, rises beyond a low range of purple hills and towers high above them, in shape and colour not unlike Mont Blanc as seen from the banks of the

Arve below Geneva, if we could only imagine the monarch of mountains deprived of his surrounding Aiguilles, and left standing alone over the vale of Chamouni.

The bird's-eye view of the great flat green plain, with rivers meandering through it, which stretches from the low range of purple hills over which Hekla rises to the foot of the heights on which we now ride, is both striking and picturesque.

About twenty volcanoes have been in action in Iceland for the last 1000 years. Of these the eruptions of Hekla have been the most frequent, although by no means so destructive as many of the others. Only attaining a height of about 5000 feet, it owes its celebrity to the frequency of its eruptions; to its rising from a plain, being visible from a frequented part of the island, and quite accessible; and also to the fact of its being well seen, from the sea, by vessels sailing to Greenland and North America. Four and twenty eruptions, of lava, sand or pumice, are recorded; the last having occurred in 1846. The intervals between these eruptions vary from six to seventy-six years, the average period being thirty-five; but some of them have lasted as long as six years at a time.

We give an account of one of these eruptions, selecting that of 1766, which was remarkable for its violence. "Four years before it took place, when Olafsen and Povelsen were there, some of the people were flattering themselves with the belief, that as there had been no outbreak from the principal crater for upwards of seventy years, its energies were completely exhausted. Others on the contrary, thought that there was on this account only more reason to expect that it would soon again commence. The preceding winter was remarkably mild, so that the lakes and rivers in the vicinity seldom froze, and were much diminished, probably from the internal heat. On the 4th April 1766, there were some slight shocks of an earthquake; and early next morning a pillar of sand, mingled with fire and red hot stones, burst with a loud thundering noise from its summit. Masses of pumice, six feet in circumference, were thrown to the distance of ten or fifteen miles, together with heavy magnetic stones, one of which, eight pounds weight, fell fourteen miles off, and sank into the ground though still hardened by the frost. The sand was carried towards the north-west, covering the land, one hundred and fifty miles round, four inches deep; impeding the fishing boats along the coast, and darkening the air, so that at Thingore, 140 miles distant, it was impossible to know whether a sheet of paper was white or black. At Holum, 155 miles to the north, some persons thought they saw the stars shining through the sand-cloud. About mid-day, the wind veering round to the south-east, conveyed the dust into the central desert, and prevented it from totally destroying the pastures. On the 9th April the lava first appeared, spreading about five miles towards the south-west, and on the 23d May, a column of water was seen shooting up in the midst of the sand. The last violent eruption was on the 5th July, the mountains in the interval often ceasing to eject any matter; and the large stones thrown into the air were compared to a swarm of bees clustering round the mountain-top; the noise was heard like loud thunder forty miles distant, and the accompanying earthquakes were more severe at

Krisuvik, eighty miles westward, than at half the distance on the opposite side. The eruptions are said to be in general more violent during a north or west wind than when it blows from the south or east, and on this occasion more matter was thrown out in mild than in stormy weather. Where the ashes were not too thick, it was observed that they increased the fertility of the grass fields, and some of them were carried even to the Orkney islands, the inhabitants of which were at first terrified by what they considered showers of black snow."[1]

This mountain, with its pits of burning sulphur and mud, and openings from whence issue smoke and flames, is associated with the old superstitions of the Icelanders as the entrance to the dark abode of Helâ, and those gloomy regions of woe where the souls of the wicked are tormented with fire. Nor are these ideas to be wondered at in connection with the terrible phenomena of such an Inferno.

As Hekla lay gleaming peacefully in the sunshine, with a heavier mantle of snow, we are told, than usual, I bade adieu to it by attempting yet another sketch from the pony's back, pulling the rein for five minutes, and then galloping on after my companions.

Having rounded the shoulder of the hill, we now lost sight of Hekla and the greater part of the plain. In a region where some brushwood and a few flowers grew among dark coloured rocks, we came upon a fine

[1] See Olafsen's Reise, th. ii. p. 138–140. Finnsen's Efterretning om Tildragelserne ved Bierget Hekla. (Copenhagen 1767). Barry's Orkney Islands, p. 13; quoted by the author of Iceland, Greenland, and the Faröe Islands. pp. 30–1.

example of ropy looking lava, curiously wrinkled in cooling, and all corrugated in wavy lines. Soon afterwards we saw a sloping mass of rock, some sixty feet square, inclined at an angle of 25°, polished smooth by the ice-drift, and deeply abraded in grooves, all running southwards. The marks were not to be mistaken, and were more distinct than those we had observed in coming.

Here I gathered specimens of geraniums and other flowers, placing them between the leaves of my pocket Wordsworth. Coming to a glade of dwarf willows, we observed bees feeding on the flowers of the flossy species, and were forthwith, even in this northern region, reminded of Mount Hybla, recalling Virgil's line,

"Hyblæis apibus florem depastâ salicti."

LAKE OF THINGVALLA.

The Professor, Mr. Murray, and I, riding together, now reached and descended the Hrafnagjà or Raven's Chasm, which has already been described. It was steeper than a stair, full of breaks and irregular turns.

At some places, the ponies drew up their hind legs and slid down. It seems more perilous to descend than to climb such places, but the ponies are very sure-footed. On a bosky slope, I pulled the bridle and made a sketch of the lake of Thingvalla, the waters of which were intensely blue.

Crossing the plain of Thingvalla, we reached our rendezvous—the Pastor's house—about nine o'clock at night, after a splendid day's ride; some of us, much to our own surprise, being not only in excellent spirits, but fresh and in good physical condition; rough-riding feats and prolonged fatigues notwithstanding. We dined on trout, soup, &c.; and at 20 minutes to 11 P.M. I wandered out, alone, to the Althing to sketch and gather flowers.

The three lost ponies, that strayed from the Geysers, have just come in. I see them now scampering before the guide and passing the waterfall of the Oxerâ, which thunders over the black rock-wall, about half a mile from the descent into the Almannagjá. The fall looks like a square sheet of burnished silver from the sacred Lögberg or Hill of Laws, on which I now sit writing, entrenched and moated round with deep volcanic chasms about two-thirds filled with clear water.

Skialdbreid—or Broadshield—Jökul, to the north-west, is mottled towards its base with black patches, but its summit and flanks are lit up with pure roseate light. Armannsfell, one of a range nearer and more to the north, is of a dark rich venetian red colour touched with bronze and exhibits a living glow, an effect I have never elsewhere seen equalled or even approached. Wherever the light falls, all is transfigured and glorious beyond description; yet there is no approach to hardness, either of line or tint, but an atmosphere of subduing softness, transparency, and purity, magically invests everything with an etherial spiritual beauty: such effects are peculiar to Iceland.

Having made a sketch of the lake, I retired to rest, the last of our party. We slept, without undressing, in our old quarters—on the floor of the pastor's parlour.

Tuesday morning.—Rose between five and six o'clock, and went out to gather ferns—*aspidium* or *crystoperis*—on the Althing. The scene around was singularly wild, and yet strikingly picturesque in its desolate strangeness; while the tender green of the valley itself afforded a refreshing rest to the eye. On returning I made a sketch of the priest's house;[1] examined the site of the little church which was being re-erected; strolled down by the river side, and performed my ablutions in it—laying my clothes in the priest's fishing coble, which was lying hauled up on the bank.

I then paused at the simple churchyard close by, and tried to conjure up life and heart histories for those who had entered this "Saula-hleith"—or soul-gate, as the churchyard is beautifully named—while hymns were being chanted over them, and who were now resting peacefully beneath the green sod.

Conversation with the pastor was again attempted to be carried on in Latin. His morning salutation was "bonus dies," or other remarks about the weather, as with ourselves. After squaring accounts, on leaving, we gave him —as a *nimbus* for the rix-dollars—a mediaeval "pax-vobiscum," in exchange for his many expressions of good-will towards us, and his rounded classical "vale!"

[1] See illustration at p. 84.

The glebe hay was being tedded, but the ground here as elsewhere is covered with little hummocks. Were it only levelled and drained, the soil, one would think, should raise turnips in quantity, and, certainly, larger hay crops would be obtained. During the short summer there is not time for the grain to ripen; but food suitable for cattle might readily be grown in the valleys; for it is chiefly by the rearing of stock, that Iceland, when she can muster the requisite enterprise and activity, will, in all probability, advance to commercial prosperity.

After sketching the gorge of the Almannagjá—see illustration, p. 81—we ascended it, crossed the lava plateau, and rapidly retraced our steps to the capital, only pausing now and again to take a sketch.

ICELANDIC FARM.

Over the last part of our journey, from the river which we forded just below the farm house on the hill, to Reykjavik, we rode like the wind—men and horses alike eager to get to the end of their journey. Our entry into the town was a regular scrimmage. It was a quarter to three P.M. when we got in, having done the distance from Thingvalla in six hours. By this time we had ceased to wonder at any feats performed by the ponies. Seldom, if ever, disconcerted, they go at anything in a most patient philosophical manner, and get over difficulties which elsewhere one would think insurmountable, and sheer madness to attempt. Thanks to mackintosh over-boots—made specially for the purpose—at the end of the journey, I was the only one of our party whose feet were dry.

REYKJAVIK.

Mr. Bushby invited us to dine with him at the hotel, and Dr. Mackinlay kindly gave us his room to dress in.

How oddly things sometimes turn up! We saw lying on the floor a box of "Brown and Polson's Patent Corn Flour," which at once suggested two very different, although not incongruous, trains of ideas; one, the contrast between the hurry and bustle of railway stations in Britain, where the corn flour is everywhere so extensively advertised, and the primitive locomotion of Iceland, in which not a single steam engine has been erected; and the other, associating the beautiful locality where the flour is made—near Paisley, at the foot of "the Braes of Gleniffer" celebrated in song by Tannahill, one of Scotland's sweetest minstrels—with some of the loveliest scenes we had lately witnessed. For here, are we not in the land of Eddas and Sagas! and is not the Poet found singing wherever there are human hearts!

A gentleman told me, that having obtained permission, he had, that afternoon, caught seventy trout in the salmon river—three of them from his pony's back; he had only to throw the fish over his head on the grass behind him, as fast as he could whip them up. He had seen a fisherman get 130 at one haul of the net. I saw the manager of the fishery, an active intelligent Scotch-man, whom, from his appearance, one would take to be the mate of a vessel. He told me he had been three years in Iceland, and had some of his family here with him.

Mr. Bushby procured us several specimens of double refracting Iceland spar, obtained from the other side of the island. It polarizes light, and is valuable in various ways, both to science and the arts.

Mr. Murray and Mr. Cleghorn set out after dinner to visit the sulphur mines of Krisuvik; I, on the principle of letting well alone, preferred remaining at Reykjavik to undergoing the fresh fatigue of such a ride immediately after the Geyser-journey. Three of us spent the evening, by invitation, at the Governor's—the Count Von Trampe. I had a long conversation with him in German, during which he mentioned that all the old Saga and Edda MSS. had been removed to Copenhagen; and, in answer to sundry enquiries, told me that the "lang spiel" is the only Icelandic musical instrument now in use. It is something like a guitar or banjo, has four strings, and is played with a little bow. The airs now played are chiefly Danish dance music, and other foreign melodies.

The Icelanders, like the natives of Madagascar, have adopted the music of our "*God save the Queen*" as their national air. The words to which it is sung were composed in the beginning of the present century, by the late Biarni Thorarensen, Governor of the northern province of the island, when he was a student at the university of Copenhagen. The song is called "Islands Minni," or the "Remembrance of Iceland;" and finely illustrates the intense love of country displayed by Icelanders, who, wherever they may travel or sojourn, always sooner or later return home though but to die; for to them, as their own proverb has it, "Iceland is the best land on which the sun shines." We here give the words of this national song, which, calling up

MUSIC IN AN ICELANDIC HOME.

in foreign lands memories of sweet home, is no less to the Icelander, than is the *Ranz de Vaches* to the

Swiss when far away from the one chalet he loves best in the world, perched, it may be, on the lofty mountain side, or lying peacefully in some green sunny valley.

ISLANDS MINNI.

I.

Eldgamla Isafold,
Astkæra fósturmold,
Fjallkonan fríd!
Mögum thín muntu kær,
Medan löud girdir sær
Og gumar girnast mær;
Gljár sól á hlíd.

II.

Hafnar úr gufu hér
Heim allir girnmunst vér
Thig thekka ad sjá;
Glepur oss glaumurinn,
Ginnir oss sollurinn,
Hlær ad oss heimskinginn
Hafnar slód á.

III.

Leidist oss fjall-laust frón,
Fær oss opt heilsutjón
Thokulopt léd;
Svipljótt land synist mér
Sífelt ad vera hér,
Sem neflaus ásynd er
Augnalaus med.

IV.

Ödruvís er ad sjá
A thjer hvítfaldinn há
Heid-himin vid;
Eda thær krystalls ár,
A hverjar sólin gljár,
Og heidar himin-blár,
Há-jökla rid.

v.

Eldgamla Isafold,
Astkæra fósturmold,
Fjallkonan fríd!
Agætust audnan thér
Upp lypt, bidjum vir,
Medan ad uppi er
Oll heimsins tíd! [1]

From the literal prose-rendering into English which
follows, the reader will be able to gather how beautiful
such thoughts must be, when clothed in the flowing
rhythmic music of the original stanzas.

THE REMEMBRANCE OF ICELAND.

I.

Old land of ice,
Dearly beloved native land,
Fair maid of the mountains!
Dear thou shalt be to thy sons
As long as land is surrounded by sea;
As men love women;
Or sun-gleam falls on the hill-side.

II.

Here, from the midst of Copenhagen's smoke,
We all yearning after home
Long, dear one, again to behold thee.
The noisy din irks us;
Revelry tempts us in vain;
And the fool jeers contemptuously at us
In the streets of Copenhagen.

III.

We are tired of a mountainless land;
We are constantly losing our health
In this smoky thick atmosphere;
I find this country everywhere
To be destitute of fine features,
A land like a face without nose,
And even without eyes.

1 See note at foot of page 65.

IV.

How different it is to see
Thy high-peaked head-dress of snowy white [1]
Reaching the cloudless sky;
Or the crystal rivers
Which sparkle in the sunshine;
And the bright blue heavens
Over the jökul's brow.

V.

Old land of ice,
Dearly beloved native land,
Fair maid of the mountains!
The best luck attend thee
Ever, we pray,
As long as shall last
All the years of the world!

One or two old Icelandic airs linger amongst the people, but are seldom heard; and as there was—so I understood the Governor to say—no musical notation to hand them down, little reliance can be placed on their accurate transmission.

I was introduced to the Compte d'Ademas of the *Artemise* frigate, an officer who speaks English well. He is Lord Dufferin's cousin. There were several other French officers present. After leaving the Governor's, we called for M. Rändrop, the state's apothecary, who received us in the wonted hospitable Icelandic manner. Madam Rändrop kindly played to us on the pianoforte "Robin Adair," "Cheer Boys," "Fin chan dal vino," "Hear me, Norma," a Danish dance, and an Icelandic song. Her two daughters, the Misses Müller, are learning English, and her son is going south by our steamer to attend the university at Copenhagen.

[1] Alluding to the old Icelandic female head-dress which is now again being introduced—See illustration p. 68.

The *Arcturus* having left the bay and gone somewhere for cargo, and the few bedrooms upstairs at the hotel being all occupied, as it was late, we resolved to sleep down stairs on the narrow sofa-seat which runs round the assembly room.

Through a large door, that opened into the billiard-room, came the loud clicking of ivory balls, noisy vociferations from the French sailors, and strong fumes of tobacco; notwithstanding which, we somehow contrived to fall asleep, and knew no more till the morning, when we beheld blue-eyed flaxen-haired Thea, the maid-of-all-work, standing before us. She was clad in a close fitting dress of home-made stuff, wore the common little jaunty black cap with its silver ornament and long silk tassel flowing down at the side of her head, and her waist-belt was covered with richly-wrought filigreed bossy silver ornaments.

She brought in a cup of coffee and milk and a biscuit, depositing them on a little table which she placed beside my long narrow couch. This good old Norse custom is called "the little breakfast;" and, from the experience of years, I can testify that in no way does it interfere with or spoil the regular breakfast which follows, while the benefit at the time is undeniable.

Then followed water, soap and towels, indicating that we were expected to get up; and as breakfast was to be served in the apartment where we lay, Thea's hint was speedily taken.

After breakfast I called for Mr. Sivertsen, who procured for me some coarse mits, made with two thumbs but no finger-divisions. These are the customary wear of the fishermen, who, when the line cuts the one side, are thus enabled to turn them and use the other. I also obtained a curious snuff box like a bottle,[1] made of walrus-tooth; a collection of stuffed birds, with a large black skua, a pair of Richardson's skua-gulls, a pair of jerfalcons, an eider duck and drake, a puffin, an arctic gull, and a pair of pheasant-tailed ducks among them; also silver bracelets and brooches of exquisite workmanship. These trinkets are made of Danish dollars by native silver-smiths, who have certainly arrived at great proficiency in their art.

I found that the few English Testaments I had brought with me to give away, were greatly prized by those who were acquiring our language; the cheapest edition of the New Testament in Icelandic costs between three and four shillings.

Last night Captain Launay, of the *Agile* French war brig, had called at the hotel and invited us to visit him, on board his vessel, to-day at 11 o'clock. At the appointed time we went down to the jetty and found a ten-oared boat waiting for us. Our party consisted of Dr. Mackinlay, Captain Forbes, Mr. Haycock, Rector Jonson and his daughter, Professor Chadbourne, and myself. We were kindly received and shown over the brig; everything on board was neat and clean; the sailors were, for the most part, diminutive in size, like Maltese, and, although lithe and agile, wanted the physical build and stamina of British sailors. The men were at mess and seemed to be well cared for.

In the captain's cabin, cakes, bonbons, and champagne were produced, and we were entertained by the officers with that frank and graceful hospitality peculiar

[1] See illustration at p. 53.

to the French. Captain Launay showed us collections of
geological specimens from Faröe, from the east of
Iceland, and also from the neighbourhood of Reykjavik;
all kept distinctly separated, and laudably labelled as
such specimens ever ought to be. He offered me what
of them I wished, and then addressing Professor Chadbourne, added, "Take all, and leave me one, I am only
an amateur"! He gave me some Faröese sea-weeds of
his own preserving, and I also accepted one or two little
geological specimens as mementos of a pleasant hour
spent with one who is deservedly a favourite with all
who know him.

The sailors, he told me, called him Captain Long-life,
because he has been five years in the north without
losing a man. His present crew is a hundred, but
during that period, he has, one way and another, passed
a thousand men through his hands. This happy result
he attributes partly to the regular use of lime juice,
which he flavours and renders palatable by mixing it
with a little brandy or rum. The addition of the spirits
adds nothing to its virtue, probably the reverse, but the
sailors like it so, and are thus induced to take it. In
many ships, he added, the men, if not watched, throw it
over their heads into the sea.

A boat came alongside with an invitation from Captain
Véron for us also to visit his frigate the *Artemise*.
It has a crew of 250. The men were at mess between-
decks; and, both seats and tables being swung, the perpendicular ropes made the whole look not unlike the
floor of a great factory. An officer took me over the
ship and through the stores. What an immense establishment is a war ship!

The French officers are well paid, and have a handsome allowance per day for mess, over and above their
pay.   On this station they have double pay, are put to
little expense, consequently save money fast, and get
leave of absence now and again to go home and spend
it.   Here we were again offered champagne but declined
it; and, at half-past one P.M., were rowed ashore in a
ten oared gig, much pleased with the kind frank atten-
tions of all the officers.

When we landed I called for Mr. Sivertsen, and afterwards visited the library with Dr. Mackinlay.   The Rev.
Olaf Pálsson dean and rector of the cathedral, and Mr.
Jón Arnason, secretary to the Bishop and also librarian,
were there before us by appointment and kindly gave
us every information we required.   There were no manu-
scripts to be seen here older than the fifteenth century,
and these were chiefly genealogies, or translations of
mediæval tales or romances such as "Charlemagne."
We saw a fine folio edition of Snorro Sturleson's writings, and hastily looked over the work on Iceland got up
by the French expedition under Gaimard.   It embraces
views of places, natural history, manners and customs,
costumes &c.   Some views of localities we had visited
were very good, but others were inaccurate and careless,
being only modified compositions instead of faithful
representations of the places indicated.   Ere leaving, I
received several original little works, in Icelandic, both
from the dean and the librarian; those from the former
were inscribed in English "with the author's best
respects;" and those from the latter with a legend
of similar import in Icelandic.

As the althing or parliament, which ceased to meet

at Thingvalla in A.D. 1800, was now assembled here, we went to see it. The place of meeting is an oblong hall in the same building as the college. You enter by the side, and see, facing you, a raised platform where the president and two or three officials sit at a table covered with papers and writing materials. Portraits in oil of the King and Queen of Denmark hung behind them. On two rows of seats, like school forms with simple spar backs, sit the members, forming an oblong square around the table; visitors find places outside this square. There are several writing desks and other conveniencies in the room.

The most of the deputies were sturdy intelligent looking men—peasant-farmers dressed in brass buttoned wadmal jackets, and wearing cow-skin shoes. On rising to speak, many of them expressed themselves in an animated manner, which seemed to us, with the aid of Mr. Brynjúlfsson's explanations and interpretations, to be at once fluent, pointed, eloquent, and effective.

The population of Iceland is, as already stated, 64,603. Parliament meets every second year, and is composed of a deputy from each of the eighteen syssels or counties into which the island is divided, and six deputies, generally officials, nominated by the King. The members are elected by household suffrage, but, on account of the great distances, and the bad roads, few people care to vote. Dr. Mackinlay mentioned one case, at last election, where a member had only one single vote—and that his own!! This indifference to matters political, as contrasted with the stirring old times when the Althing was supreme—being then both deliberative and executive, "parliament and high court of justice in one"—may be accounted for, by the fact that it does not now possess legislative power. The result of its deliberations is merely a petition to the King, suggesting that certain things should be done; and only under certain circumstances, can they levy taxes or recommend them.

The island is divided into three governments, each government being in civil matters quite independent of the others. The governor or stiftsamptsman who resides at Reykjavik, is at the head of the civil administration, "conducts all public affairs, presides in the supreme courts of justice, watches over the execution of the laws, the collecting and expenditure of the public revenue, and, along with the Bishop, directs the school, and appoints the clergy" throughout the whole island. The governor is sometimes a native of the island, though oftener a Dane. "He continues in office five years, with a salary of about £300 per annum, and is entitled to promotion on his return to Denmark. Under him are the amtmen, of whom there ought to be four, but as the governor holds this office in the southern province, and the northern and eastern are united, there are only two others. These have the superintendence of the inferior officers, and nearly the same duties in their province as the governor exercises in relation to the whole island. Subordinate to them are the sysselmen or sheriffs, nineteen in number, who are empowered to hold courts, appoint justices of the peace and notaries, and to administer the laws concerning inheritances. They are chosen by the crown from among the principal proprietors in the district. Under these are the hreppstiorar or bailiffs, who assist the sheriff in preserving the peace and public order, and have at the same time, the charge of the poor.

"All causes civil and criminal, come in the first instance before the sysselman in the Heradsthing, one of which is held regularly, once in twelve months, though extraordinary sessions are also called. This court consists of the sheriff as judge, with four assistants named meddomsmen. The landfoged or steward, who is receiver-general of the island, and police-master of Reykjavik, holds a similar court in that town. From their decision there is an appeal to the highest tribunal, instituted in A.D. 1800, on the suppression of the althing, and which consists of the governor as president, who takes no part in the proceedings, a chief-justice, two assessors, a secretary, and two public pleaders. Cases are here decided according to the native laws, or Jonsbook, introduced in A.D. 1280, and the latter royal ordinances; and from their judgment the last appeal lies to the supreme court of Copenhagen. The high moral character of the people renders the last court nearly a sinecure,—not more than six or eight cases, public or private, occurring annually. The crimes are mostly sheep-stealing and small thefts, and the only punishments inflicted in the country are whipping or fines. Those condemned to hard labour are sent to Copenhagen; and a peasant, being capitally convicted many years ago, for murdering his wife, it was found necessary to carry him to Norway for execution.

"The taxes collected in the island, being very inconsiderable, impose little burthen on the inhabitants. They are principally levied on property according to several old customs; and payment is chiefly made in produce of various kinds, which is converted into money by the sysselman, and transmitted, after deducting a third for his own salary, to the landfoged or treasurer. The whole amount does not exceed 50,000 rix-dollars, and does not even suffice for the support of the civil government of the island."[1]

The machinery of civil government is well arranged; but the people are peaceable, and to a large extent govern themselves; thus rendering the duties of the officials very light. In reference to this pleasant state of matters, Dr. Mackinlay quaintly remarked, "Each country is presided over by a sysselman or sheriff, who, besides his judicial duties, has to discharge the duties of lord lieutenant and revenue officer, postmaster, poorlaw guardian and head constable. As the average population of each syssel is only 3700, he has, after discharging all his duties, time enough on hand to be his own clerk and message boy!"

At five o'clock, Dr. Mackinlay, Mr. Haycock, Dr. Livingston, Professor Chadbourne, and myself, dined at the hotel, with Gísli Brynjúlfsson, Mr. Bushby, and Captain Forbes; it was our last dinner at Reykjavik. The *Arcturus* is to sail with us to-night at ten o'clock for the east of the island. All last things have a touch of sadness about them; we have been happy together, and shall not likely all meet again.

Mr. Murray and Mr. Cleghorn have not yet returned from Krisuvik. Gísli Brynjúlfsson the poet is an M.P., and at present here to attend the althing. He is

[1]Hassel, vol. 10. p. 231-233. Mackenzie, p. 312-323 Henderson, vol. 1. p. xxvi. Barrow, pp. 293-305. Iceland, Greenland, and the Faröe Islands, pp. 209-10.

employed, as already mentioned, by the government at Copenhagen in connection with Icelandic antiquities and literature, and has a work on these subjects in preparation. He speaks English fluently, and gave us much interesting information.

After dinner Dr. Mackinlay called with me for Mr. Jón Gudmundsson, editor of the "Thiöthölfr," a Reykjavik newspaper—a quarto sheet of 8 pp.—in which, along with other news, the proceedings of the althing now sitting are reported in a condensed form. No particular time is fixed for publication, so that it appears at irregular intervals when there is news to communicate. Mr. Gudmundsson is an advocate, and holds an official appointment in the althing. He presented us with several numbers of his paper. The type is clear and the paper good, so that it and another Reykjavik newspaper the "Islendingur," a folio of 8 pp.,—both printed at the same government office—are without exception the most beautifully printed newspapers I ever saw anywhere.

In Mr. Gudmundsson's house we saw medallions of Finn Magnusen, Finnsen, aud other distinguished Icelanders. He was exceedingly polite and courteous, but, as we knew he must be much occupied at present, we made our visit a short one.

We then saw Dr. Hjaltalin, chief physician of the island, and well known for his antiquarian and scientific acquirements. He and Rector Jonson are good, tall, portly specimens of humanity. The latter good-naturedly told me that when some one called him a John Bull, although he did not quite understand the phrase, he knew that it somehow associated him with England, and, for that reason, felt "flattered—very much flattered!"

Our friends returned while we were making calls, and describe their moonlight ride of thirty miles to Krisuvik as more like a wild dream of chaos than a reality. Their path lay among lava chasms, along the tops of narrow lava ridges, irregularly jugged like a saw; through huge lava blocks, like ten thousand Stonehenges huddled together; over volcanic sand and cinder heaps; over hollow lava domes, and through great burst lava bubbles, or extinct craters. Lava everywhere, parts seemed like a troubled sea which had been suddenly spelled into stone, and then roasted, baked and cracked. This scene has been aptly characterized by an old traveller as "a congealed pandemonium." In a boggy valley were seen several boiling mud-caldrons, which exhale sulphurious fumes. These gases condense in the atmosphere and deposit a crust of sulphur, in layers of various thickness, on the coloured clay banks on the side of the hill. Many jets of steam and smoke rose around; while on their right lay the lovely blue lake of Kleiservatn. Mr. Bushby had kindly furnished them with a letter to his agent, which procured for them such shelter and creature comforts as his iron house could afford.

It was now about 9 o'clock; and, not without sincere regret, on pushing off from the shore, did we bid adieu to those kind-hearted, learned, yet simple-minded gentlemen at Reykjavik, who had done so much to make our visit to their island a pleasant one.

While some ponies were being taken on board from a large boat alongside, the steam was suddenly blown off; the noise frightening them, one jumped into the sea and swam ashore, a distance of a mile, with a boat after it. However it was got on board again, none the worse for its adventure. It turned out to be a pony which Mr. Murray had purchased, and was taking south with him to Long-yester.

Mr. Bryujúlfsson had accompanied me to the steamer, and, before starting, Mr. Arnason also came on board to bid us another adieu!

ORÆFA JÖKUL, THE HIGHEST MOUNTAIN IN ICELAND.

JÖKUL-RANGES AND VOLCANOES ON THE SOUTH COAST.

At ten o'clock P.M., *August* 3, the anchor was heaved and we sailed for the east of the island.

The bay at Reykjavik is very lovely. Every crevice of the Essian mountains is distinctly shown; while the positive colours and delicate tints of these and other heights rising far inland, which the eye takes in, in sweeping round the semicircle from Snæfell to Skagi, are bright, varied, and beautiful beyond description. Deep indigoes dashed with purple, violet peaks, pale lilac ranges; and, relieved against them, cones of dazzling snow and ice glittering like silver, side by side with rosy pinks and warm sunny browns, all rising over a foreground of black lava. The sky overhead is blue; and the northern horizon lit up with a mellow glow of golden light.

The frigate *Artemise*, the brig *Agile*, the Danish schooner *Emma*, and several trading vessels lying at anchor, animate the scene.

Snæfell Jökul—rising to the north-west on the extreme of yonder narrow ridge that runs out due west into the sea for nearly fifty miles, separating the Faxa from the Breida fiord—dome-shaped, isolated and perpetually covered with snow, is now touched with living rosy light.

At its foot lie the singular basaltic rocks of Stappen, somewhat like the Giant's Causeway, or the island of Staffa in the Hebrides. Indeed, stapp is the same word as staff, and indicates the character of the columnar formation.

For the first time, since leaving home, we see the stars. One or two, only, are shining in the quivering blue overhead, with a quiet, subdued, pale golden light. I made a sketch of Snæfell as it appeared from the quarter deck

SNÆFELL JOKUL—FROM FIFTY MILES AT SEA.

of the steamer at a distance of fifty miles; it seemed a low cone rising from the sea. As the evening was calm and beautiful, ere retiring, we walked the deck till a late

L

hour, musing on the structure and marvellous phenomena of this half-formed chaotic island, where Frost and Fire still strive for the mastery before our very eyes.

August 4.—On getting upon deck, I found we were past Cape Reykjanes, and making for the Westmanna Islands. Eldey—the rock like a meal-sack—lies, in the distance, far astern.

My place at table is between Dr. Mackinlay and Mr. Haycock, the latter being next the chairman Rector Jonson who is going to Copenhagen; Mr. Murray, Mr. Cleghorn, Professor Chadbourne and Dr. Livingston sit opposite. The Danes are all congregated at the other end of the table with the captain.

Half-past three P.M. Saw Eyafialla Jökul, and Godalands Jökul, Myrdals Jökul, and Kötlugjá. These form part of the most southern range of snow-mountains in the island, and rise distinctly over a dark greenish and purple range of hills, away to the east on our port bow. Eyafialla is the second highest mountain in Iceland, being next in height to Oræfa Jökul. It has a distinct crater. Only one violent eruption, that of A.D. 1612, is recorded previous to A.D. 1821. "But on the night between the 20th and 21st December, of that year, the lofty Eyafialla Jökul, of which the movement of A.D. 1612, was the only one formerly known, burst its icy covering, and began to cast out ashes, stones, and dust, accompanied with a strong flame. It continued till January throwing out great quantities of pumice ashes, which covered all the surrounding fields; and in February 1822, a lofty pillar of smoke still rose from the crater. In June of the following year it again began to burn, and on the 26th of the same month, destroyed a part of the adjacent land; but after pouring out some streams of water, in the beginning of July, it was once more quiet. In this month also the Kötlugjá, after sixty-eight years repose, threw out sand and ashes, covering nearly one hundred square miles of ground."[1]

Kötlugjá—the gjá, fissure, or chasm of Kötlu—is not a separate mountain with a crater, but simply a yawning rent, so large as to resemble an extensive valley, situated on the north-west shoulder of Myrdals-Jökul, which is a lofty ice-mountain. From its inaccessibility it has never been explored, having been only examined from a distance. The rent is visible from the sea.

Records of volcanic eruptions occurring throughout the island have, in general, been carefully kept by the Icelanders from the earliest times; but in this case, from the proximity of numerous other volcanic vents, and the distance of the spectators, along with the long continued and intermittent nature of single eruptions—sometimes lasting for years—there appears to be some confusion in the various accounts, which renders it difficult to reckon the number of

KÖTLUGJÁS ERUPTIONS.

The first outbreak, which, by the way, is the earliest recorded date of an eruption in the island—being before Elldborg to which that honour is usually assigned—occurred in the year A.D. 894, and the last in A.D. 1823.[2]

[1] "Iceland, Greenland, and the Faröe Islands," p. 37.
[2] Since our visit, there has been another eruption of Kötlugjá in 1860, the particulars of which have been collected by Lauder Lindsay,

The number of them during that period is reckoned by
the best authorities at fourteen, the longest interval between two eruptions being 311 years, and the shortest 6.
As its devastations have only been less terrible than
those of Skaptár, we shall now, after presenting a concise
table of dates, glance at the various eruptions of Kötlugjá, extracting or briefly condensing from reliable
sources, dwelling more particularly on those of A.D. 1625,
and 1755, two of the most fearful and destructive.

Esq. M.D., F.L.S. &c., and published in the Edinburgh "Philosophical
Journal" for January. From his interesting and admirable scientific
paper, which treats the subject largely, we learn that this eruption,
like that of 1823, was "mild and innocuous." It began on the 8th, and
continued to the 28th or 29th of May, and was preceded for several
days by earthquakes. On the morning of the eighth a dark cloud was
seen to rise from the mountain, which at the same moment sent forth
an enormous flood of water, with very large pieces of ice, running with
the water-stream into the sea. Some of the pieces of ice were so large
that they were stranded at a twenty fathom depth in the sea. On the
12th of May the flames could be seen from Reykjavik, although this
town is no less than about eighty English miles distant. During the
evenings flashes of lightning were seen in the same direction. On the
16th May, the smoke was about twenty-four thousand (?) feet high; it
was sometimes of a dark colour, but at other times it resembled steam.
At this time the fire was seen from several places at a distance of
about 80 English miles. The wind being northerly during the eruption, the sand and ashes fell chiefly in Myrdals-sand, which was the
direction also taken by the waterfloods. Sulphur was found floating
in the sea, and the fish disappeared from certain parts of the neighbouring coasts. A large quantity of cinders was mixed with the water-
floods. Cinders and balls of fire, as well as smoke, were thrown up;
but the cinders and ashes, from being carried by the wind partly into
the sea and partly to the neighbouring snow-fields, did comparatively
little damage to the lowland farms; although the well-known devastations of former eruptions, especially those of 1665 and 1755, gave rise
to extreme alarm and the most serious apprehensions among the poor
inhabitants.

For the table, and the collecting of many of the facts and paragraphs which follow relating to Kötlugjá, I am indebted to my friend Dr. Lauder Lindsay.

1st eruption A.D.	894.	Interval since previous eruption.			
2d	„	934.	„	„	40 years.
3d	„	1245.	„	„	*311 „
4th	„	1262.	„	„	17 „
5th	„	1311.	„	„	49 „
6th	„	1416.	„	„	105 „
7th	„	1580.	„	„	164 „
8th	„	1612.	„	„	32 „
9th	„	1625.	„	„	13 „
10th	„	1660.	„	„	35 „
11th	„	1721.	„	„	61 „
12th	„	1727.	„	„	†6 „
13th	„	‡1755.	„	„	28 „
14th	„	1823.	„	„	68 „

The first eruption, in A.D. 894, destroyed the pasture lands between the hill called Hafrsey, and the Holmsâ river. Eight farms were abandoned, and the district of country in question is still almost entirely a sandy desert.

The second, A.D. 934, was also a formidable one, and formed the extensive sandy desert now known as the Solheima-sand, a tract about twenty miles long; and formed altogether of volcanic sand, ashes, or lapilli, and pumice.

The third, in A.D. 1245, covered a tract of country, though of what extent we are not informed, with sand and ashes to the depth of six or eight inches.

* Longest interval. † Shortest interval. ‡ Most important eruption.

The fourth, A.D. 1262, or, according to some writers, 1263, was attended by such an ejection of dust and ashes, that the sun could not be seen at mid-day in serene weather. During this eruption, the large river called Fulilækr, the Jökulsá—or Jökul river—which divides the Skoga-sand from the Solheima-sand, suddenly made its appearance.

The fifth, in A.D. 1311 (some say 1332), appears to have been more destructive to life than any of the previous ones. Many farms were destroyed in the district called Myrdals-sand; several sand-hills and other hills were formed, and several marshes sprang into existence. It vomited ashes and sand during the greater part of the winter, and, melting the ice about the crater, the inhabited tract in the vicinity was inundated, and all the inhabitants except two perished in the flood. Another account states that this eruption was known as "*Sturluhlaup*," from only *one man* of the name of Sturla having been saved, of those overwhelmed by the volcanic ejections.

The sixth, A.D. 1416. The lava or waterfloods took the direction of Hjörleifshöfdi, an isolated hill and promontory on the coast of the Myrdals-sand, considerably to the south-east of Kötlugjå.

The seventh, A.D. 1580. During this eruption it is stated that Myrdals Jökul was rent asunder, and as the name Kötlugjå is now first given to the crater or fissure of eruption, it is probable that at this date the chasm was first recognised or discovered, if not formed. This eruption was characterized by fire, darkness, and a rain of ashes, as well as by waterfloods; one of which latter went eastward toward the monastery of Thyckvaboe, and another southward to Myrdal. Many farms were destroyed, but there appears to have been no loss of human life.

The eighth, in 1612, was attended, it is conjectured, by a subsidence to some extent of the Fall-Jökul, which is situated between Eyaffialla and Myrdals Jökul, as well as of the lower lands between Langanes and Thorsmerkr. The accompanying fire was such, that the eruption was visible extensively in the north of Iceland.

The ninth, in A.D. 1625, was "one of the grandest and most devastating eruptions of Kötlugjá that has ever occurred. Its historian is Thorsteinn Magnússon, at the time sysselman or sheriff of Skaptafells-syssel (or district), who lived in the monastery of Thyckvaboe. His account was published in Copenhagen in A.D. 1627. According to him, 'at daybreak on the second of September it began to thunder in the Jökul; and about 8 o'clock A.M. floods of water and ice were poured down upon the low country, and carried away upwards of 200 loads of hay[1] which lay in the fields about Thyckvaboe. These floods continued to be poured forth like a raging sea till past one o'clock in the afternoon, when they gradually diminished, but were succeeded by terrible darkness, earthquakes, thunder, flames, and showers of sand. Nor was it in the immediate vicinity of the crater alone that the fire appeared, but down in the inhabited tract, at the distance of nearly twenty miles from the mountain, igneous

---

[1] 'In estimating the seriousness of such a loss, it is necessary to bear in mind that the hay harvest is, so far as the vegetable kingdom is concerned, the *only* harvest in Iceland; and that hay is almost the sole provender for horses, sheep, and cattle during three-fourths of the year.'

vapours were seen attaching themselves to the clothes of the inhabitants. (?) This dreadful scene continued, with little variation, till the 13th of the month. It was frequently so clear at night that the mountains, with all their clefts and divisions, were seen as distinctly at the distance of twenty miles as they were in the clearest day. Sometimes the flames were pure as the sun, sometimes they were red, and at others they discovered all the colours of the rainbow. The lightenings were visible now in the air, and now running over the surface of the ground; and *such as witnessed them were more or less affected in such parts of their bodies as were uncovered.* [!] These flashes were accompanied by the loudest claps of thunder, and darted backwards and forwards; now to the ground, and now into the air, dividing sometimes into separate bolts, each of which appeared to be followed by a separate report; and after shooting in different directions, they instantly collected again, when a dreadful report was heard, and the igneous appearance fell like a waterspout to the ground, and became invisible. While the showers of sand lasted, it was frequently so dark in the day time that two individuals holding each other by the hand could not discover each other's face.' Dr. Hjaltalin states that the water-floods, bearing large masses of ice, 'surrounded the monastery of Thyckvaboe, with its adjacent farms, one of which was overflowed by the stream; but the people saved themselves on a high hill, where the flood could not reach them. The flood was followed by such heavy shots and continual thunder, that the people thought the heavens would burst to pieces, and they were surrounded with continual flashes of lightning. The pasturages were so covered with ashes and pumice, that cattle, horses, and sheep could not get any food, and were seen running about in wild confusion. During the eruption such a darkness prevailed sometimes that days were darker than nights; aud it is related that showers of ashes from this eruption reached the town of Bergen in Norway, which is the greatest distance to which volcanic ashes were ever thrown from Iceland.' The account in the 'Islendingur' of June 16, p. 45, mentions further, that the mixed water and ice flood flowed in cascades and waves over Myrdals-sand; that the inhabitants fled to the heights for safety; that the depth of the water-flood, which surrounded the monastery of Thyckvaboe, was such that a large ocean-vessel might have sailed between the byres and the principal building, and that there was an excessive falling of sand in the district to the north-east of Kötlugjá, called the Skaptártunga. This eruption thus lasted for about twelve days, wholly destroying many farms, and partially destroying or rendering temporarily useless others. The damage done was greatest in the low lands to east, north-east, and south-east of Kötlugjá.

The tenth, A.D. 1660—commencing on 3d November—"appears scarcely to have been less formidable than the preceding eruption. Water-floods overwhelmed and destroyed the farm and church of Höfdabrekka, which latter was cast into the sea immediately adjoining, apparently by an earthquake-shock. Only such articles were saved from the building as could, at the moment, be snatched away by the clergyman Jón Salamonsson. The quantity of sand, ashes, and sulphur, thrown out and deposited on the coast about Höfdabrekka was such,

that what formerly was a depth of twenty fathoms of
sea water, became at once dry land. Such is the
account in the 'Islendingur.' Dr. Hjaltalin says ,the
clouds of pumice, ashes, and sand, rendered the
atmosphere, in the vicinity of Kötlugjá, very dark
during nine days. Many farms were destroyed.
Flames and ashes were ejected during the greater part
of winter. Henderson asserts, that 'the quantity of ice,
&c., carried down by the inundation, was so great, that
where it was deposited, it rose to the height of forty-nine
fathoms above the surface of the former depositions.
The church of Höfdabrekka' constructed wholly of wood,
and of limited dimensions, 'was observed to swim
among the masses of ice, to a considerable distance in
the sea, ere it fell to pieces.' The volcano appears, with
some intermission, to have erupted sand the two
following years."

The eleventh, A.D. 1721, began at nine A.M. on the
11th May. Dr. Hjaltalin says "the narrative of this
eruption proceeds from certain of the inhabitants of the
north of Iceland, who observed the phenomena from
the distance of about 100 English miles! These distant witnesses, state that the eruption was preceded
by heavy shots, like shots of artillery, lasting less or
more for several days, and distinctly heard by them in
the north of the island. These sounds were followed
by a heavy fire—which expression seems translateable as
vivid flames—also visible at the great distance above
named. The flames or fire were followed by clouds of
ashes, so dense and so extensive, as to have produced
complete darkness for some hours, at the remoteness of
80 or 100 miles." "The 'Islendingur' refers to an earth-

quake chiefly felt in Myrdal, but extending east-ward to Lidu, and west-ward to Fljótshlíd. About noon of the same day—11th May—the earth became fissured at various points; loud sounds were heard, and lastly, flames, with steam or smoke, were seen to issue from Kötlugjá, A water-flood now descended from the volcano, bearing huge pieces of ice, resembling in bulk small islands; which icebergs sailed along as rapidly as a ship in a good breeze. These icebergs were borne by the flood from Höfdabrekka eastward to Hjörleifshöfdi and Hsfrsey. One village was destroyed in the east of the Myrdals-sand district." Again, Henderson states, p. 213,[1] the "inundations lasted nearly three days, and carried along with them such amazing quantities of ice, stones, earth, and sand, that the sea was filled with them to the distance of three miles from the shore. The sun was darkened by the smoke and ashes which were thrown into the air; sand and pumice were blown over almost the whole island; and the ice and water desolated a considerable tract of grass land, over which they flowed."

The twelfth, A.D. 1727, is believed to have been of little intensity or importance.

The eruption which follows—the thirteenth, that of 1755—is the "most celebrated of all the outbreaks of Kötlugjá, on account alike of its grandeur, its duration, and its frightful results—an eruption which has since caused Kötlugjá to be dreaded by the Icelanders as one of their most dangerous volcanoes, if not their most

[1] Founding his statements on the manuscript of the Surgeon Sveinn Pálsson, and on Horrebow's Natural History of Iceland—p. 12: London 1758.

dangerous one." It began about noon on the 17th of October, and "continued, with intermissions, till 25th August 1756—its duration, therefore, being nearly a year. The 'Islendingur' gives a very short reference merely; but the accounts of Dr. Hjaltalin and of Henderson are comparatively full. According to Dr. Hjaltalin, the eruption was preceded by a series of earthquakes, beginning in September; they were especially severe in the north-east of Iceland, near Cape Langanes, about 150 or 180 miles distant from Kötlugjá. In this district they overthrew several farms; and in a milder degree they were felt over a considerable extent of country. The eruption itself began at ten A.M. of 17th October, about a fortnight prior to the earthquake which destroyed Lisbon. Vivid flames shot towards the sky, accompanied by severe earthquakes, sounds like thunder, and lightnings. The volcano was enveloped in smoke or steam; showers of ashes and pumice fell constantly, while volcanic bombs were hurled high into the air. The latter must have been of great size, for they were seen bursting, and the accompanying detonating reports were heard at a distance of upwards of a hundred miles. The days, it is said, were darker than the nights; and the flames and bombs gave so unearthly a character to the scene, that the poor inhabitants fancied that the day of judgment had arrived, and that our globe was bursting into atoms. Over large tracts of counrty, the soil was covered with sand and ashes to a depth of two or three feet; cattle, horses, and sheep, consequently died in great numbers. This devastation caused a famine and pestilence among the inhabitants, who perished by the hundred. The eruption was violent for fourteen days. The water-floods over-flowed the district of Myrdals-sand, which is about twenty miles long and sixteen broad. Five parishes were more or less devastated, and fifty farms were destroyed. These were the more local disasters; but, in addition to this, the sand and ashes were spread over a' great portion of the island, producing fatal epidemics and epizöotics,[1] and it is said even the wild-fowl fled from many parts of the island. The earthquakes were characterized by distinct wave-like motions of the land, which fluctuated like an agitated ocean, and the same earthquake-waves were propagated from the coasts outward to sea, to the serious damage of the shipping." Henderson says—vol. 1. p. 314—"The inhabitants of the track about Kötlugjá were first apprised of the impending catastrophe on the forenoon of the 17th October, by a number of quick and irregular tremifactions, which were followed by three immense floods, from the Jökul, that completely overflowed Myrdals-sand, and carried before them almost incredible quantities of ice and gravel. Masses of ice, resembling small mountains in size, pushed one another forward, and bore vast pieces of solid rock on their surface. After the rocking had continued some time, an exceedingly loud report was heard, when fire and water were observed to be emitted alternately by the volcano, which appeared to vent its rage through three apertures situated close to each other. At times the column of fire was carried to such a height that it illuminated the whole of the surrounding atmosphere, and was seen at the distance of one hundred and eighty miles; at other times the air was so filled

---

[1] From the Greek ἐπι and ζωον—a term applied to diseases among animals; *e.g. murrain*, in which cattle are preyed upon by parasites.

with smoke and ashes that the adjacent parishes were enveloped in total darkness.   Between these alternations of light and obscurity, vast red-hot globes were thrown to a great height, and broken into a thousand pieces. The following night presented one of the most awful and sublime spectacles imaginable.   An unremitting noise, like that produced by the discharge of heavy artillery, was heard from the volcano.   A fiery column of varie-gated hues rose into the atmosphere; flames and sparks were scattered in every direction, and blazed in the most vivid manner."

"The eruption continued with more or less violence till the 7th of November, during which period dreadful *exundations of hot-water* were poured forth on the low country; and the masses of ice, clay, and solid rock, that they hurled into the sea, were so great that it was *filled to the distance of more than fifteen miles;* and, in some places, where it was formerly forty fathoms deep, the tops of the newly deposited rocks were now seen towering above the water.   A violent eruption happened again, on the 17th of November, when the volcano remained inactive till the following year, during which it emitted fire and water five times—viz., on January 15, June 28 and 29, and August 12 and 25."

"The principal damage occasioned by these eruptions, consisted in the destruction of the pasture-grounds throughout the most part of the syssel—or district. Numbers of the cattle were carried away by the deluge; and the mephitic substances, with which everything was impregnated, brought on a raging mortality in different parts of the country.   On the breaking forth of the water, a number of people fled for refuge to an insulated mountain called Hafrsey, where they were obliged to stay seven days without either meat or drink; and were exposed to the showers of stones, fire, and water which fell around them. The lightning, which was very violent during the eruption, penetrated through solid rocks, and killed two people and eleven horses, three of which were in a stable. One of the persons killed was a farmer, whom it struck dead as he left the door of his house. What is remarkable, his upper clothes, which were of wool, bore no marks of fire, but the linen he had under them was burned; and when he was undressed, it was found that the skin and flesh of his right side were consumed to the very bone. [!] His maid-servant was struck with the lightning at the same time; and though her clothes were instantly changed, it continued to burn in the pores of her body, and singed the clothes she put on. [!] She died a few days afterwards, having in the meantime suffered inexpressible pain."

This eruption, Henderson very truly remarks, becomes the more noteworthy from "the terrible convulsions to which at the same time a great part of the terrestrial globe was subjected. Not only were the British isles rocked by repeated and violent shocks of an earthquake, houses thrown down, rocks split, and the waters of the sea and lakes[1] heaved up; but in Norway, Sweden, Germany, Holland, France, and Italy, the same phenomena were experienced. Spain and Portugal, however, suffered most from the shocks. Numerous villages, convents, and churches were demolished; the largest moun-

---

[1] 'The celebrated agitation of the waters of our own Loch Ness occurred contemporaneously with the great earthquake of Lisbon, here also referred to.'

tains shaken from the foundations, and the low grounds inundated by the swelling and overflowing of the rivers. Lisbon, in particular, exhibited a scene the most tragical and melancholy. The most ponderous edifices were heaved up and shaken; steeples, towers, and houses thrown down; the ground and streets danced under the feet of the inhabitants; and many thousands of them were buried in the ruins. Nor was the earthquake confined to Europe. It stretched over into Barbary, and destroyed upwards of a dozen of cities on the coasts of Africa. Its concussions were also felt in Persia, in the the West Indies, and in America."[1]   Sir George S. Mackenzie and Sir William Hooker[2] both also describe this eruption in their respective works of travel, but the incidents do not differ from those given above. The latter writer characterizes the sounds accompanying the eruption as "most frightful and horrible roarings." The illuminations at night were so vivid, "that heaven and earth seemed to be equally in a state of conflagration." On the 19th of October a column of smoke issued from the volcano, which column was black by day; but the smoke was intermixed with balls and sparks of fire, which by night lighted up the whole of the Myrdal district, while the country to the east thereof was in darkness both day and night. "Ashes fell like rain" in Faröe, 300 miles distant, and subterranean noises were heard as far as the Guldbringé and Kiosar syssels—80 to 90 miles distant."

[1] Stukesley's "Philosophy of Earthquakes," 3d ed., London 1756, 8vo, pp. 9–30.

[2] "Journal of a Tour in Iceland in the Summer of 1809," 2d ed., 2 vols., London 1813, by Sir William Jackson Hooker, K.H., D.C.L., L.L.D., &c., the present distinguished Director of the Royal Botanic Garden at Kew.

The fourteenth, A.D. 1823, began on the 1st and ended on the 26th July. The phenomena were, as usual, chiefly water-floods, showers of ashes, slight earthquakes, and vivid lightnings, which latter struck several persons. Only one farm, Solheimar, was destroyed, and comparatively little damage was done elsewhere; altogether the eruption was one of the mildest and most innocuous hitherto recorded of Kötlugjá.

These glimpses of the recorded volcanic history of that one spot on which we now gaze, will convey to the reader some idea of the terrific visitations to which the islanders are exposed; even when there are not lava streams licking up rivers, pastures, farms, and people in their fiery floods, filling up whole valleys or rushing out into the sea and forming capes, hissing, the while, louder than the Midgard Serpent, which encompasses the whole earth.

White fleecy clouds come and go, at times muffling the summit of these jökuls, which are deemed the most picturesque in Iceland, if we except Snæfell on the west coast, and Oræfa on the south-east.

After passing the Westmanna islands and the east-most mouth of the Markarfliót river, which sweeps round the north and west sides of Eyafialla Jökul, the south-east mountain ranges, on which we have long been gazing, begin; the general character of the coast, north of this point, having been low like the Guldbringé syssel. This district has been rendered classic ground, as the scene of Njal's Saga,[1] and we only wish it were permitted us to land and visit Bergthorsknoll and Lithend, to cross

---

[1] See Dasent's admirable translation of "Burnt Njal," since published.

M

the rivers, scamper over the plains, or scale the Three-corner mountain.   It is now clear, and one can take in the general character of the whole district at a glance.

The colour of the sea now assumed a light green aspect, broken here and there by white crested waves. Snow patches lay on the rugged purple hills; these, again, were touched with lines of intense fiery gold, actually excandescent.   Sea-birds flitted past like white gleams; and, altogether, the scene, flooded with golden light, presented a magnificent study of colour.   I made jottings of the outlines, tints, and atmospheric effects, for a water colour drawing; to be painted "some day"—that unattainable period when so many things are to be done, but which ever recedes from us like the horizon line; luring us on and on, and cheating us from day to day with a vague phantom shadow of

"Something evermore about to be."

The Skogar-foss—force or waterfall—yonder, falling sheer over the rock cliffs into the sea, gently sways to and fro in the wind.   It falls from so great a height that it appears to lose itself in vapour or dust, like the Staubach.   There is an old tradition that an early colonist—Thrasi—before dying, buried a chest of gold and jewels in the deep rock-basin into which this magnificent sheet of water tumbles.[1]

---

[1] Mr. Brynjúlfsson had the following lines—intimating the hopelessness of searching for the treasure concealed below—repeated to him, when recently visiting the locality.   They are thus literally rendered by him into English.

"Thrasa kista aúdug er   "Thrasi's chest wealthy is
  Under forsi Skoga   Under foss of Skogar;
  Hver sem thángast fyrsti fer   Whosoever thither first goes
  Fiflskú hefir nóga.."   Foolishness has enough."

Sun-gleams rest on the snow-mountains and play on the ice of the glaciers. These are very numerous near the coast, the ice being generally of a light whity-green colour and corrugated in wavy lines.

As the weather is clear and bright, we see the coast near Portland to more advantage than on our first approach to the island. The wild fantastic promontories, rock-islets, and needle shaped drongs—serrated, peaked and hummocky—resemble the ruins of old castles and cathedrals. The likeness of one of them to Iona, already remarked upon, is now even still more apparent. Behind these rocks is a low range of hills, beyond which rise the jökuls.

The summits of these mountains are white with perpetual snow. The shoulders shade downwards into pale green ice, which terminates abruptly at the edge of a dark rugged precipitous line of rock that descends sheer into the valley behind the low range of hills next the sea. The precipice looked as if the sides of the mountains had, in some way, been sliced down, say from a third of their height, leaving the snowy summits and icy shoulders untouched.

Glaciers were formed, wherever the nature of the slope would admit of them. In some instances they seemed to approach the brink of the precipice and overhang it; but more frequently they chose places where rents, chasms, irregularities, or depressed spaces, occurring between any two mountains in the range, broke the wall, and thus afforded an incline plane all the way down to the valley.

Many whales continue to sport round the vessel, spouting up jets of water, tumbling about and showing the whole of their large tails. At times they leap nearly altogether out of the sea, and fall with a great splash. They often remain perfectly motionless for a considerable time. When diving down, both the rounded shape of the fish, and the peculiar parabolic motion with which it rises and falls, make the ridge of the back with its dorsal fins resemble the segment of a great black revolving disk, like a monster saw-wheel. Gulls, skuas, and pheasant-tailed ducks are flying about.

A lot of beer-drinking and meerschaum-smoking Danes are on board, going to Copenhagen. The smell of tobacco is felt everywhere, above, below, and at all hours. Their voices are frequently heard during the day calling for "snaps." They consider a glass of this spirit indispensible for breakfast, and take it every morning to begin with. However, the hours passed very pleasantly on shipboard. The following

ICELANDIC STATISTICS

will interest the reader. From the last census—1855— we learn that the population of the island is 64,603; of that number 52,475 live by farming, and 5,055 by fishing, thus accounting for nearly three-fourths of the whole population. In exact figures the number is only 923 short of that proportion.

There were then in the island 65 persons deaf and dumb, and 202 blind. Curious to observe that, although there previously had been and again may be, there was not then a single watchmaker on the island. The extreme paucity of common tradesmen—less than 11 to the 1000—indicates a very primitive pastoral state of society amongst the islanders; home wants being generally supplied by home skill. The following table is constructed, from data contained in the census, to show at a glance the various occupations of the Icelanders, and also what relative proportion these bear to each thousand of the population.

	Total numbers in the Island at census in 1855.		Proportion to each 1000 of the whole population.
Clergymen, professors and teachers at the college, and employés at churches	2,365	...	36·61
Civil officers	454	...	7·03
Do. out of office	140	...	2·17
Farmers who live by agriculture	52,475	...	812·27
Farmers who depend chiefly on the fisheries	5,055	...	78·25
Tradesmen as follows:			
Bakers	10	...	0·16
Coopers	35	...	0·55
Gold and silversmiths	80	...	1·24
Carpenters	61	...	0·94
Blacksmiths	80	...	1·24
Masons	6	...	0·09
Millers	4	...	0·07
Turners	8	...	0·13
Boat builders	38	...	0·59
Shoemakers	18	...	0·28
Tailors	27	...	0·41
Joiners	174	...	2·69
Saddlers	46	...	0·71
Weavers	20	...	0·30
Men who live by other industrial occupations	103	...	1·59
Merchants and innkeepers	730	...	11·30
Pensioners, and people living on their own means	356	...	5·51
Day labourers	523	...	8·09
Miscellaneous occupations not classed	586	...	9·07
Paupers	1,207	...	18·68
Prisoners	2	...	0·3
	64,603		1000

There are only sixty-three native Icelandic surnames.
Few people have got any; the custom is, after telling
one's own christian name, when asked whose son are
you? to answer in old Hebrew fashion, son of, or
daughter of so and so. There are 530 men's christian
names, and 529 women's names in use; so that there
need be no lack for choice of names in a large family.
Many of them, slightly modified in spelling, are familiar
to us, but chiefly as surnames, *e.g.* Kettle, Halle, Ormur,
Gils, Olafur, &c.

The number of individuals bearing certain names, is
all duly recorded in the last census. I note a few of
them, from which the reader may infer that Casa's droll
extravaganza, depreciating the name John under its
various forms, is as applicable to Iceland as to Italy;
and that Sigridur, Kristin, and Helga, are favourite names
among the ladies.

The figures in the following list indicate the total
number of persons, in the whole island, who bear these
respective names.

Andros, 136; Ausumunder, 125; Bjarni, 869; Einer,
878; Eiriken, 351; Gísli, 681; Gunnar, 150; Halldor,
428; Johann, 494; Johannus, 498; Jón, 4827; Magnus,
1007; Odin, 169; Olafur, 992; Thordur, 445; Thorwaldsen, 106 &c.

Female names:—Anna, 869; Elin, 438; Elizabeth,
194; Gróa, 269; Halldóra, 515; Helga, 1135; Johanna,
630; Kristin, 1615; Rosa, 269; Sigridur, 2641; Lilja,
120; Soffia, 182; Thorbjörg, 436; Sessilja, 326 &c.

Half-past 6 P.M. Looking back to Portland Huc,
over the light-green sea with its white crested waves,

the reddish brown fantastic islets, and the singular arched opening in the rock—Dyrhólaey—show distinctly and beautifully against the amber light of the horizon.

As we paced the deck, talking about the old Norse language—which is still spoken in Iceland as it used to be in the eighth and ninth centuries in Norway, Sweden, and Denmark, in the Orkney, Shetland, and Faröe islands, in the two northern counties of Scotland, and in other Scandinavian settlements along the British coast—Dr. Mackinlay remarked, that "so well had the language been preserved, an Icelander of the present day had no difficulty in understanding the most ancient writings of his country." This can be said of no other tongue in western Europe.

To this—the very language of the Vikings—both the old lowland Scotch, and, at a further remove, our modern English, chiefly owe their directness, expressiveness, and strength.

Many words, which we now use with a secondary or restricted meaning, still retain their primitive signification in Icelandic. Thus the word "smith"—a contraction for smiteth—which with us is restricted to a worker in metals, in Icelandic still retains its old sense of handcraftsman. Hence the Icelander not only talks of a goldsmith as a guldsmidr, a silversmith as silfursmidr, but of a saddler as södlasmidr, a cooper as a koparsmidr, a shoemaker as a skörsmidr, a joiner as a trésmidr, a builder as a husasmidr, a printer as a prentsmidr, a blacksmith as a jarnsmidr, a cabinet-maker as a skrinsmidr, a watchmaker as an ursmidr, and, in a metaphorical sense, of a poet or ode-writer as an odarsmidr; just as the Anglo-Saxons talked of a warrior as a war-smidr.

Over a narrow strip of low sand-beach, the near snow-mountains and icefields, like frosted silver burnished in parts, now lie gleaming with dazzling brightness in the sun; coloured here and there with living gem-like streaks of opal, amber, crimson, and orange which glow yet more intensely, as if the snow and ice had been magically touched with an unextinguishable pencil of fire.

Portland point is left astern, and over it, dark clouds, of a leaden hue and ruddy edges, came down to within

PART OF MYRDALS JOKUL AND KOTLUGJA RANGE.

a short distance of the transparent glowing horizon. The coast-range and islets, off the point, are deep purple, relieved against a narrow golden belt of light below the leaden cloud. In it, hang motionless a few cloud streaks—light, fleecy, purplish gray—and, lower down, others of only a lighter amber than the pure ether in which they float.

The sea is of a light sap green; the level sun-glare slants across the wake of the steamer, and touches the crested waves; while a line of light, like a silvery mist, marks the edge of the sea, by running along the coast at the foot of the snow-capped hills. Sea-gulls flying about are following the vessel, and screaming with delight or expectation. All is a perfect study of colour—warm purples, glowing ambers, fiery crimsons, and cool greens —each heightened by neutral tints in the clouds, and crests of white foam, little more than a ripple, on the green sea. I walked the deck for two hours with the captain, and turned in at eleven o'clock.

Friday morning. We are passing Oræfa Jökul, which, by the latest measurement, rises 6,405 English feet above the sea level, and is the highest mountain in the island. It is an immense mass, covered with snow and ice, and exhibiting glaciers creeping down to the sea. Sometimes the internal heat of this volcano melts and

ORÆFA JOKUL.

cracks the surface ice-mail, so that it splinters and rushes down the sides as an avalanche of ice and water, filling up hollows and valleys. When in action it only ejects ashes and pumice; never lava.[1] By the side of the

[1] There was a slight eruption of this mountain on March 23, 1861, which only lasted a few days. The smoke and sulphurous gases which it exhaled tarnished metal at 50 miles distance.

mountain is a gently sloping snow-field, with several pointed black peaks rising abruptly out of it. This field stretches away far inland. Dr. Mackinlay tells me that, from the land-side, Oræfa appears a double-peaked broad shouldered mountain; one of the peaks or ridges presenting a deep scarped side like that of Salisbury Crags.[1]

With but few interruptions, a chain of snow-mountains stretches across the island, from Snæfells Jökul in the west, to Thrandar Jökul in the east; while the central desert or plain, running across from sea to sea between this range and that on the south-east, is nearly 100 miles broad, from 2000 to 2200 feet above the sea level, and only 400 or 500 feet from the snow-line. The south-east corner of the island is an enormous unexplored snow or ice plateau, called Klofa or Vatna Jökul, of about 2400 square miles, chiefly covered with, or at all events surrounded by ranges of jökuls, over which Oræfa, the most southern jökul of this unexplored region and the king of Iceland mountains, keeps watch and ward.

Away to the north-west, bounding this icy region on the west, rises Skaptár Jökul, by far the most destructive volcano in the island.[2] And "in no part of the world," remarks Dr. Lindsay, "are volcano phenomena on so gigantic a scale as in Iceland. In it there are lava streams fifty miles long, twelve to fifteen miles broad and six hundred feet deep. Portions of these streams

[1] See illustration, p. 160.

[2] See illustration p. 134, where Skaptár is represented as rising in the distance, over a hill-range on the other side of a level plain, which in the wood-cut resembles and might be mistaken for water.

sometimes form hills as high as Arthur's Seat or Salisbury Crags; and such is the persistence of the heat, that rents in the lava have been found still smoking, or filled with hot water, so long as eleven years after an eruption. In no part of the world of the same extent, are there so many widely separate vents or foci—about twenty—of subterranean igneous action. The boiling springs which are most numerous, show of themselves that such action is going on under the whole island. The calculations of Professor Bischoff show, that the mass of lava thrown up by the eruption of Skaptár Jökul, A.D. 1783, was greater in bulk than Mont Blanc. A larger mass of lava by far, than was ever thrown out from a single volcano, at any time, in any part of the world."

As a particular example of the ravages produced by these terrible convulsions of nature may give the reader a clearer and more vivid idea of their action, than any general description, we shall select the

ERUPTION OF SKAPTAR JÖKUL,

in 1783; it having been not only very violent, but the one of which we possess the fullest and most authentic accounts.

"The preceding winter and the spring of that year had been unusually mild, and nothing seemed to foretell the approaching danger, till towards the end of May, when a light bluish fog was seen floating along the ground, succeeded in the beginning of June by earthquakes, which daily increased in violence till the 8th of that month. At nine in the morning of that day

numerous pillars of smoke were noticed rising in the hill
country towards the north, which, gradually gathering
into a dark bank, obscured the atmosphere, and proceed-
ing in a southerly direction against the wind, involved
the whole district of Sida in darkness, showering down
sand and ashes to the thickness of an inch. This cloud
continued to increase till the 10th, when fire-spouts
were observed in the mountains, accompanied by earthquakes. Next day the large river Skaptaá, which in the
spring had discharged a vast quantity of fetid water,
mixed with gravel or dust, and had lately been much
swollen, totally disappeared. This incident was fully
accounted for on the 12th, when a huge current of lava,
burst from one side of the volcano, and rushed with a
loud crashing noise down the channel of the river, which
it not only filled, but even overflowed, though in many
places from four to six hundred feet deep and two
hundred broad. The fiery stream after leaving the hills,
threatened to deluge the low country of Medalland,
when a lake that lay in its way intercepted it during
several days. But at length the incessant torrents filled
the basin, and proceeded in two streams, one to the
east, where its progress was for a short time interrupted
by the Skalarfiall, up which, however, the accumulating
flood soon forced its way, rolling the mossy covering over
the mountain before it like a large piece of cloth. The
other current directed its progress towards the south,
through the district of Medalland, passing over some old
tracts of lava, which again began to burn, whilst the air
in its cavities escaped with a strange whistling noise, or
suddenly expanding, threw up immense masses into the
air to the height of more than 120 feet. The waters of

the rivers, swollen by the melting of the Jökuls in the interior, and intercepted in their course by the glowing lava, were thrown into a state of violent ebullition, and destroyed many spots spared by the fire. In this district, the liquid matter continued to flow to the 20th of July, following principally the course of the Skaptaá, where it poured over the lofty cataract of Stapafoss, filling up the enormous cavity the waters had been hollowing out for ages. During the whole of this eruption, the atmosphere was filled with mephitic vapours, or darkened with clouds of ashes, by which the sun was either concealed from the miserable inhabitants, or appeared like a blood-red globe, adding to their terror and consternation.

"The molten elements had so long confined their fury to the Skaptaá, that the inhabitants of the eastern district on the Hverfisfliot, though much incommoded by the showers of ashes, hoped to escape its more immediate visitations. But on the 28th of June, a cloud of sand and smoke caused so thick a darkness, that in the houses at noon, a sheet of white paper, held opposite the window, could not be distingushed from the black walls, whilst red-hot stones and dust burnt up the pastures, poisoned the waters, and threatened to set fire to the dwellings. On the 3d of August a thick vapour rising from the Hverfisfliot, the entire disappearance of its waters, and a foaming fire-stream, which on the 9th rushed with indescribable fury down its bed, overflowing the country in one night to the extent of more than four miles, converted the fearful anticipations of the natives into dreadful realities. The eruptions of sand, ashes, pumice, and lava continued till the end of August, when the volcano appeared completely exhausted; but flames were still seen in February, 1784, and thick clouds of smoke, even in July of that year.   The whole catastrophe closed in August with an earthquake of such extreme violence that men were thrown to the ground.

"The immediate source whence this enormous mass of matter issued is entirely unknown, being situated in that great central desert of sand and snow which none of the natives have ever penetrated; and no traditions of any former occurrence of this kind have been preserved. Some persons who went up into the mountains during the continuance of the eruption were, in consequence of the thick smoke, compelled to return, and some subsequent attempts met with no better success.   It is not even known whether the current that flowed from the Skuptaà and that in the Hverfisfliot proceeded from the same crater; it is, however, probable their sources were different though closely connected.

"The extent of the lava can only be accurately known in the inhabited districts.   The stream that flowed down the Skaptaá is calculated at about fifty miles in length, by twelve or fifteen at its greatest breadth: that in the Hverfisfliot at forty miles in length by seven in breadth. In the narrow channel of the Skaptaá it rose to 500 or 600 feet; but in the plains its extreme height does not exceed 100, and in many places is only eight or ten feet. From its immense thickness, it was a long time in cooling, being so hot in July 1784, twelve months after the eruption, that Mr. Stephenson could not cross it, and even then sending up a thick smoke or steam.   In the year 1794 it still retained an elevated temperature, emitting vapours from various places, and many of its

crevices being filled with warm water. This long reten-
tion of heat will appear more extraordinary, when we
consider the numerous globular cavities and fissures it
contained, permitting a free circulation of the water and
atmosphere.

"The destructive effects of this volcano were not confined to its immediate vicinity, vast quantities of sand
and ashes being scattered over the remoter parts of the
country, and some were conveyed to the Faröe islands,
a distance of nearly 300 miles.[1] The noxious vapours
that for many months infected the air were equally per-
nicious to man and beast, and covered the whole island
with a dense fog which obscured the sun, and was perceptible even in England and Holland. The steam rising from the crater, or exhaled from the boiling waters,
was condensed in the cooler regions of the atmosphere,
and descended in floods that deluged the fields and con-
solidated the ashes into a thick black crust. A fall of
snow in the middle of June, and frequent showers of
hailstones of unusual magnitude, accompanied with tremendous thunder-storms, tearing up huge fragments of
rock, and rolling them down into the plains, completed
the scene of desolation. The grass and other plants
withered, and became so brittle that the weight of a
man's foot reduced them to powder; and even where the
pastures seemed to have recovered, the cattle refused to
touch them, dying of actual starvation in the midst of
the most luxuriant herbage. Small unknown insects
covered many of the fields, while other portions of the
soil, formerly the most fertile, were changed by the ashes
into marshy wastes overgrown with moss and equiseta.

[1] This also happened during the eruption of Hekla in 1693.

A disease resembling scurvy in its most malignant type attacked both men and cattle, occasioned in the former no doubt by the want of food, and the miserable, often disgusting, nature of that which alone they could obtain. Many lived on the bodies of those animals which had perished from hunger or disease, whilst others had recourse to boiled skins, or substances still more nauseous and unwholesome. The numerous earthquakes, with the ashes and other matter thrown into the sea, caused the fish to desert many parts of the coast; whilst the fishermen, seldom daring to leave the land enveloped in thick clouds during most of the summer, were thus deprived of their usual stock of winter provisions. We cannot better conclude this frightful catalogue of evils, than by the following summary of the numbers of men and cattle more or less immediately destroyed by it in two years. The most moderate calculation makes these amount to 1300 human beings, 19,488 horses, 6,801 horned cattle, and 129,937 sheep." Stephenson makes these numbers still higher and says, "9,336 men, 28,000 horses, 11,461 cattle, and 190,488 sheep."[1]

Fine dust and vapour from this terrific eruption overspread Asia, Europe, and America during the whole summer. Franklin speculated on the cause of this haze, and Dr. Mackinlay reminded me that Cowper, who frequently refers to it in his letters, has, in the second Book of the "Task," a beautiful allusion to it, and also

[1] "Greenland, Iceland, and Faröe," pp. 38–42: chiefly abridged from Stephenson's "Account of the Eruption," published at Copenhagen in 1785, which will be found translated in Hooker's Journal, vol. ii., 124–261. See also Henderson, vol. i., pp. 272–290; and Gliemann, pp. 107–109.

to the earthquake in Calabria which occurred nearly at the same time as the Skaptár eruptions:

"Fires from beneath, and meteors from above,
Portentous, unexampled, unexplained,
Have kindled beacons in the skies; and th' old
And crazy earth has had her shaking fits
More frequent, and foregone her usual rest.
Is it a time to wrangle, when the props
And pillars of our planet seem to fail,
And Nature, with a dim and sickly eye,
To wait the close of all?"

A.D. 1784, the year after the outbreak of Skaptár, which left the whole island in mourning, was almost as memorable for earthquakes, not only in Iceland, but in many parts of the world widely separated from each other, as 1755 had been in connection with the eruption of Kötlugjá.

Most of the Icelandic mountains are volcanic, and, from the native history, we learn the frequency with which they have manifested this character. Let us glance at the following brief sketch of their

VOLCANIC HISTORY,

chiefly compiled by the author of "Iceland, Greenland, and the Faröe Islands."

Of these mountains, this writer says, "most of them seem now to be in the state of intermittent activity, in which more or less violent paroxysms occur at intervals of longer or shorter duration; and, but for the uncertainty of these periods, we might consider some as in a state of complete repose. These alternations of movement and rest seem common to the separate members and to the

N

whole system; there being many years in which the island remains undisturbed, whilst at other epochs it appears as if entirely devoted to the fury of contending elements. The most terrible of the volcanoes known in ancient times were Hekla, Oræfa-Jökul, and the Köt-lugjá; to which have recently[1] been added Krabla, Leirhnukr, and Skaptáfells, which commenced only in the 18th century. The earliest record of such an occurrence is that of Elldborg,[2] in the western part of the island, said to have happened in the 9th or 10th century. This was followed by the eruption from the mountains in Guldbringé syssel in the year 1000, at the time when the althing was deliberating as to the reception of the Christian religion. In the 11th century Hekla appeared in a state of violent commotion, which extending, in the middle of the 12th, to many others, devastated the land from north to south, and was accompanied by destructive earthquakes. In the beginning and at a later period of the 13th century, the south-western quarter was particularly excited; whilst in the middle of the succeeding one, the island was desolated by the most terrible convulsions, concluding in 1391 with a violent earthquake, felt over the whole country. From this date till the beginning of the 16th, the volcanoes were comparatively quiet; but at that period, and in the end of the century, they raged both in the south and the north. The 17th was again an interval of repose, in which only the southern ones were active; but the eighteenth age proved that their energies had undergone no diminution, by eruptions even more violent than those of the fourteenth. Between 1720 and 1730 the same

[1] Second ed. published in 1841.   [2] Should be Kötlugjá. A.J.S.

mountains were in incessant action, accompanied by earthquakes; whilst in the north, Krabla and Leirhnukr began their devastations. In the years 1753 and 1755 the Skeideræ and Kötlugjá Jökuls poured out every variety of volcanic matter. In 1766 Hekla again commenced, and the destructive outbreak of the Skaptár in 1783 closed these frightful scenes. From that time till 1821, with the exception of some slight agitations, and probably a few inconsiderable eruptions in the desert part of the country, no displays of volcanic action occurred."

Eyafialla Jökul continued in eruption from A.D. 1821 till 1822. In July 1823 it again began to burn. In the same month Kötlugjá covered nearly 100 miles of ground with sand and ashes. "In July 1825, both sides of the island were visited by earthquakes, accompanied by destructive hurricanes and floods; whilst on the 13th of February 1827, there was an eruption of the Skeideræ Jökul."

The subjoined list of Icelandic volcanoes, with the dates of their eruptions, is transcribed from the same source, and presented to the reader, not by any means as complete, but as the best to which I at present have access. It will aid him in realizing the fearful results of these terrific energies so frequently at work.

"Hekla, 1004, 1029, 1105, 1113, 1157, 1206, 1222, 1294, 1300, 1340, 1374, 1390, 1436, 1510, 1554, 1583, 1619, 1625, 1636, 1693, 1728, 1754, 1766.

Guldbringu Syssel, 1000.

Eyafialla Jökul, 1821.

Solheima Jökul, about 900, 1245, 1262, 1717.

Kötlugjá or Myrdals-Jökul, 894, 1311, 1416, 1580, 1625, 1661, 1721, 1727, 1755, 1823.

Skaptár-Jökul, 1783.

Sida-Jökul, in tenth century, and in 1753.

Skeidaræ-Jökul, 1725, 1727, 1827.

Oræfa-Jökul, 1362, 1720, 1727, 1755.

Hnappafell's-Jökul, 1332, 1772.

Heinabegr's-Jökul, 1362.

Trolladynger, 1151, 1188, 1340, 1359, 1475, 1510.

Herdubreid, 1340, 1510, 1717.

Krabla, and Leirhnukr, 1725—1730.

Grimsvatn, 1716.

Elldborg, end of ninth or beginning of tenth century.

Submarine eruption, Breida fiord, 1345.

Submarine Reykjanes, 1211, 1226, 1238, 1240, 12—, 1340, 1422, 1583, 1783, 1831."

Here are records of nineteen vents and seventy-seven eruptions. "These have occurred in about ten centuries, or, on an average, one in thirteen years. The most violent paroxysms seem to have occurred in 1340, 1362, 1725—1730, and 1754—1755. To complete this view of internal activity, we may add, that the following years were distinguished by violent earthquakes; 1181, 1182, 1211, 1260, 1261, 1294, 1300, 1311, 1313, 1339, 1370, 1390, 1391, 1552, 1554, 1578, 1597, 1614, 1633, 1657, 1661, 1706, 1755, 1784, 1789, 1808, 1815, 1825."

ENTRANCE TO REYDARFIORD.

THE EAST COAST. BREIDAMERKR—SEYDISFIORD.

Sailing north-east along the coast, we see the Breida-merkr ice-plains, and the mouth of the river Jökulsá, which is only a mile or two long. Dr. Mackinlay informs us that the most dangerous rivers in Iceland are the shortest. They spring, full formed, from the bosom of the thick-ribbed ice. The Jökulsá, which crosses Brieda-merkasandr, is one of the most dreaded of these. It springs from Breidamerks-Jökul, which, however, is not a snow-mountain, but only a high field of ice projected southward into the plain from the great snow-range to the north. Some years it is eight or ten miles from the sea, in others only one; the length of the river varies accordingly. It is half a mile broad. Sometimes this river gets dammed up, then bursts from caverns of ice with a noise like thunder, carrying along with it masses of ice with uncontrollable fury to the sea. Sunshine melting the ice swells such rivers more rapidly than rain. The near view of this cold icy region—so dreary, lone and still—made one almost feel cold, although the sun was bright and the thermometer, at noon, stood at 100 degrees.[1]   The dazzling whiteness of the snow and the ice-blink, made our eyes ache.   It was literally

> "A waste land where no one comes
> Or hath come since the making of the world."

As we approach Hornafiord the character of the mountains changes; instead of great white massive

NEAR THE ENTRANCE TO HORNAFIORD.

ranges, many isolated, sharp-pointed, rugged peaks, called horns, now rise.   They are almost free from snow, and of richly varied tints, chiefly lilacs and browns, glowing in the sunshine.

The general character of the mountain-ranges at this point, and indeed along the entrances to the fiords of the east coast, as far as Seydisfiord, resembles Goatfell and the Holy Island in Arran—firth of Clyde—only it is higher, wilder, even more serrated, and, in addition, ex-

[1] At night it sunk to 50°.

hibits many curious fantastic pointed rocks or *drongs*. Fleecy clouds often rested on the peaks, or rolled, incense-like, among them.

The western half of the island is diversified by a great network of lakes, on whose lonely waters, Dr. Mackinlay remarked, "thousands of milk white swans sport in the summer sunshine," while the eastern half is broken up by isolated volcanoes whose smouldering fires are capped with snow.

The western coast is scooped out into two enormous gulfs, the Faxa and Breida-fiords; while that portion of the east coast, to which we have referred, viz.: from Hornafiord to Seydisfiord, is all along closely indented with little fiords or arms of the sea. These run inland for a distance of from ten to eighteen miles, and average say about two miles in breadth. They are separated from each other by lofty mountain ridges, such as we have described, running far out into the sea, and ending in sheer precipitous headlands or lofty horns. Let the reader lay his hand flat down on this page with his fingers stretched apart, let him then suppose each of the fingers to represent a mountain range, and the interspaces fiords, and he will be able to form an idea of the way in which the coast is indented. At Reydar and Berufiords, these ridges appear to be about 2000 feet high, with many sheer precipices, half that height, from which a stone could be pitched into the sea. It will thus be seen, that the fiords are shut in on both sides by steep mountain ridges like walls of rock, the summits of which are often veiled in dark clouds, and in some places are covered with perpetual snow. These rocky heights are as bare as if they had newly been splintered—not a tree or shrub on their sides—and the lone stillness of the fiords is only broken by the wild "water lapping on the crag," the cataract roaring and leaping down rock gulleys, or the streamlet trickling down the broad stair-like ledges of the trap, dripping from step to step like a white glassy fringe. These fiords appear to have been rents formed when the island was first heaved up; and, where the arm of the sea terminates, they are continued further into the interior as green valleys down which rivers flow. In places where mountain-tracks are utterly impracticable, these river-courses serve for bridle-paths in passing from one valley or fiord to another.

The tender herbage affords delightful pasture for sheep; fish, chiefly cod, are to be had in abundance in the fiords, and the streams abound in trout. Vessels can sail up and find sheltered havens in which to lie, thus affording water carriage for the exchange of commodities, and bringing the advantages of the coast to the interior.

In the country one never meets anything approaching to a village. It is a populous district where you see a farm in a valley, another group of turf hovels, called a *thorpe*, a few miles further up, and perhaps, a homestead of some kind perched on the green slope of a neighbouring hillside. Should there be, in addition to these, a black wood building near the edge of the water, with a white flagstaff before it—it is a merchant's factory and gives to the place the importance of a market-town.

It was now between 2 and 3 o'clock in the morning, but as the sky was clear and lovely, and we were sailing along a coast, the striking features of which, although singularly picturesque, we had never seen described.

in books, I remained on deck most of the night, and only, from a forced sense of duty, lay down for a short time without undressing.

These fiords on the east coast are very similar in character; most of the features we have noted being common to them all. I shall therefore simply enumerate, in their order, the names of those we passed between Hornafiord and Seydisfiord, a distance of about 100 miles, for the first 75 of which the steamer's course lay north-east, and for the remaining 25 nearly due north:— Skardsfiord, Papafiord, Lonfiord, Altafiord, Hamarsfiord, Berufiord, Stödvarfiord, Faskrudsfiord, Reydarfiord, Nordfiord, and Mjofifiord.

On Saturday morning, between 5 and 6 o'clock, we entered Seydisfiord, sailed up to the head of it and dropped anchor, having now reached the extreme point of our destination.

This lonely fiord on the north-east of Iceland, is land-locked like Lochgoil or Teignabraich in Scotland. The valley at the head, with hills on either side, makes a bend to the north, so that there are high hills all round us. Those on the south—our left hand side— sweep round, forming an amphitheatre, till they are apparently met by those of the north-side; the fiord is thus shut in on the west, and the continuation of the valley, beyond it, shut out.

The hill-sides are terraced with sixteen or eighteen trap-steps, which run in regular horizontal layers and yet further complete the resemblance of the head of the fiord to a great amphitheatre. From these steps, water, glassy-white, may be seen trickling down, every little way, all round; with here and there a mountain cataract

which has made a deep gully for itself. The hill-range
on the left, which sweeps round and bounds the view, is
capped with a series of singular rocky cones, occurring
at regular intervals, and in shape resembling the chimneys of a glass work. They are mottled with snow-
patches; mist streaks float athwart them; while in the
west, not only those chimneys, but the top of the ridge
itself is now hid from view, muffled up in dense clouds
which form the curtain of the amphitheatre. A river
flows into the fiord from the valley, which, although
green and yielding a hay-crop, is marshy and much in
want of draining. From the sloping nature of the
ground, this could easily be done at little expense, and
would, we doubt not, prove a highly remunerative
investment.

MR. HENDERSON'S FACTORY AT SEYDISFIORD.

Near the beach are three stores, or factories as they
are called; two belong to Danes, and the other to Mr.

Henderson, one of the owners of the *Arcturus*, who has been here for sometime but is going south with us to-night. The factories are one-storey houses, built of wood. A traffic in produce, chiefly fish and wool, is carried on with the farmers, whose sod-covered dwellings are sparsely scattered along the neighbouring coast, or in valleys above the fiords. Customers are sometimes attracted from much greater distances; we saw long strings of ponies riding down water-courses, and crossing the shoulders of bare hills where one would think there was scarcely footing for a goat.

Before breakfast Dr. Mackinlay and I had a swim in the fiord, and found the water much warmer than we anticipated; indeed, it was pleasanter in this respect than the last bath I had in the sea at Teignabraich. We then breakfasted with Mr. Henderson, who gave us a most cordial welcome. The steamer was several days later in arriving than the time he had expected her, so that he had almost begun to despair of her ever coming for him, and was conjuring up gloomy visions of being obliged to winter here, and fancying all sorts of things. Now, for him, all was changed and bright. I tried to masticate a bit of raw dried stock-fish, which the Ice-landers commonly use, eating it as we do bread. I also tasted "snaps," of which the Danes are so fond, for the first and last time; it seemed like a mixture of gin and kirchen-wasser, flavoured with coriander seed. The breakfast before us was a most substantial one, there being no lack either of welcome, which is the best of cheer, or of mutton, fish, beer, coffee, milk, and stale black rye-bread. Be it remembered that this breakfast was neither Icelandic, Danish, nor Scotch; but, exhibiting some of the characteristics of all three, seemed marvellously adapted to our present requirements in this distant habitat.

We stepped into the store, and saw exposed for sale hardware and soft goods of all kinds. In a corner were standing lots of quart-bottles gaudily labelled "essence of punch," whatever that may be. Mr. Henderson showed me some specimens of double refracting calc, or Iceland spar, which is obtained in the neighbourhood. It only occurs in one place of the island, filling a fissure of greenstone from two to three feet wide and twenty to twenty-five feet long, on the north bank of the Reydar-fiord, about a thousand feet above the sea level. There, a cascade rushes over the rock, bringing down fragments of the spar from time to time. The mass itself gets loosened, bit by bit, through the action of frost on the moisture which enters edgeways between the laminae, wedging them apart in the direction of the cleavage of the crystals. Transparent specimens more than a few inches in size are rare and valuable. Mr. Henderson presented me with a beautiful large semi-transparent chalcedony weighing 1 ℔ 7 oz., and some pebbles.

His partner, Mr. Jacobson, an Icelander, also gave me a young raven to make a pet of. It was this year's bird and quite tame. I called it Odin; and, having got hold of an old box, improvised a door from a few spars, that it might have a sheltered place to roost in at night till it got to the end of its voyage.

I now wandered up the valley, for an hour or two, alone, and sat down on a slope, on the right side of it, to look around me and rest. The river, near where I sit, flashes down over a steep rock and forms a fine waterfall, the roaring of which is echoed from the chimney-capped amphitheatre of hills opposite. Beneath the fall, it flows peacefully along, runnelling and rippling on, to the blue fiord, through the quiet green valley. White streamlets of water trickle down the trap hill-sides, every forty or fifty yards; the whole producing a continuous quiet. murmur or undertone, not unlike that from the wings of an innumerable swarm of gnats playing in the sunshine on a warm summer's day, but ever broken in upon by the clear liquid tinkle of the streamlets nearest us, heard drip, dripping, with a clear metallic sound which might be compared to the chirp of the grasshopper. This solitary glen, now lying bathed in light, is fanned by the gentle breeze, fragrant with the smell of tedded hay, and richly variegated with wild flowers—harebells, buttercups, wild thyme, cotton-grass, and forget-me-nots —a gathered bunch of which is now lying beside me on a moss-cushioned rock. Quietly musing here on all, of strange or new, I have seen since leaving home, and dwelling more particularly on the great kindness I have received at all hands, I feel grateful to God, who has hitherto opened up a way for me and given me friends amongst strangers wherever I chanced to wander.

We saw specimens of surturbrand, which crops out on the top of a steep mountain, at the mouth of the fiord, on the north side, and obtained a few more geological specimens and plants.

After dinner, I strolled for a quarter of a mile up the valley with Mr. Henderson and Dr. Mackinlay, to visit the farm behind the store. It consists of a group of hovels, the walls are stone and turf, the gables wood, and the roofs covered with green sod. The entrance is a

dark muddy passage leading into a ground-floor apartment as dark and muddy, where, in winter, cattle are
kept. The kitchen is a dirty, smoky, sooty hole, with
fish hanging in it to smoke and dry; a pot of seal-
blubber stands steaming in a corner. The fire is raised

FARM HOUSE, SEYDISFIORD.

on a few stones above the floor, like a smithy-forge;
while there is a hole in the roof for the smoke. Picking
our way through another long passage, dark and dirty,
we found a trap-ladder and ascended to a little garret,
where I could only walk erect in the very centre.
The apartment was floored and fitted up with bunks all
round the sides and ends. In these box-beds, at least
seven people—men, women and children—sleep at night,
and sometimes a few more have to be accommodated.
The little windows in the roof are not made to open, and
no regard whatever is paid to ventilation. Dr. Mackinlay
prescribed for an old man we found lying ill in this

abominable fetid atmosphere, where his chances of re-
covery were very slight. He was an old farm servant
about whom nobody seemed to care anything.

In a little apartment shut off from this one, and in
the gable portion of the building which in this case
constitutes the front of the house, an old woman at the
window sits spinning with the ancient distaff,[1] precisely
as in the days of Homer.

To amuse the farmer's daughters I showed them my
sketches, with which they seemed much interested.

SEYDISFIORD, LOOKING EAST TOWARDS THE SEA.

I understood part of their remarks, and could in some
degree make myself understood by them, with the few
Danish and Icelandic words I kept picking up. On
receiving a little money and a few knick-knacks, they,
all round, held out their hands and shook mine very
heartily. This, the Icelanders always do, on receiving a
present of anything however trifling.

[1] See illustration D at p. 53.

After sketching the farm-house, I took two views of Mr. Henderson's store; one of them from a height behind, looking down towards the fiord, and the other from the brink of it, looking up the valley. In the latter, a part of the same farm-house appears, and thus indicates its exact position.[1] With the assistance of these three sketches taken together, the reader will be enabled to form some idea, of the appearance presented by this arm of the North Sea.

We sailed from Seydisfiord at half-past six P.M. on Saturday night, direct for the Faröe islands.

There is a singular cone-shaped mountain called Brimnæs Fjall at the mouth of the fiord, showing masses of clay-rock alternating with and pushing up trap, which is deposited in thin layers of perpendicular structure. Several pillars or shafts are left standing singly on the very summit, and present a very curious appearance, distinctly relieved against the amber light of the sky. At Dr. Mackinlay's request I made a sketch of it.

BRIMNÆS FJALL.

A vessel of Mr. Henderson's, which had been given up as lost, now unexpectedly came in sight, which necess-

<hr />

[1] Compare illustrations pp. 202, 206, and 207.

itated Mr. Jacobson and a young Iceland lad, who were *en route* to Copenhagen, to get on board her and return to Seydisfiord to look after her cargo, evidently much to their disappointment.

The wild scenery of the coast, especially at Reydarfiord, was strikingly picturesque.[1]

Mr. Murray, Professor Chadbourne, Mr. Henderson and I walked the deck till a late or rather an early hour, and watched the fast receding mountain-ranges of Iceland—pale lilac, mauve, or deep purple—and the distant horns, shading through similiar tints from rose to indigo, all distinctly seen athwart the golden light of the horizon which for hours has been ebbing slowly and softly away, but is now on the turn, and about to flow again.

Sabbath, August 7. The weather is fine; no land or sail in sight all day; whales playing about the ship. Had many pleasant deck-walks and talks, and several quiet hours, sitting perched on the stem, reading, or watching the prow, below, cutting and cleaving through the clear green water like a knife.

Monday morning, August 8. We are sailing between two of the Faröe islands, bright sunshine lighting up all the regularly terraced trap-rocks, caves, and crevices of this singular group.

I have now got a pet to look after, and, without Shakspere's authority for it, we know that   .

"Young ravens must have food."

The last thing I did last night was to shut *Odin* in his box, and the first thing this morning to let him out

[1] See illustration p. 197.

O

again and give him the freedom of the ship. The bird
knows me, is pleased when I scratch his head, and confidingly runs hopping to me for protection when the
boys about the ship teaze him more than he likes. His
fellow traveller, a young Icelandic fox brought on board
at Reykjavik to be sent to the Marquis of Stafford, also
runs about the ship during the day. At first we had
some misgivings on the subject; for

> "Treason is but trusted like the fox—
> Who ne'er so tame, so cherished, and locked up,
> Will have a wild trick of his ancestors."

However, these fears were soon dissipated; for *Odin* can
hold his own, and when the fox, approaching furtively,
uses any liberty with his tail feathers, he suddenly gets
a peck from the bird's great formidable beak, which he
does not seem much to relish. The salutary fear continues for a short time, is forgotten, and again the dab
comes as a reminder. We were often greatly amused,
watching their individual habits and droll ways, when
the one intruded upon the other. It was half play, half
earnest, a sort of armed neutrality with a basis of mutual
respect.

On the west coast of Stromoe is the roofless ruin of
the church of Kirkuboe. It was begun in the twelfth
century, but never finished. It is built of stone, has five
large windows and several small ones below; a little
farm house or hut, with red tiles on the roof, stands near
it. What a strange lonely place for a church! Thorshavn lies on the other—the east—side of the island. It
is only five miles distant as the crow flies, but as we
have to sail round the south point, and Stromoe is
twenty-seven miles long, we do not reach it till near noon.

On landing, Mr. Haycock accompanied me to call for Miss Löbner, who has been poorly ever since her sea voyage. Her mother presented wine, cake, coffee &c., and was most hospitable. None of us being able to speak Faröese, at first we felt a little awkward; but a brother of the old lady's who speaks English soon came to the rescue and acted as interpreter. With justifiable pride, they again showed us their flower and kitchen garden. I got the whale-knives, caps, shoes, gloves &c., which had been made or procured for me during my absence in Iceland. Ere leaving, Miss Löbner appeared to say adieu! and insisted on my accepting several other specimens of Faröese workmanship as remembrances of Thorshavn. No people could have been kinder.

Again, wandering about, we explored the town, looked at the church, stepped into the stores, passed the governor's garden, and wandered a mile or two in that direction in order to obtain a view, and get quit of the fishy smells which superabound in Thorshavn.

On our return we called for Mr. Müller, who presented me with a copy of the gospel of St. Matthew in Danish and Faröese, arranged in parallel columns. I understood him to say that this was the only book ever printed in the Faröese dialect, and that it is now out of print and very rare. It bears the date of 1823.

Here we saw an old man 76 years of age, an Icelander who has been in Faröe for the last 40 years. He had spent several years in England, and told me that, in 1815, he saw our regiments land at Liverpool after the battle of Waterloo. He speaks English fluently.

A Thames fishing smack, and a sloop from Lerwick, are lying in the bay. Piping and dancing goes merrily on, on board the latter, relieved by intervals of music alone. In one of these, we heard "The Yellow Hair'd Laddie," rendered with considerable taste, although, doubtless, several "improvements and additions" were made on the original score.

We took some Faröese boatmen into the saloon of the steamer, and I shall not soon forget the look of wonder and utter astonishment pourtrayed on their countenances, as they gazed on the mirrors and everything around, or were shown things with which they were not familiar and heard their uses explained. They were greatly pleased with my life-belt. Dr. Mackinlay showed them a multiplying-glass, and, as it was handed from one to another—each man first making the discovery of what had so inexplicably excited the wonder of the last looker—the queer exclamations of amazement accompanied by inimitable pantomimic gestures reached their culminating point, and were irresistibly droll.

The weather is all we could desire. The sailors are

NAALSÖE—FARÖE.

singing some curious Danish songs, with the time well marked, as they heave the anchor; and at 20 minutes past 6 o'clock P.M. we are steaming out of the bay. The evening is lovely, and the Thermometer, on the deck, stands at 68°. Thorshavn soon disappears, and we leave

ENTRANCE TO THE SOUND LEADING TO THORSHAVN.

the Faröe islands astern, relieved against an amber sky, Dimon being the most striking and conspicuous of the group. A few stars shone overhead, and I walked the deck till midnight.

Tuesday, August 9. At breakfast, tasted a whale-steak which Miss Löbner had yesterday sent on board for me, with particular instructions to the stewardess to have it properly cooked. The flesh looked and tasted like dry tough beef, with a slight flavour of venison. The blubber, however was too strong for any of us to do more than merely satisfy—not gratify—our curiosity.

The day was lovely. Professor Chadbourne invited me to visit and spend a month with him during his holiday. Indeed, cordial, pressing invitations, all round, were the order of the day. As fellow-travellers we had been happy together, and felt sorry at the near prospect of our little party being broken up and scattered; for several valued friendships had been formed.

Between three and four o'clock in the afternoon, the thermometer indicated 98° in the sun and 75° in the

shade.   Dr. Mackinlay showed me an old Danish dollar
he had got, in change, at Reykjavik; it bore the date of
A.D. 1619, the year of the landing of the Pilgrim Fathers
from the *May Flower*.   Part of the day was spent in
writing out these pages from my diary.   In the evening
we saw, far to our left, faint and dim on the horizon
line, the north-west islands of Shetland; and by a quarter
to 8 o'clock P.M. were sailing twenty miles to the west
of Fair Isle, which lies between Orkney and Shetland.
Both groups are in sight.   We have not seen a sail since
we left Faröe, and now, what we at first fancied to be one,
off the north end of the Orkneys, turns out to be a light-
house, rising apparently from the sea, but in reality from
low lying land which is yet below the horizon.

The sunset to-night is gorgeous; cavernous recesses
opening through a dense purple cloud-bank into glowing
regions of fire; while broad flashing gleams ray out on
every side athwart the sky, as if from furnace-mouths.
Then we have moonlight on a sea smooth as glass, and
not even a ripple to be seen.   The Orkney light-house,
now gleaming like a setting star, is left far astern.   The
phosphoresence along the vessel's side and in her wake
is most brilliant; while, seething, electric-like, from the
screw, it rivals the "churned fire-froth" of the demon
steed.   The moon, half-hid, is at times deep crimson and
again bright yellow.   Many falling stars are shooting
"madly from their spheres;" not that our music lured
them, although, "on such a night" of nights, when all is
harmonious, we cannot but sing.   Mr. Murray gives us
"Home, sweet home" and "The last rose of summer,"
and ere retiring at midnight, all of us join together in
singing the "Spanish Chant."

Wednesday morning, August 10.   We are off Inverness; wind a-head and rising. Professor Chadbourne to-day gave me an oak-leaf which he plucked from the tree, at Upsala, planted by Linnæus with his own hands. Wrote as long as the heaving of the ship would admit of it, then arranged botanical specimens and read Wordsworth. The wind is blowing so fresh, off Peterhead, that, with full steam, we are not making above one and a half knots; and at times can scarcely keep any way on. Passed the Bell-Rock; the sea still rising. Went to bed at 11 o'clock P.M.; vessel pitching a good deal.

Thursday morning, August 11.   Rose at four o'clock and was on deck ere the *Arcturus* dropt anchor in Leith Roads.   But as we cannot get our traps on shore till the custom-house officer comes at nine o'clock to overhaul them, we remain and breakfast on board,   The examination made, at half-past ten o'clock A.M., we landed by a tug steamer, and made for our respective railway stations, each, on parting, bidding the other "a bright adieu!" in the hope that it might only be for "a brief absence!" "Odin" was in good feather: his owner sunbronzed and strong.

At length, comfortably ensconsed in the fast express, I lay back in the corner of a compartment, closed my eyes and resigned myself to see pleasant pictures and dream waking dreams—of snow-jökuls, volcanoes, glaciers, and ice-fields; of geysers, mud-cauldrons, and sulphur-pits; of lava plains, black, wierd and blasted, or dreary wastes of ice; of deep rapid rivers, flashing waterfalls, leaping torrents; of frightful chasms, rugged cliffs, and precipitous mountains mirrored in deep blue fiords; of pathless stony deserts, enlivened at times with oasis-like spots of tender green herbage and bright coloured flowers; of wild break-neck rides, over bare rocks, among slabs and lava-blocks of all shapes and sizes and lying in every conceivable direction; through volcanic sands and scoriæ; by red and black vetrified craters, or across dangerous fords; of multifarious scamperings too, and mud-plashings over hill and dale; or wild rides down rocky steeps, not on a phantom steed, but on a sure-footed Iceland pony; of pleasant companionship by the way; of cordial welcome and great kindness received, in quiet homesteads, and at all hands from the people, wherever we went; then again of Frost contending with Fire, and of all the varied and marvellous phenomena of Iceland, that singularly interesting island in the lone North Sea.

STROMOE—FARÖE.

APPENDIX.

APPENDIX.

I.

ICELANDIC STORIES AND FAIRY TALES

TRANSLATED INTO ENGLISH BY THE REV. OLAF PALSSON, DEAN AND RECTOR OF REYKJAVIK CATHEDRAL. REVISED AND EDITED BY DAVID MACKINLAY AND ANDREW JAMES SYMINGTON.

STORIES OF SÆMUNDUR FRODI, CALLED THE LEARNED.[1]

I. THE DARK SCHOOL.

Long, long ago, when Trolls and Giants lived among men, there was a famous school where curious youths were taught the mysteries of witchcraft. France and Germany both claim the honour of it, but no one knows where it really was.

It was kept in a dismal cavern, deep underground, into which no ray of sunlight ever entered. Here, the scholars had to stay no less than seven winters; for it took them all that time to complete their studies. They never saw their teacher from one year's end to another. Every morning a grey grizzly hand, all covered with hair,

---

[1] Sæmund Frodi, like other learned men of those days, was supposed to be in possession of magic powers. He was the Friar Bacon of Iceland; and these stories in which his name figures, handed down by tradition, are still often told in Iceland by the fireside on the long winter evenings. Curious to observe, that, in most mediæval stories of this kind, Satan is always outwitted and gets the worst of it. A.J.S.

pushed itself through the cavern wall and gave to each one his lesson book. These books were written all over with letters of fire, and could be read with ease, even in the dark. The lessons over, the same grizzly hand again appeared to take away the books and bring in the scholars' dinner.

At the close of winter, the scholars who had then got through their seven years apprenticeship were dismissed. The great iron door was opened, and the master stood watching those who went out; for he had stipulated that the scholar who walked hindmost, in passing through, was to be seized by him and kept as a thrall. But who was this strange school-master? Why, Old Nick himself. No wonder, then, that each of the scholars struggled hard to be first in passing the fatal threshold.

Once on a time, there were three Icelanders at the dark school; Sæmund Frodi, afterwards parish priest at Oddi, Kalfar Arnason, and Halfdan Eldjarnsson, afterwards parish priest at Fell, in Slettuhlid. They were all dismissed at the same time. Sæmund, to the great delight of his companions, offered to walk hindmost in going out of school, so he dressed himself in a long loose cloak, which he took care to leave unbuttoned, and bidding good bye to school-fellows left behind, prepared to follow his countrymen. Just as he was putting his feet on the first step of the stair which led up from the school door, Old Nick, who was watching hard by, made a clutch at the cloak and called out,

> "Sæmund Frodi, pass not the door,
> Thou art my thrall for evermore."

And now the great iron door began to turn on its hinges;

but, before Old Nick had time to slam it too, Sæmund slipt his arms out of the sleeves of his cloak, and sprung forward out of the grasp of his enemy.

In doing so, the door struck him a heavy blow on the heel, which gave him a good deal of pain, when he said,

> "The door hath swung too near the heel,
> But better sore foot than serve the Deil."

And so Sæmund outwitted Old Nick, and got away from the dark school along with his two friends. Since then, it has become a common saying in Iceland, when a person has had a narrow escape from danger, that "the door swung too near his heels." [1]

II.—SÆMUND GETS THE LIVING OF ODDI.

At the time Sæmund, Kalfur, and Halfdan came out of the dark school, there was no priest at Oddi, for the old priest had just died. All three of them would fain have the living, and so each went to the king to ask it for himself. The king knew his men; and so he sent them all away with the same answer, that whoever reached Oddi first, should be made priest of that place.

Thereupon Sæmund summoned Old Nick and said to

---

[1] This story may explain the origin of the Scotch proverb, "Deil tak' the hindmost."—There is another version of Sæmund's mode of escape; viz.: That when he was about to be seized, pointing to his shadow on the wall, he said, "I am not the hindmost, dont you see him that is coming behind me?" Old Nick then caught at the shadow, and thought it was a man; but Sæmund got out, and the door was slammed on his heels. But after that time, it is added, Sæmund was always without a shadow, for Old Nick would not let his shadow free again. Here, in this old-world story, we have the germ of Chamisso's "Shadowless Man." A.J.S.

him, "Now, I'll make a bargain with you, if you swim
with me on your back across to Iceland, and land me
there without wetting my coat-tail, I'll be your servant
as long as I live." Old Nick was highly pleased with
the offer and agreed at once. So, in less than no time,
he changed himself into a seal, and left Norway with
Sæmund on his back.

Sæmund took care to have his prayer book with him,
and read bits out of it every now and then while on the
way. As soon as they got close to the shores of Iceland,
which they did in less time than you would think, he
closed the book and suddenly struck the seal such a
heavy blow on the neck with it that the animal went
down all at once into deep water. Sæmund, now left
to himself, struck out for the shore and got easily to
land. In this way Old Nick lost his bargain, and
Sæmund got the living of Oddi.

III. THE GOBLIN AND THE COWHERD.

When Sæmund was priest of Oddi, he once had a
cowherd—a good servant withal, but greatly addicted to
swearing. Sæmund often reproved him for this, but all
his reproofs were of no avail. At last he told him, he
really ought to leave off his bad habits, for Old Nick
and his servants lived upon people's curses and wicked
words. "Say you so?" said the cowherd, "if I knew for
certain that Old Nick would lose his meals by it, I would
never say a bad word more." So he made up his mind
to mend his ways.

"I'll soon see whether you are in earnest or not," said
Sæmund, and so, he forthwith lodged a goblin in the

cowhouse. The cowherd did not like his guest, and no wonder: for he was up to every kind of mischief, and almost worried the life out of him with his wicked pranks. The poor cowherd bore up bravely for a time, and never let slip an oath or angry word. The goblin got leaner day by day, to the intense delight of the cowherd, who hoped, bye and bye, to see an end of him.

One morning, on opening the byre door, the poor cowherd found every thing turned topsy-turvy. The milk pails and stools were broken in pieces and scattered about the floor; and the whole of the cows—and there were many of them—tied tail to tail, were straggling about without halters, and goring each other. It needed but half an eye to see who had done the mischief. So the cowherd in a rage turned round to the goblin who, shrunk and haggard, lay crouched up in a corner of a stall, the very picture of wretchedness, and poured forth such a volley of furious curses as would have overwhelmed any human being in the same plight. The goblin all at once began to revive; his skin no longer shrivelled looked smooth and plump; his eye brightened up, and the stream of life again flowed joyously through his veins.

"O, oh!" said the cowherd, as he suddenly checked himself, when he saw the wonderful effect his swearing had on the goblin, "Now I know for certain that Sæmund was right." And from that day forward he was never known to utter an oath. As for the goblin, he soon pined away again and has long since been beyond troubling anybody. May you and I, and all who hear this story, strive to follow the good example of Sæmund's cowherd!

IV. OLD NICK MADE HIMSELF AS LITTLE AS HE WAS ABLE.

Sæmund one day asked Old Nick how little he could make himself. "Why," replied he, "as for that I could make myself as small as the smallest midge." Thereupon Sæmund bored a tiny hole in the door post, and asked him to make good his boast by walking into it. This he at once did; but no sooner was he in, than Sæmund stopped the hole with a little plug of wood, and made all fast.

Old Nick cursed his folly, cried, and begged for mercy; but Sæmund would not take out the stopper till he promised to become his servant and do all that he was told. This was the reason why Sæmund always had it in his power to employ Old Nick in whatever business he liked.

V. THE FLY.

As might be expected, Old Nick always harboured a great ill will against Sæmund: for he could not help feeling how much he was in Sæmund's power. He therefore tried to revenge himself on various occasions; but all his tricks failed, for Sæmund was too sharp for him.

Once, he put on the shape of a little fly, and hid himself—so he thought, at least—under the film that had gathered on the priest's milk jug, hoping that Sæmund would swallow him unawares, and so lose his life. But Sæmund had all his eyes about him; so instead of swallowing the fly he wrapped it up in the film, covered the whole with a bladder, and laid the package on the altar. There, the fly was obliged to remain till after the

service, when Sæmund opened the package and gave Old
Nick his liberty. It is told, as a truth, that old Nick
never found himself in a worse case than when lying on
the altar before Sæmund.

VI. THE GOBLIN'S WHISTLE.

Sæmund had a whistle of such wonderful power, that,
as often as he blew it, one or more goblins appeared before him, ready to do his bidding.[1]   One day, on getting
up, he happened to leave the whistle under his pillow,
and forgot all about it till the afternoon when the house-
maid was going to make his bed.   He charged her, if
she found anything unusual about the bed, she was on no
account to touch it, or move it from its place.   But he
might have saved himself the trouble of speaking; for,
as soon as the girl saw the whistle, she took it up in her
hand, and looked at it on every side.   Not satisfied with
much handling it, she put it to her mouth and blew it
lustily.   The sound of the blast had not died away before
a goblin stood before her, saying, "what will you have
me to do?"   The girl was not a little startled, but had
the presence of mind to conceal her surprise.

It so happened that the hides of ten sheep, that had
been killed that day, were lying on the ground in front
of the parsonage.   Recollecting this, the girl replied to
the goblin, "Go and count all the hairs that are on the
ten hides outside, and, if you finish your task before I
get this bed made, I'll consent to marry you."   The

---

[1] The reader will here be reminded of Aladdin's Lamp, Genii, and of
the East, from whence these Stories also originally came in the days
of Odin.

goblin thought that a task worth undertaking for such a prize; and hurrying out, fell to counting the hairs with all his might. The girl who did not like the idea of being the wife of a goblin, lost no time, you may be sure, in getting through with her work; and it was well she bestirred herself; for, by the time the bed was made, the goblin had almost finished his task. Only a few hairs of the last hide remained uncounted, but they were enough to make him lose his bargain. When Sæmund afterwards learned how prudently the girl had got out of her scrape, he was very well pleased.

ICELANDIC FAIRY TALES.

BIARNI SVEINSSON AND HIS SISTER SALVÖR.[1]

Once on a time, a worthy couple, Sveinn and his wife, occupied a farm, on the shores of the beautiful Skaga-fiord, in the north country. They were in easy circumstances and were blessed with two fine children, a son and daughter, who were the joy of their hearts. Biarni and his sister Salvör—for these were the names of their children—were twins and greatly attached to each other.

[1] To the right understanding of the story of "Biarni Sveinsson," it must be remembered that a superstition prevailed amongst the Icelanders regarding the central deserts. These, they believed, were inhabited by a strange mysterious race of men who held no intercourse with the other inhabitants, and were said to be in the habit of kidnapping women from the country. This belief may have had its origin in the fact, that, in former days, some few outlaws and their families took refuge in the deserts, and lived there for a time in order to escape the hands of justice. A. J. S.

In the spring of the year,[1] about St. John's day, when these two had reached the age of twenty, the people of Skagafiord were arranging a party to make a journey to the mountains of the interior, to gather Iceland-moss for making porridge. Sveinn promised to let his son go with the party. As soon as Salvör knew that, she felt a great desire to go too; and so she went to her parents to ask their consent. This was not so easily got, as they did not wish to part with both their children at once; and besides, they knew she was ill fitted to bear the hardships and fatigues of mountain travelling. But she fretted so much at the thought of being left behind, that, at last, they consented to let her go.

The night before the moss-gatherers were to leave, Sveinn the farmer dreamed that he had two beautiful white birds, of which he was very fond, and that all at once, to his great grief, the hen-bird disappeared and could nowhere be found. On awaking in the morning, he could not help thinking that his dream betokened no good to his darling Salvör, so he called her to him, and after telling her his dream, he said to her, "Salvör dear! I cannot bear to part with you, you must stay at home with your mother and me, for I would never forgive myself if any ill befel you by the way." Salvör who had been in great glee at the prospect of riding, day after day, up the romantic valleys to the south of Skagafiord, and there tenting out amidst the mountains, was neither to hold nor to bind, when she found that, after all, she would have to stay at home; she wept with vexation and distressed herself so much that her father could not bear it, and again gave an unwilling consent

[1] In Iceland vegetation is late.

to let her go. So she accompanied her brother and the rest of the party to the mountains.

The first day after getting there, she gathered Iceland moss with the others, but during the night she fell suddenly ill and was unable to leave her tent on the following day. Biarni stayed with her, and did all that a brother could do to help and comfort her. For three whole days he was her companion, but, on the fourth day, he left her for a time in charge of a friend, while he himself joined the moss-gatherers. After partly filling his bag, he sat himself down by a large stone, and, resting his head on his hand, brooded over his sister's unhappy fate; he feared she was going to die among the mountains.

By and by he heard a great tramping of horses, and, on looking about, he saw two men riding towards him at a quick pace. One of them wore red coloured clothes, and had a red horse; the other who was younger, was dressed in black, and was mounted on a black horse. On reaching the place where Biarni was sitting, they dismounted and saluted him by name.

"What ails you Biarni," said the elder of the two strangers." For a time Biarni answered not a word, but on being pressed to do so, he opened up his heart to them and told all about his sister's illness.

"My companions are going to return home, but I must stay to watch over Salvör; and who knows how soon she may die in my arms."

"You are in a hard case Biarni," said the other, "and I am sorry for you, but wont you leave your sister with me, and I will take good care of her."

"No, no," said Biarni, "that I dare not do, for I know

neither who you are, nor where you come from. But will you tell me where your home is?"

"That's no business of yours," said the other, rather gruffly, and then, taking from his pocket a silver-gilt box set with precious stones, added, "Won't you sell me your sister for this box."

"No," said Biarni, "nor for a thousand like it. I would not give her to you for any money."

"Well! well! there is no help for it, you will at all events accept this box, as a token that you have met with men among the mountains."

Biarni took the offered gift with pleasure, and thanked the giver. The two men then bade him farewell and rode away, while he returned to the tent. Next morning his companions went away home, leaving him alone with his sister. Though she was now a little better, he dared not sleep, for he was afraid lest the strangers should come and steal her away. But, after watching a whole day and night, he felt overcome with fatigue; so he lay down, and folding his arms round her waist to protect her, fell into a sound sleep. But, when he awoke, his sister was gone, and was nowhere to be found. He spent a whole day sorrowfully wandering from spot to spot, looking and calling for her, but it was all in vain. He then turned his back on the mountains, and with a heavy heart went home, and told his parents what had happened.

"Woe is me," said Sveinn, "what I feared most has come to pass, but God's will be done!"

There was great grief in Skagafiörd when the news spread from farm to farm; for Salvör, with all her waywardness, was a promising girl, and was every body's favourite. A party of young men returned to the mountains to look for her, but nowhere was the least trace of her to be found.

And now ten years had passed away. By this time Biarni was married and settled on a farm, not far from his father's. During autumn all his sheep went amissing, and his shepherd could not discover what had become of them though he searched diligently for them three whole days. On learning this, Biarni bid his wife provide him with a week's supply of food, and an extra pair of shoes; "for," said he, "I shall go to the mountains myself to look for the sheep." His parents, who were still alive, urged him to stay at home; for they feared that, if he went to the mountains, they might never see his face again.

"I must go," said he to them, "I cannot afford to lose the sheep. But be of good heart, and do not begin to weary for me till the week is over."

He then went away on foot, and did not leave off walking for three days. At the end of that time he came to a cavern, where he turned in and lay down to sleep. On waking, he could not see a yard before him; for a thick fog which rested on the ground. He continued his journey, but soon lost his way. Towards evening the fog cleared off, and he found himself in a spacious valley, not far from a large well built farm house. It was the hay season, so that all the people of the farm were busy in the meadow. On getting near the house, he noticed, in particular, two women and a girl who were tedding the hay. "God's peace be with you," said he, on reaching the spot; and then, telling them of his mishaps, he asked permission to stay all night under their roof. They gave him a hearty welcome, and the girl went with him to the house. She was of more genteel appearance than the rest—young and handsome —and, as Biarni thought, bore some resemblance to his long lost but well remembered sister. This unexpected circumstance renewed his old griefs, but he did what he could to seem cheerful before his young hostess. She led him through several apartments to a large well furnished room, where everything was neat and tidy. Here, she drew in a chair, and kindly asked him to sit down and rest, while she brought in supper. He had not long to wait; for she soon placed upon the table a plentiful supply of meat and wine.

After supper, she showed him to the little room where he was to sleep for the night; she then took away his wet clothes, wished him a kind good night, and left the room.

As Biarni lay in bed, he fell a-wondering where he was, and how the sight of the girl should have so waked up the sad memories of the past. He fell asleep thinking of these things, but was soon awakened by the sound of singing in a room over his head. It was the family at evening worship, as is the custom of the country. He heard both men and women singing, but one voice sounded clear above all others, and thrilled to his very heart, so strongly did it remind him of his sister Salvör. Thoughts of the past filled his mind and kept him awake for hours, but he fell asleep again, and slept on, till he was roused up in the morning by the girl. She brought with her a suit of fine clothes, and bade him put them on.

"To-day is Sunday," she added, "and you must stay here till to-morrow." She then left the room.

While Biarni was putting on his clothes, a little boy in a green coat, and very nicely dressed, came into the room and wished him good morning. "What has brought you here, so far away from home?" said the little fellow to him.

"I have come to look for some sheep that I have lost."

"Well, I have not seen them in this valley. But I hope you wont go to look for them to-day. Father is going to hear service in the church, and you must be there too."

Before Biarni had time to reply, some one called the boy away, saying, "Sveinn, come here, and don't plague the stranger with your nonsense."

At breakfast, Biarni was waited on by the girl who had treated him so well the evening before.

Towards mid-day, people began to come from far and near, to join in the public service in the church close by. The boy came for Biarni, and led him by the hand into the church and showed him to a seat. On looking about, what was his surprise to see by his side the man in the red clothes whom he had seen, ten years before, among the mountains! But, his surprise was greater still, on discovering that the clergyman who conducted the service, was no other than the man in the black dress who had travelled with the other. The church was full of people. Most of the men were tall and strongly built, but had something forbidding about their looks. Some wore brown knitted garments of undyed wool. Biarni said nothing to his neighbour, but took out the gilt box and offered him a pinch of snuff. This he took, but without seeming to recognize Biarni.

By and by, Biarni saw, seated just in front of the pulpit, a comely well dressed woman who seemed the very picture of his sister. When their eyes met, she was overcome with emotion and began to smile and weep by turns. Biarni now felt confident that it was indeed his beloved sister Salvör whom he now saw before him.

The service decently performed to the end and the blessing pronounced, the boy again took Biarni by the hand and led him out. In passing the church door, an old ill looking man, who sat there, tripped Biarni up and made him fall. On this, the man in the red clothes came forward and chastised the offender, while Biarni went with the boy into the farm house. The two men whom Biarni had met among the mountains, shortly after came in and saluted him.

"Do you know us, Biarni!" said they to him kindly.

"Yes," replied he. But not another word could he utter for emotion.

A moment after, the woman, he had seen in the church and taken for his sister, entered the room. She flew into his arms and pressed him to her bosom saying,

"Before we were born we lay in each other's arms, I was taken weeping from thy embrace, and now I return laughing to thy arms, my brother."

It was a joyful meeting.

When Biarni recovered himself, he told his sister about his parents, and also all that had happened in Skagafiord since her departure. The man in red clothes then addressed himself to Biarni, and said,

"Whilst thou wert asleep among the mountains, I took thy sister away from thee and gave her in marriage to this man in the black dress, who is my son. He is the clergyman of the valley and I am the sysselman. It was I that took away the sheep and led thee astray to this place, that brother and sister might meet again. To-night thou must stay here with thy sister. To-morrow I shall give thee back thy lost sheep and go with thee part of the way to Skagafiord."

Biarni spent a happy evening with Salvör. In the morning he took leave of her with many tears, and departed under the guidance of her husband and of her father-in-law, who gave him back his sheep, and helped him to drive them. On reaching the inhabited part of the country, his new friends parted with him and bade him an affectionate farewell; but not before they had made him promise to leave Skagafiörd and live with them.

"You must come and settle in the valley beside us," said they to him, "we shall return next summer and lead you and your friends to your sister's home."

On getting to Skagafiörd, Biarni told his wife and mother all that had happened to him, when away, and also the promise he had made to remove to the mountains; but charged them to say nothing to the neighbours about it. His parents were rejoiced to learn that Salvör was still alive, and promised to go with him and his wife.

In June of the next year, three men, from the mountains, rode up one night to Biarni's house. The night following, Biarni, and his parents, and all his household went away with them and in due time reached the valley where Salvör lived. How it rejoiced Sveinn and his wife to see again their long lost daughter! They settled in the valley and died there, at a good old age.

Biarni lived there too, for many years, but he could never forget the beautiful Skagafiörd; so when age came upon him, he returned to his old home, and spent his latter years among the friends of his youth.

UNA THE FAIRY.

Many many years ago, a strapping young fellow, called Geir, was settled in the farm of Randafell, on the south slope of the Eyafialla mountains, near the sea-coast. Every thing prospered with him; for he was active and industrious, and scorned to eat the bread of idleness. His wife was as industrious as himself, but unfortunately, she took ill and died, shortly after their marriage. At the hay-making season, which came on soon after, he missed his wife greatly; for the maid servants were too few to look after the house and make the hay.

One day, when they had a good deal more work before them than they were able to get through, a strange woman made her appearance in the hay field, and, without so much as saying, "by your leave," began at once to handle the rake; and cleverly she handled it, too, for she got through more work than any two of them. She was young and handsome, but silent as the grave. Not a word could Geir, or any one else, get out of her the live long day. At night she disappeared, no one knew where; but, when morning came, there was she, first in the field, ready to take her place among the women.

Things went on in this way till the end of the harvest, when Geir went up to her, and thanked her kindly for the help she had given them.

She took what he said in good part, and no longer refused to talk with him. They had a long chat together, but Geir was not made a bit the wiser, as to where she lived, or whose daughter she was. She told him, however, that her name was Una.

"Una," said he to her at last, "I am greatly in want of a housekeeper; I dont know any body so likely to suit as you; will you take the situation?"

"I have no objection to do so," she replied, "when do you want me?"

"The sooner the better."

"Well, I shall come with my luggage to-morrow, and take up my abode with you." She then disappeared.

Next morning, she walked into the farm house, and set down a large chest, full of clothes, which she had brought with her. This she put out of the way in the closet, and then began to bustle about the house, looking after household duties.

And now things began to prosper again with the Randafell farmer. Una was a capital manager, and soon became famous all over the country side for her good butter, and her well ordered house. Geir was delighted with his housekeeper; but one thing distressed him—he could not persuade her to go to church.

When Christmas Eve came round, Geir and all the servants went to church, to the vesper service. Geir was anxious that Una should go too. But no! she would not budge, excusing herself by saying, that she was needed at home to look after the house. It was morning before the church goers got back, for the church was a good three hours' ride from Randafell. On returning they found Una busy preparing the Christmas feast. The ordinary work of the house was done, so that they had nothing to do but to take a few hours rest, before sitting down to enjoy themselves.

By the time the third winter came round, Geir began to think of taking a wife, and who so likely to suit him as Una! And so thought all the neighbours too. Many a talk they had about her, when gathered together in the churchyard, on the Sundays, waiting the arrival of the clergyman. After discussing her good qualities, "Isn't it strange," the one would say to the other, "that we can't find'out who Una is, or where she comes from?"

"Aye! that is true," another would say, "but isn't it stranger still, that all the time she has been at Randafell, she has never once entered the church door?"

Geir was very fond of her, but could not make up his mind to ask her to marry him, so long as she refused to bend her knee in prayer to God.

On the third Christmas Eve, Geir set out, with all his household, to the midnight service in the church. Una as usual remained at home. When they were on the road, Geir's serving man suddenly complained of severe pain. He lay down on the spot, and said he would rest there till he got better; so Geir and the others went on without him.

As soon as they were out of sight, the man got up to his feet, mounted his horse and rode back again to the farm. His sickness was only feigned, in order to get the chance of finding out what could tempt Una always to stay at home, at a time when every true hearted Icelander made a point of joining his neighbours, in the house of God, to commemorate the anniversary of that blessed night when Christ was born in Bethlehem.

On reaching the farm, he unsaddled the horse, and

slipped quietly in, taking care to hide in a dark corner where he could see all that was going on, without being himself seen. Una was busy sweeping and cleaning the house; and so cleverly did she go about her work that everything was put to rights in a very short time. After washing herself, she went to the store-closet and put on a dress which the man had never seen till now, and which was more befitting a king's daughter than a poor farmer's housekeeper. Never before had Una looked so handsome and beautiful.

She now took out of her chest a piece of red cloth, which she put under her arm. Shutting her chest and the closet door, she left the house and ran down the meadow, till she came to a pool of water. Here she spread out the red cloth, and placed herself upon it. At this instant the man, who had been breathlessly following her, came up, and unseen by her just succeeded in getting his foot on a corner of the cloth. And now they sunk down and down into the earth, with a feeling as if they were going through smoke. By and by they landed on a green plain, not far from a splendid farm house. Una took up the cloth, put it under her arm, and went up to the house. The man walked softly behind, taking care to keep out of her sight. A great many people came out of doors to welcome Una, who seemed rejoiced to see them, and saluted them kindly.

Great preparations were going on inside for a feast. The guest chamber was swept and garnished, and the table laid. As soon as the people took their places several dishes were brought, and abundance of good wine. The serving man, who had slipped in with the others unknown to Una, took his place among the guests.

Among other things he was presented with a fine rib of smoked mutton, which he took and preserved, for he had never seen so fat a rib before. After supper the people amused themselves with games of different kinds, and were all very happy.

Just as day began to break, Una told her friends, she would have to go away, as her master, the peasant, would soon be back from church. So she took a kind leave of every one, and walked to the spot where she had alighted, on coming down.

The man followed her, and again succeeded in getting his foot on the cloth, without being seen. So they ascended together through the dark earth, till they came to the pool of water again. Una took up the cloth, and went straight to the store-room to change her dress. After that she went into the house, to await the return of the peasant, and make ready the Christmas feast.

The serving man had, meantime, taken up his place at the spot where he had been left behind the night before. When the farmer came up he asked him how he was.

"I am almost well again," said the man, "and quite able to go home with you."

So they all rode together to Randafell.

Una received them with a smiling face, and told them that the feast was quite ready. So they were not long in taking their places. As is usual on such occasions, the principal dish was smoked mutton. As this happened to be very fine, the farmer took up a large rib, and holding it up said,

"Have any of you ever seen such a rib as this"

"I think I have; what think you of that," said the

serving man, as he held up before them the rib he had got the night before.

As soon as Una saw this, she changed colour, went out without saying a single word, and was never afterwards seen.

GILITRUTT.

Once on a time, a smart active young peasant occupied a farm under the Eyafialla mountains. As his pasture land was good, he kept many sheep. These yielded him no small store of wool, and yet, it was no easy matter for him to keep a coat on his back; for the wife whom he had lately married, though young and healthy, was lazy to a degree, and gave herself little concern about the affairs of the house. Her husband was greatly dissatisfied, but could not induce her to mend her ways.

At the close of summer he gave her a large bundle of wool, and told her to be sure to spin it and work it up into coarse wadmal during the winter months. "Very well," she said, "I'll see about it bye and bye;" but at the same time looked as if she would far rather have nothing to do with it. She let it lie in a corner untouched, spite of the hints she got every now and then, from her husband. It was mid-winter before she fully made up her mind to set to work; and then she began to perplex herself, as to how she could get so much wool worked up, before the close of winter.

Just then, an ugly old woman came to the door, begging for alms.

"Can you do any work for me in return," asked the peasant's wife.

"Perhaps I can," replied the old woman.

"But what kind of work would you have me to do?"

"I want you to make some coarse cloth for me, out of this wool."

"Very well, let me have the wool then."

And so, the peasant's wife handed the large bag of wool to the old woman, who, without more ado, tossed it up on her back, at the same time saying,

"You may depend on my coming back with the cloth, the first day of summer."

"But what payment will you ask for your work when you bring the cloth," said the peasant's wife.

"I wont take any payment; but you must tell me what my name is, in three guesses."

The peasant's wife, too lazy to spin and weave for herself, agreed to this strange condition, and so the old woman departed.

As the winter months passed on, the peasant often asked what had become of the wool.

"Give yourself no concern about it," said the wife, "you'll have it back, all spun and woven, by the first day of summer."

As he never could get any other answer, he at last ceased to talk about the wool. All this time his wife was trying to find out the old woman's name, but all her efforts were unavailing. By the time the last month of winter came round she became so anxious and uneasy that she could neither eat nor sleep. Her husband was greatly distressed at the change which had come over her, and begged her to let him know what ailed her. Unable longer to keep the matter secret, she told him the whole.

He was very much startled at what he heard, and told her how very imprudent she had been, as the old woman was, most certainly, a witch, and would take her away if she failed in her bargain.

A day or two after this conversation, he had occasion to go up the adjoining mountain. He was so bowed down with grief, at the thought of losing his wife, that he scarcely knew what he was about; and so wandered from the road, till he came to the bottom of a lofty cliff. While he was considering how he could get into the right road again, he thought he heard a sound as of a voice inside the hill. Following the sound he discovered a hole in the face of the cliff. On peeping through this hole, he saw a tall old woman sitting weaving with the loom between her knees; and, as she beat the treadles, every now and then breaking into a snatch of song,

"Ha! Ha! and Ho! Ho!
The good wife does not know
That Gilitrutt is my name."

" Aha!" muttered the peasant to himself, if she does not know now, she will know bye and bye;" for he felt quite sure that was the same old hag who had so imposed on his poor foolish wife.

All the way home, he kept repeating the word *Gilitrutt*, and, as soon as he got in doors, he wrote it down on a piece of paper, that he might not forget it. But he did not, at that time, give his wife the least inkling of what had befallen him. The poor woman grew more and more sorrowful, as the days passed on; and, when the closing day of winter came, she was so woe-begone that she had not the heart even to put on her clothes. In the course of the day, her husband enquired if she had found out her visitor's name yet.

"Alas, no! Would to God I could find it out! for I am like to die of grief."

"There is no occasion for that," he replied cheerfully, "I've found out the name for you; so you need not be afraid to meet the old hag." With that, he handed her the piece of paper, and at the same time told about his adventure on the mountain. She took the paper, with a trembling hand, for at first she feared that the news was too good to be true; and, though her husband's story comforted her not a little, she could not get rid of a suspicion that the name might not be the true one.

She wanted her husband to stay indoors the next day, so as to be present when the old woman called.

"No! no!" said he, "you kept your own counsel when you gave her the wool, so, you must do without me when you take in the cloth, and pay her the wages agreed on."

He then left the house.

And now came the first day of summer. The peasant's wife was in the house alone, and lay a-bed, listening with a beating heart for the first sound of the old hag's footsteps. She had not long to wait; for, before the morning passed, a trampling noise was heard, and in stalked the old woman with a bundle on her back, and a scowl on her face. As soon as she got within the room, she threw down the big bundle of cloth, and, in an angry tone, called out,

"What is my name now? What's my name?"

The peasant's wife, who was almost dead with fear, said "Signy!"

"That my name! That my name! guess again, good wife."

"Asa," said she.

"That my name! That my name! No indeed. You must guess again; but remember this is your last chance."

"Are you not called Gilitrutt?" said the woman timorously.

This answer came like a thunderbolt on the old hag, who fell down with a great noise on the floor, and lay there for sometime. She then got up, and, without speaking a word, went her way out of the house, and was never more seen in the country-side.

As for the peasant's wife, she was full of joy at her deliverance, and, ever after, was a changed woman. She became a pattern of industry and good management, and henceforth always worked her own wool herself.

HILDUR THE FAIRY QUEEN.

Once on a time a farmer settled in a mountainous part of the country, but the particular spot is not mentioned, nor has his name come to us; but we do know that he was a bachelor, and had a housekeeper named Hildur.

Who Hildur was, neither the farmer nor any of the neighbouring gossips could find out: but as she took good care of the household and discharged her duties faithfully, she was allowed to keep her own secret. All the servants liked her, and the farmer thought himself very fortunate in having fallen in with such a housekeeper. She was of a quiet disposition, but always kind and obliging.

The farmer's affairs were in a flourishing state: his sheep throve and multiplied, and he had nothing to annoy him except this, that he had great difficulty in getting shepherds to enter his service. The cause of this was not that the farmer treated his shepherds badly, but that, one after another, they were found dead in bed, on Christmas morning.

In olden times, it was the custom for the Icelanders, on Christmas Eve, to meet together at midnight for public worship; and any one who absented himself from church, on that occasion, was considered as much to blame as if he were keeping away on Christmas day itself. Those living up among the mountains, and who had long weary roads to go, had often great difficulty in getting to church in time; especially those who were not able to leave home before the Pleiades could be seen in the south-eastern heavens.

In this farm, the shepherds did not usually get home from work before that time, so that they generally missed the opportunity of attending the Christmas Eve service. Hildur never went on those occasions, as she preferred staying at home to watch the house—as is customary for some one to do on Christmas Eve—and attend to the preparations for the Christmas feast. She was always busily occupied in this way till the night was far advanced, so that the church-goers were back from the services and asleep in bed, before she retired for the night.

As often as Christmas morn came round, the farmer's shepherd, whoever he might be, was found dead in bed. This strange fatality was well known over all the country side. No wonder, then, that shepherds were afraid of entering the farmer's service, even though offered better wages than they could get elsewhere. No mark of violence was ever seen on the body of the unfortunate shepherd, so that no blame could be attached either to the farmer, or to any one in the house. At last the farmer declared that he could not find it in his heart to engage shepherds, with the prospect of certain death before them, and that he would, for the future, leave his sheep to take care of themselves.

When things had reached this pass, there came to him, one day, an active hardy man, who offered his services as shepherd.

"I am not so much in want of your services as to be willing to take you."

"Have you engaged a shepherd for next winter?" asked the stranger.

"No, I have not," replied the farmer, "but surely you have heard how sad has been the end of all that have been before you."

"Oh yes, I've heard all about it; but their fate will not hinder me from taking care of your sheep, if you are only willing to engage me."

At last, the farmer complied with his entreaties, and engaged him as shepherd. He soon shewed that he was in every respect fitted for the place. He was kind and obliging; and both able and willing to lend a hand at any farm work, so that he soon became a favourite with everybody.

Till Christmas-tide, nothing extraordinary happened. On Christmas Eve, the farmer went to church as usual with his domestics. The housekeeper alone stayed at home, and the shepherd was left in charge of the sheep. Towards evening the shepherd came in from his work, and after partaking of dinner, lay down to rest in bed. He took care, however, not to drop asleep; for, though free from fear, he thought it only prudent to keep awake.

When the night was advanced he heard the church-goers come in, and take some refreshment before going to bed. Up till this time, he had not remarked anything unusual; but when the others had fallen asleep, he felt languid and weary. He was afraid lest he should be over-powered with sleep, and did his best to keep awake. A little while after, some one, whom he believed to be the housekeeper Hildur, stealthily approached the bed-side. Thinking he was asleep, she began to try to put some-thing in his mouth. He felt certain that it must be a magic-bridle, and so, pretending to be quite unconscious of what was going on, he let himself be quietly bridled.

As soon as the bridle was on, she led him out very easily; mounting on his back, she rode away at a smart pace till they reached a yawning chasm in the earth. Then she dismounted beside a stone, and letting go her hold of the bridle, disappeared into the chasm. The shepherd did not want to lose sight of her, and so tried to follow; but he soon found that that was out of his power, so long as he had on the bridle. By dint however of rubbing his head against the stone, he got rid of the bridle, and leaving it behind, he threw himself into the chasm into which Hildur had sprung.

As far as he could judge, he had not gone very deep down till he saw Hildur again. She was then landed on a fine level meadow, along which she was walking quickly. From what he saw he came to think that all was not right with Hildur, and that she was not the woman she had seemed to be in the farmer's house. In order to keep her from seeing him as he followed her over the plain, he took out of his pocket a stone which had the wonderful property of making him invisible so long as he held it in his hand. With this stone of darkness in his left-palm, he made after her as fast as he could, and kept close behind her the rest of the way.

After walking some distance over the plain, there appeared in sight ' a splendid palace of great size, towards which Hildur directed her steps. A great crowd of people came out to meet her. Foremost among them was a man dressed in purple and gold, who bade her welcome, at the same time calling her his beloved wife, and embracing her very affectionately. Those who attended him saluted her as their queen, and received her with every mark of respect. By the king's side were two children, of eight or ten years of age, who ran joyfully into Hildur's arms, and called her mother.

On entering the palace, Hildur was very honourably received. She was dressed in a royal robe, and had rings of gold put upon her hand. The shepherd followed the crowd into the palace, and took up his place where he could see all that was going on without running the risk of being found out. The furniture was rich and gorgeous beyond conception, so that he was completely dazzled with the sight.

In the principal saloon a table was set out and a feast prepared, the splendour of which cannot be described.

Hildur then made her appearance, magnificently attired, and sat down on the throne beside the king, while the other guests took their places on each side.

At the close of the feast, the table was removed, and soon the guests began to pass the time in dancing, or other amusements. The king and queen paid no heed to what was going on, but sat alone, engaged in a close conversation which seemed to the shepherd to be at once kind and sorrowful.

While the king and queen were thus occupied, three children, younger than those before mentioned, came forward, and their mother Hildur, who received them kindly, took the youngest on her knee and fondled it. But, as the child was restless and uneasy, she set it down again. She then drew a ring from her finger, and gave it to the child as a plaything. The child amused itself for some time with it, and then dropped it on the floor. The shepherd, who was standing close by, at the time, hastily snatched it up and put it into his pocket, without being observed by any one. As soon as the ring was missed, a careful search was made for it, but, to the great astonishment of everybody but the shepherd, it was nowhere to be found.

As the night was now far advanced, the queen— Hildur—began to prepare for her departure. Those present were sorry to see this, and begged her to stay longer with them. The king also added his entreaties, but all without effect. Before this time, the shepherd had noticed an ill-looking woman, who sat all alone in a corner of the room. She was the only one that had failed to give Hildur a joyful welcome to the palace, or ask her to prolong her stay. As soon as the king saw that Hildur was bent on going, he stepped up to this old woman, and said, "Take back your words, mother! at my humble entreaty, so that my queen may no longer be bound to absent herself from home, and from those nearest and dearest to her."

The old woman replied angrily, "All my words shall stand, I will by no means retract them."

With a sorrowful heart, he went back to the queen, and, folding his arms around her, begged her in words of kindness not to leave him again.

"Alas," said she, "I cannot stay here, in consequence of the spell by which your mother has bound me, and who knows if I shall ever see you more."

She then told him she had killed so many men it could no longer be concealed, and that she would certainly be punished, even though what she had done was sore against her will.

While she was lamenting her unhappy lot, the shepherd, seeing how matters stood, made the best of his way out of the palace, and went straightway to the bottom of the chasm. He reached the top, with the greatest ease. After that, he put the stone of darkness in his pocket, and putting the bridle in his mouth again, waited patiently on Hildur. It was not long before Hildur made her appearance, looking very sorrowful. Taking a hold of the bridle, she mounted on his back and rode quickly back to the farm.

On her arrival she laid the shepherd quietly in bed, and unbridled him, and then slipped away to her own bed, where she ' lay down to sleep. Although the shepherd had been all this time wide awake, he feigned sleep so well that Hildur was quite deceived. After she had gone to bed, he was no longer on his guard, but fell asleep, and as might be expected slept till it was broad day. The farmer was astir early in the morning, for he was anxious to know if this Christmas, like so many that was gone, was to be a season of mourning in place of a season of rejoicing. The most of the servants got up early too, but, while they were dressing, he went quietly to the shepherd's bed, and touching him with his hand, found that he was alive and apparently well. This rejoiced the heart of the farmer, who falling down on his knees, praised God loudly for his great goodness. The shepherd, shortly after, got up in the best of health. As soon as he was dressed, the people of the house gathered about him, to ask if anything unusual had befallen him during the night.

"Nothing," said he, "except that I had a very wonderful dream."

"What kind of a dream?"

The shepherd began with the tale, as it is here told; how Hildur came to his bed and bridled him; and every thing exactly, as far as he could recollect. When he had done, all were silent except Hildur, who said,

"If you tell the truth, show us some token to prove what you say."

The shepherd, noways daunted by this demand, shewed them the ring, which he had picked up from the floor of the fairy palace during the night, and said,

"Though I am not bound to bring forward proofs, I can easily do so, for there is token sufficient that I have been with the fairies. Is not that your ring, Queen Hildur?"

"To be sure it is," replied Hildur "and may good fortune ever attend you, for you have delivered me from the spell by which my cruel mother-in-law bound me, and through which I have been compelled to do so many bad deeds which my soul abhorred."

Then queen Hildur told her story as follows. "I was a fairy maid of low degree, but the present fairy king fell in love with me. The marriage was so displeasing to his mother, that she became furious with rage and told him that he would have to part with me soon, and that, after that, we could enjoy each other's society only at rare intervals and for a short time together. But me she bound with such a spell, that I was forced to become a servant in the world of woe, and, every Christmas Eve, to kill a man. I was to bridle him when asleep, and ride on his back along the same road that I took with the shepherd last night in going to meet the king. This I was to do till I was convicted of murder and put to death, unless, before that, I should fall in with a man so courageous as to dare to go with me to the world of Fairies', and then be able to show plain proofs that he had been there and seen what was done. Now, it is clear that all the other shepherds of this farmer have suffered death for my sake, but, as it was not in my power to prevent it, I hope their deaths will not be laid to my charge. This stout-hearted man is the first who dared to venture into the dark road that leads to Fairyland. I shall yet reward him for delivering me from the spell of my cruel mother-in-law. I thank you all for your kindness to me, during the years I have been among you. But I must stay here no longer, for I long for my proper home."

After these words Queen Hildur disappeared, and since then, she has never once been seen in the world of mankind.

Of the shepherd, it is told, that he married and settled down on a farm, in the following spring. He was generously treated by the farmer, who, when they parted, stocked his farm free of all cost to him. Ere long he became noted as one of the best farmers of the neighbourhood, and was often called upon for his advice and assistance in matters of difficulty. He was beloved by all, and successful beyond all his expectations in whatever he undertook. None of his neighbours could boast of such thriving flocks and herds as his. But his wonderful good fortune did not make him proud, for, as he often said, he owed all his success to Hildur the Fairy Queen.

A CLERGYMAN'S DAUGHTER MARRIED TO A FAIRY MAN.

In a certain district of Iceland, there lived a clergyman who had a daughter in the early bloom of womanhood. One day, when the conversation turned on the subject of elves or fairies, the young woman happened to say,

"I should like to be married to a fairy man, if he were only a brave one."

Her father was very angry at her words, and gave her a good scolding and a box on the ear besides. Shortly afterwards, a child about the parsonage saw a man ride up to the door of the house, and then dismount. Watching his opportunity, the man stepped indoors, and soon reappeared, leading the clergyman's daughter by the hand. Before he could be prevented, he mounted on horseback and rode off with her. Her sorrowful parents searched for her throughout all the neighbouring country, but nowhere could she be found.

It is told, that three winters after this time, a shepherd who had been long in the clergyman's service, and had loved his daughter dearly, one day lost his way and all

the sheep.   After wandering about for hours, he found
himself at the door of a farm house he had never before
seen.   The farmer, a fine manly looking fellow, came out,
and after listening to his story offered him a bed for the
night.   He accepted the offer gladly, but at the same
time lamented over the loss of the sheep.

"Don't bother yourself about them to-night," said the
farmer, "be sure they will turn up again;" and with
that he led him to a room up stairs.   There he saw an
old man and woman, and two children who were playing
on the floor.   But, besides these, he saw the clergyman's
lost daughter who was now the wife of the man who had
asked him in.

The shepherd was entertained with the best that was
in the house; and when bed-time came, was shown to a
private sleeping room.   The clergyman's daughter then
went to him, and handing him a leather bag, asked him
faithfully to deliver to her mother some valuables she
had put in it.   She also bade him tell her mother that
though her husband was a fairy man, he did not hinder
her from saying her prayers every night.   On the shepherd asking her if ever she went to church, she said
she was there just as often as himself, and that she
always sat under the pulpit, with her husband, beside
the altar.

"How does it come that nobody ever sees you in
church?"

"Oh, the reason is," she replied, "that we always leave
the church before the blessing.   But dont tell anybody
what I have now mentioned.   Only deliver the leather
bag to my mother; for if you blab what I've told you, be
sure you will be an unfortunate man."

He gave her a promise of secrecy; on that, she left the room. On getting up in the morning, he was glad to learn that his lost sheep had turned up. The farmer, who had fed them on hay during the night, delivered them up to him, and put him on the right road. He got home with the sheep in safety, and after a very short journey; but he never could tell which way he came. As for the promise of secrecy, he paid no attention to it; but on the contrary gave a full and exact account of everything he had seen and heard.

Now, the clergyman, who was anxious to find his daughter, bethought himself of a plan, and that was, to pronounce the blessing before she could have time to get out of church. So he went round among his parishoners, and told them not to be shocked if they should hear him the next Sunday pronounce the blessing at an earlier stage of the service than usual. When next Sunday came, his daughter occupied her customary seat, though not visible to any one in the church. In the middle of the service the clergyman stopped and pronounced the blessing. His daughter, thus caught unawares, was obliged to discover herself. He did what he could to induce her to stay, but all in vain.

"If you try to force me," said she, "the consequences will be very serious; and besides, it would not be right in me to leave a husband who has always treated me so kindly."

Of the shepherd, it is told, that he was from that day unfortunate in all that he had to do with. But one cannot be sorry for him, as he brought his troubles on his own head through his want of truthfulness.

THE CLERGYMAN'S DAUGHTER IN PRESTSBAKKI.

In Prestsbakki, in the Skaptáfells district, there once lived a clergyman, named Einar. He was well to do in the world, and had a numerous family. No one cared less about fairy tales than he did. In fact, he used to speak of fairies as if there were no such beings. In his idle moments he would tauntingly dare them to shew themselves to him; and then, as they did not choose to obey his orders, he would boast that there were no fairies to come.

Well, on one night while asleep, he dreamed that a man came to his bedside and said to him,

"You have provoked the fairies long, but now they will have their revenge. From this time forward you shall not dare to deny their existence. I will take away your eldest daughter, and you shall never see her more."

And sure enough, in the morning, when the clergyman awoke, he found that his eldest daughter, who was twelve years of age, had disappeared. Search was made for her in all directions, but nowhere could she be found. As time passed on, she often made her appearance among her brothers and sisters, while they were playing in the meadows. Again and again, they tried to prevail on her to go home with them; but, just as she seemed willing to do so, she always became invisible. When asked as to her welfare, she always said that she was in good health, and kindly treated by her new friends. Her father frequently saw her in his dreams, and to him she told the same story, only adding that she was to be married, bye and bye, to the fairy clergyman's son. Some time after she appeared to her father again in a dream, and invited him to come to her marriage, which was to take place on the following day. This was the last time he ever dreamed about her, and never after did she show herself among her brothers and sisters.

THE CHANGELING.

It was a common belief, in olden times, that the fairies often took away infant children who happened to be left alone, and changed them for decrepit old men or women who were made to appear as children. These changelings, however, neither grew nor spoke after the manner of children, and were very apt to become idiots. It once happened that all the people of a certain farm were working in the meadows, except the mistress of the house who was at home looking after the house and her little son, a boy three or four years old. Up to that time the boy had thriven amazingly. He could talk well, and was a clever promising child. As there was no one to assist the mother with the household work, one day, she was obliged to leave the boy by himself for a short time, while she went to wash the milk pails in a brook close by. On returning soon after, she was surprised to find the boy, at the door, weeping and howling in a strange uncouth way, very different from his wonted manner. Usually he was very quiet, gentle and obedient, but now she could not get a word out of him. Time passed on, but the child remained silent, restless, and thoroughly untractable. His body ceased to grow, and his behaviour was like that of an idiot. His mother could not account for the strange change that had come over him. In the midst of her grief, she at last bethought herself of going

R

to take the advice of a neighbour woman who was
famous for her prudence and skill. The neighbour
listened attentively to all she had to say about the boy,
and then said to her,

"Don't you think, good wife, that the boy is a
changeling? for, it seems to me, that the fairies must
have taken away your own boy the day you left him
alone, and have put another in his place."

"How could I find out, if what you say is true?" said
the surprised mother.

"Oh, very easily, just go home, and take the first
opportunity of leaving the boy alone beside something
that is likely to call forth his surprise. When his eye
catches what you have put purposely in his way, if
nobody is within sight, he is sure to make some remark
about it to himself. You must listen to what he says,
and if you find anything strange or suspicious about it,
go in at once and flog him without mercy, till something
comes out of it."

The boy's mother thanked her neighbour humbly for
her advice, and went away home to put it into practice.
The first thing she did on returning was to place the
little porridge pot in the middle of the kitchen floor.
She then bound a great many sticks together, so as to
make a long rod, and fastened the spurtle to one of the
ends. The rod was so big, that when the spurtle rested
in the pot, the upper end was away up the chimney.
Leaving it in this position, she went away and fetched
the boy to the kitchen, and then left him all alone. On
going out, she drew the door behind her; but not so
closely as to prevent her from peeping in to see what
was going on.

As soon as the boy thought he was alone, he began to trip round the pot, wondering greatly what could be the meaning of the long spurtle. At last he said, "Well, old as I am, and I am no chicken now, as my grey beard and my eighteen children in Fairyland can testify, I never, in all my born days, did see such a long spurtle for such a little porridge pot.

This was enough for the mother, who was not long of making her appearance in the kitchen with a good sized stick in her hand. Seizing hold of the changeling, she flogged him unmercifully for a long while, spite of his heart-rending cries.

Bye and bye a strange old woman walked in, holding on her arms a little boy whom she fondled kindly. Addressing the farmer's wife, she said, "Why should you treat my husband so cruelly. Your conduct is a sorry recompense for the care I have bestowed on this little boy of yours." So saying, she laid the little boy at his mother's feet, and took her husband away with her.

The fairy man and woman were never more seen again. The now recovered boy remained with his parents, and grew up a fine manly youth, the joy of his mother's heart.[1]

[1] These popular northern fireside stories and tales are partly gathered from direct oral narration, and partly taken from a small volume, "Islenzk Æfintyri," the collection of Messrs. M. Grimson and J. Arnason, published in Icelandic, at Reykjavik, in 1852.

II.

SPECIMENS OF ICELANDIC POEMS.

In the "Völuspá,"[1] from the older Edda, we have a sublime description of chaos; of creation; an account of a period of strife, crime, and suffering; dire conflicts between the powers of good and evil; of the destruction of the world of Odin and the dissolution and conflagration of the universe; of the Regnarök or twilight of the Gods; of the renovated world, the descent of Baldur the Good, the punishment of the wicked, and the happiness of the good in Gimlé or Heaven. From this poem— the most remarkable in the whole range of Scandinavian mytho-cosmogony—the following verses are extracted:

"It was time's morning
When Ymer lived.
There was no sand, no sea;
No cooling billows;
Earth there was none,
No lofty heaven;
Only the Gulph of Ginunga,
But no grass.

 . . .

The sun knew not

Where was his dwelling;
The stars knew not
That they had a firmament;
The moon knew not
What powers she possessed.

 . . .

The tree Yggdrasil
Bears a sorer burden
Than men know of.
Above the stags bite it;

[1] Völu-spá or spae, the Prophesy—wisdom, oracle, or mystic song— of Volu (Volu is the genitive of Vola). Scoticê, Vala's spae, as in the word *spae*-wife. One of these Valor, or Northern sybills, whom Odin consulted in Neifelhem, when found in the tomb where she had lain for ages, is represented as saying—

"I was snowed over with snows,
And beaten with rains,
And drenched with the dews;
Dead have I long been."

On its sides age rots it ;
Nighögg gnaws below.

. . . .

There saw she wade
In the heavy streams
Men—foul perjurers,
And murderers.

. . . .

Brothers slay brothers :
Sisters' children
Shed each other's blood.
Hard is the world ;
Sensual sin grows huge.
There are sword-ages, axe-ages,
Earth-cleaving cold ;
Storm-ages, murder-ages,
Till the world falls dead,
And men no longer spare
Or pity one another.

. . . .

Mimer's sons play,
But the world is kindled
By the ancient
Gjallarborn.
Loud blows Heimdall,
His sound is in the air :
Odin talks
With the head of Mimer.

Quivers then Yggdrasil,
The strong-rooted ash :
Rustles the old tree
When Jötun gives way.
All things tremble
In the realms of Hel,

Till Surtur's son
Swallows up Odin.

Garmer he shouts
By the Gnipa-hall
The band must burst
And the wolf fly.

Hrymer drives eastward,
Bears his shield before him ;
Jormungaud wolters
In giant fierceness.
The waves thunder ;
The eagles scream ;
Death rends the corpses
And Nagelfar gives way.

Köl hies eastward ;
Come must Muspel's
Folk to the sea.
Loke rows afar ;
All the children of madness
Follow the wolf,
Bileist's brother
Journeyeth with them.

Surtur fares southward.
With flickering flames
From his sword
God's sun flashes.
Break the stone mountains;
The weird women flee,
Men throng Hel's dread roads,
And Heaven is rent."

Then Surtur flings fire over the world.

"The sun grows dark.
Earth sinks in the sea.
From heaven vanish

The lustrous stars.
High from the flames
Rolls the reck ;

High play the fires
'Gainst heaven itself.
. . . . .
Up, sees she come
Yet once more,
The earth from the sea,
Gloriously green.
. . . . .
Then comes the Mighty One
To the great Judgment—
The great above all—

He who guides all things.
Judgments he utters;
Strifes he appeaseth;
Laws He ordaineth
To flourish for ever.

. . . . .
In Gimlé the lofty
There shall the hosts
Of the virtuous dwell,
And through all ages
Taste of deep gladness."

The "Sólar Ljód"—"Sol" or "Sun-song"—was composed by Sæmund himself, the collector of the Edda, and a Christian priest, ages before the time of Dante.

"By the Nornors' seat
Nine days I sate,
Then to horse was lifted.
The sun of the giant race
Gleamed sadly
Out of heaven's weeping clouds.

Without and within
Seemed I to journey
Through the seven worlds
Above and below.
Better path I sought
Than there was to find.

And now to be told is
What first I beheld
In the home of torture.
Scorched birds were flying—
Wretched souls in myriads,
Thick as mosquito legions.

Flying saw I
Hope's dragons
And fall in drear waste places.

They shook their wings
Till to me seemed that
Heaven and earth were rent.

The stag of the sun
Southward saw I journey.
His feet stood
On earth, but his huge antlers
Traversed the heavens above
him.

Northward saw I ride
The sons of the races;
Seven they were together.
From the full horn they drank
The purest mead
From wells of heavenly strength.

The winds stood still,
The waters ceased to flow.
Then heard I a dread cry.
There for their husbands
False vengeful women
Ground earth for food.

Bloody stones
Those women dark
Dragged sorrowfully,
Their gory hearts
Hung from their breasts
Weighed with heavy weights.

Many men
Along the burning ways
Sore wounded saw I go.
Their visages
Seemed deeply dyed
With blood in murder shed.

Many men
Saw I amongst the dead
Without one hope of grace.
Pagan stars there stood
Over their heads
All scored with cruel runes.

Men saw I too
Who enviously had scowled
Upon the good of others.
Bloody runes
Were on their breasts
Ploughed out by hands of men.

Men saw I there
All full of woe,
All mazed in wondering.
This do they win
Who to eternal loss
Love this world only.

Men saw I too   .
Who sought always to snatch
From others their possessions.
In throngs they were,
And to the miser's hell
Bore groaning loads of lead.

Men saw I next
Who many had bereaved
Of life and goods,
And through the hearts of these
For ever fiercely ran
Strong venom snakes.

Men too I saw
Who never would observe
Sabbaths and holy days.
Their unblessed hands
Fast rivetted together
With ever burning stones.

Men too I saw
Who with huge brag and boast
On earth did vaunt themselves.
Here their clothes
Were vilely squalid
And with fire enwrapt.

Men saw I too
Who with their slanderous breath
Had blasted others.
Hel's ravens
Remorselessly their eyes
Tore from their heads.

But all the horrors
Thou canst not know
Which Hel's condemned endure.
Sweet sins
There bitterly are punished,
False pleasures reap true pain.

———

Men did I see
Who the Lord's laws

Had followed stanchly.
Purest light
For ever growing clearer
Passed brightly o'er their heads.

Men did I see
Who with unwearied zeal
Did seek the good of others.
Angels read
The holy books
Upon their radiant heads.

Men did I see
Who with sharp fasts
Their bodies had subdued;
God's holy hosts
Before them all bow'd down
And paid them highest homage.

Men did I see
Who had their mothers
Piously cherished,
And their place of rest

Amid heaven's beams
Shone gloriously.

Holy maids there were
Who their pure souls
Had kept unsoiled by sin,
And souls of those
Who their rebellious flesh
Did ever sternly quail.

Lofty chariots saw I
Travel through heaven
Having access to God;
And they were filled with those
Who causelessly
Had on the earth been slain.

Father Almighty !
Illustrious Son!
And Holy Spirit of Heaven.
Thee do I implore,
Who didst make all things,
To keep us from all sin ! "

Sæmund concludes this remarkable poem with these strophes:

"This song
Which I have taught thee
Thou shalt sing unto the living.
The Sun's song,
Which in its solemn theme
Hath little that is feigned.

Here do we part,
But part again to meet
On the Great Day of men.

Oh, my Lord !
Give the dead rest,
Comfort to those who live !

Wonderful wisdom,
To thee in dream is sung,
'Tis truth which thou hast seen !
And no man is so wise
Of all who are created
As, ere this, to have heard
One word of this Sun's Song !

From the heroic poems relating to Sigurd and Bryn-hild—the originals from which the German "Niebelungen lied" is taken—the following passage is extracted. In it Gudrun, in conversation with Thjodreck, describes her youth before the murder of Sigurd: "A maid was I amongst maidens; my mother reared me lovely in bower. Well loved I my brothers, till me Gjuké apportioned with gold, with gold apportioned and gave me to Sigurd. So raised himself, Sigurd, over the sons of Gjuké, as the green lily above the grass grows; or the high-antlered stag, above other beasts; or the fire-red gold above the silver grey. My brothers were incensed that I should have a husband more illustrions than any. Sleep they could not, nor decide on anything, before they Sigurd had caused to perish. Grangé (Sigurd's steed) galloped to the *Ting* (assembly of the people), wild was his neighing, but Sigurd himself was not there. All the horses were covered with sweat, and with blood of the contenders.

"Weeping I went to speak to Grané, the blood sprinkled; of his master I asked him; then hung down Grané mornfully his head, for the creature knew that his lord was not living. Long did I wander, long was I confused in mind before of the Prince I could ask after my King."

The "Hávamál"—Odin's High Song"—displays a shrewd insight into human nature, and contains many maxims, both of a moral and social kind, which one would scarcely expect to find embodied in the heathen ethics of an ancient Scandinavian Scald. The whole poem is here presented to the reader.

HÁVAMÁL.

I.

"In every corner
Carefully look thou
Ere forth thou goest;
For insecure
Is the house when an enemy
Sitteth therein.

II.

Hail him who giveth!
Enters a guest.
Where shall he be seated?
Yet, ill shall fare he
Who seeks his welfare
In other men's houses.

III.

Fire will be needful
For him who enters
With his knees frozen.
Of meat and clothing
Stands he in need
Who journeys o'er mountains.

IV.

Water is needful,
A towel and kindness
For this guest's welcome;
Kind inclinations
Let him experience;
Answer his questions.

V.

Good sense is needful
To the far traveller;
Each place seems home to him.
He is a laughing-stock
Who, knowing nothing,
Sits mid the wise.

VI.

With the deep thinker
Speak thou but little;
But guard well thy temper;
When the noble and silent
Come to thy dwelling,
Least errs the cautious.

VII.

Good sense is needful
To the far traveller;
Least errs the cautious;
For a friend trustier
Than good understanding
Findeth man never.

VIII.

A cautious guest
When he comes to his hostel
Speaketh but little;
With his ears he listeneth;
With his eyes he looketh;
Thus the wise learneth.

IX.

Happy is he
Who for himself winneth
Honour and friends.
All is uncertain,
Which a man holdeth
In the heart of another.

X.

Happy is he
Who prudent guidance
From himself winneth;
For evil counsel
Man oft receiveth
From the breast of another.

XI.

No better burden
Bears a man on his journey
Than mickle wisdom.
Better is she than gold
Where he is a stranger ;
In need she is a helper.

XII.

No better burden
Bears a man on his journey
Than mickle wisdom.
No worse provision
Takes a man on his journey
Than frequent drunkenness.

XIII.

Ale is not so good
As people have boasted
For the children of men.
For less and still less,
As more he drinketh,
Knows man himself.

XIV.

The hern of forgetfulness
Sits on the drunkard,
And steals the man's senses.
By the bird's pinions,
Fettered I lay,
In Gunlada's dwelling.

XV.

Drunken I lay,
Lay thoroughly drunken,
With Fjalar the wise.
This is the best of drink,
That every one afterwards
Comes to his senses.

XVI.

Be silent and diligent,
Son of a Prince,
And daring in combat;
Cheerful and generous,
Let every man be,
Till death approaches.

XVII.

A foolish man fancies
He shall live for ever
If he shuns combat.
But old age will give
To him no quarter,
Although the spear may.

XVIII.

The fool stares about
When he goes on a visit,
Talks nonsense or slumbers.
All goes well
When he can drink,
For then the man speaks his mind

XIX.

He, he only
Who has far travelled,
Has far and wide travelled,
Knoweth every
Temper of man,
If he himself is wise.

XX.

If cups thou lackest
Yet drink thou by measure :
Speak what is seemly or be still.
No one will charge thee
With evil, if early
Thou goest to slumber.

XXI.

The gluttonous man,
Though he may not know it,
Eats his life's sorrow:
Lust of drink, often
Makes the fool, foolish
When he comes mid the prudent.

XXII.

The flocks they have knowledge
When to turn homeward
And leave the green pastures;
But he who is foolish
Knoweth no measure,
No bounds to his craving.

XXIII.

An evil man
And a carping temper
Jeer at all things.
He knows not;
He ought to know,
That himself is not faultless.

XXIV.

A foolish man
Lies awake the night through
And resolves on many things.
Thus is he weary
When the day cometh;
The old care remaineth.

XXV.

A foolish man
Thinks all are friendly
Who meet him with smiles;
But few he findeth
Who will aid his cause,
When to the Ting he cometh.

XXVI.

A foolish man
Thinks all are friendly
Who meet him with smiles.
Nor knows he the difference
Though they laugh him to scorn
When he sits 'mong the knowing
    ones.

XXVII.

A foolish man
Thinks he knows everything
While he needs not the know-
But he knows not   [ledge.
How to make answer
When he is questioned.

XXVIII.

A foolish man,
When he comes into company
Had better keep silence.
No one remarketh
How little he knows
Till he begins talking.

XXIX.

He appears wise
Who can ask questions
And give replies.
Ever conceal then
The failings of others,
The children of men.

XXX.

Who cannot keep silence
Uttereth many
A word without purport.
The tongue of the garrulous,
Which keepeth back nothing,
Talks its own mischief.

XXXI.

Hold in derision
No one, although he
Come as a stranger.
Many a one, when he has had
Rest and dry clothing,
Thou mayest find to be wise.

XXXII.

He seemeth wise
Who in speech triumphs
O'er mocking guests.
The talkative man
Knows not at the table
If he talks with his enemies.

XXXIII.

Many are friendly
One to another;
Yet storm ariseth.
Strife will arise   .
For ever, if one guest
Affronteth another.

XXXIV.

Thou mayst dine early
Unless thou art going
Unto the banquet.
Sits he and flatters;
Hungry he seemeth,
Yet few things he learneth.

XXXV.

Long is the journey
To a deceitful friend
Though he dwell near thee.
But, direct lies the path
To a friend faithful,
Though he dwelleth afar off.

XXXVI.

Do not too frequently
Unto the same place
Go as a guest.
Sweet becomes sour
When a man often sits
At other men's tables.

XXXVII.

One good house is there
Though it be humble:
Each man is master at home.
Though a man own but
Two goats and and a straw-rick,
'Tis better than begging.

XXXVIII.

One good house is there
Though it be humble:
Each man is master at home.
The man's heart bleedeth
At every mealtime
Who his food beggeth.

XXXIX.

Without his weapon
Goes no man
A-foot in the field.
For it is unsafe
Out on the by-paths
When weapons are needful.

XL.

Never found I so generous,
So hospitable a man
As to be above taking gifts.
Nor one of his money
So little regardful
But that it vexed him to lend.

XLI.

He who has laid up
Treasures of wealth
Finds want hard to bear.
Adversity often uses
What was meant for prosperity,
For many things are contrary to
  expectation.

XLII.

With weapons and garments,
As best may be fitting
Give thou thy friends pleasure.
By gifts interchanged
Is friendship made surest;
If the heart proffers them.

XLIII.

Let a man towards his friend,
Ever be friendly,
And with gifts make return for
  gifts.
With thy cheerful friend
Be thou cheerful;
With thy guileful friend on thy
  guard.

XLIV.

Let a man towards his friend
Ever be friendly;
Towards him and his friend.
But with an enemy's friend
Can no man
Be friendly.

XLV.

If thou hast a friend
Whom thou canst confide in
And wouldst have joy of his
  friendship,

Then, mingle thy thoughts with
  his,
Give gifts freely,
And often be with him.

XLVI.

If thou hast another,
Whom thou hast no faith in
Yet wouldst have joy of his
  friendship,
Thou must speak smoothly;
Thou must think warily,
And with cunning pay back his
  guile.

XLVII.

Yet one word
About him thou mistrusteth
And in whom thou hast no re-
  liance.
Thou must speak mildly,
More so than thou meanest;
Paying back like with like.

XLVIII.

Young was I formerly;
Then alone went I,
Taking wrong ways.
Rich seemed I to myself
When I found a companion;
For man is man's pleasure.

XLIX.

The noble, the gentle
Live happiest,
And seldom meet sorrow.
But the foolish man,
He is suspicious,
And a niggard grieves to give.

L.

I hung my garments
On the two wooden men
Who stand on the wall.
Heroes they seemed to be
When they were clothed !
The unclad are despised.

LI.

The tree withereth
Which stands in the court-yard
Without shelter of bark or of leaf.
So is a man
Destitute of friends.
Why should he still live on ?

LII.

Even as fire,
Burns peace between enemies,
For the space of five days.
But on the seventh
It is extinguished,
And the less is their friendship.

LIII.

Only a little
Will a man give ;
He often gets praise for a little.
With half a loaf
And a full bottle
I won a companion.

LIV.

Small are the sand-grains,
Small are the water-drops :
Small human thoughts :
Yet are not these
Each of them equal.
Every century bears but one man.

LV.

Good understanding
Ought all to possess,—
But not too much wisdom.
Those human beings
Whose lives are the brightest,
Know much and know it well.

LVI.

Good understanding
Ought all to possess,
But not too much knowledge.
For the heart of a wise man
Seldom is gladdened
By knowledge of all things.

LVII.

Good understanding
Ought all to possess,
But not too much knowledge.
Let no one beforehand
Inquire his own fortune.
The gladdest heart knoweth it
    not.

LVIII.

Brand with brand burneth
Till it is burned out :
Fire is kindled by fire.
A man among men
Is known by his speech ;
A fool by his arrogance.

LIX.

Betimes must he rise
Who another man's life
And goods will obtain.
The sleeping wolf
Seldom gets bones.
No sluggard wins battle.

LX.

Betimes must he rise
And look after his people
Who has but few workmen.
Much he neglecteth
Who sleeps in the morning.
On the master's presence depends
half the profit.

LXI.

Like to dried faggots,
And hoarded up birch bark,
Are the thoughts of a man,
The substance of firewood
May last, it is true,
A year and a day.

LXII.

Cleanly and decent,
Ride men to the Ting
Although unadorned.
For his shoes and apparel
Nobody blushes,
Nor yet for his horse, though
none of the best.

LXIII.

Question and answer
Is a clever thing,
And so it is reckoned.
To one person trust thyself,
Not to a second.
The world knows what is known
unto three.

LXIV.

Bewilderedly gazes
On the wild sea, the eagle,
When he reaches the strand.
So is it with the man
Who in a crowd standeth
When he has but few friends
there.

LXV.

Every wise man
And prudent, his power will use
With moderation.
For he will find
When he comes 'mong the brave
That none can do all things.

LXVI.

Let every man
Be prudent and circumspect
And cautious in friendship.
Often that word
Which we trust to another
Very dear costs us.

LXVII.

Greatly too early
Came I to some places;
Too late to others.
Here the feast was over;
There unprepared.
Seldom opportunely comes an
unwelcome guest.

LXVIII.

Here and everywhere
Have I been bidden
If I fell short of a dinner.
But the fragments are easily
Left for his faithful friend
When a man has eaten.

LXIX.

Fire is pleasant
To the children of men,
And the light of the sun,
If they enjoy
Health uninterrupted,
And live without crime

LXX.

Perfectly wretched
Is no man, though he may be
    unhappy:
One is blessed in his sons;
One in his friends;
By competence one;
By good works another.

LXXI.

Better are they
Who live than they who are
    dead.
The living man may gain a cow.
I saw the fire blazing
In the hall of the rich man,
But death stood at the threshold.

LXXII.

The lame may ride;
The deaf fight bravely;
The one-handed tend the flocks,
Better be blind
Than entombed:
The dead win nothing.

LXXIII.

It is good to have a son
Although he be born
After his father's death.
Seldom are the cairn-stones
Raised by the way-side
Save by the son to his father.

LXXIV.

There are two adversaries;
The heaviness of the brain,
And death by the bedside.
He who has gold for his journey
Rejoices at night
When he grows weary.

LXXV.

Short are the boat-oars;
.   .   .   .
Unstable autumnal nights.
The weather changes
Much in five days;
Still more in a month.

LXXVI.

Little enough knows he
Who nothing knows:
Many a man is fooled by another.
One man is rich,
Another man is poor;
But that proves not which has
    most wisdom.

LXXVII.

Thy flocks may die;
Thy friends may die;
So also mayest thou, thyself;
But never will die
The fame of him
Who wins for himself good re-
    nown.

LXXVIII.

Thy flocks may die;
Thy friends may die;
So also mayst thou thyself.
But one thing I know
Which never dies,
The doom which is passed on the
    dead.

LXXIX.

I saw the well-filled barns
Of the child of wealth;
Now leans he on the staff of the
    beggar.
Thus are riches,
As the glance of an eye,
They are an inconstant friend.

S

LXXX.

A foolish man,
If he gaiu wealth
Or the favour of woman,
Grows in self-esteem,
Though he understands nothing:
Forth goes he in arrogance.

LXXXI.

Know thou, that when
Thou enquirest of the runes,
Known to the world,
What the holy Gods did,
What the great Scalds have
    written,
It is best for thee to be still.

LXXXII.

Praise the day at eventide;
The wife when she is dead;
The sword when thou hast
    proved it;
The maid when she is married;
Ice when thou hast crossed it;
Ale when thou hast drunken it.

LXXXIII.

Iu wind cut thou fire-wood;
In wind sail the ocean;
In darkness woo a maiden,
For many eyes has daylight.
In a ship man voyages;
The shield it defends him;
The sword is for slaughter,
But the maid to be courted.

LXXXIV.

Drink ale by firelight;
On the ice drive the sledge;
Sell thou the lean horse
And the sword that is rusty;
Feed the horse at home;
Bed the dog in the court-yard.

LXXXV.

The word of a maiden
No one can trust;
Nor what a woman speaketh;
For on a turning wheel
Was the heart of woman formed,
And guile was laid in her breast·

LXXXVI.

A breaking bow;
A burning flame;
A hungry wolf;
A chattering crow;
The grunting swine;
The rootless tree;
The heaving billows;
The boiling kettle;

LXXXVII.

The flying spear;
Sinking waters;
Oue night's ice;
The coiled-up snake;
The bride's fond talk;
Or the broken sword;
A bear's play;
Or a king's son;

LXXXVIII.

A sick calf;
A freed bondsman;
A false fortune-teller;
The newly-slain on the field;
A bright sky;
A smiling master;
The cry of a dog;
A harlot's sorrow;

LXXXIX.

An early sown field
Let no one trust,
Neither his son too soon;
The field depends on the weather;
The youth on his sense,
And both are uncertain.

XC.

A brother's death,
Though it be half-way here;
A half-burned house;
A steed very lively,
(For a horse has no value,
If one foot stumble),
Are not so sure
That a man may trust to them.

XCI.

Thus is peace among women;
Like a fleeting thought;
Like a journey over slippery ice,
On a two-years-old horse
With unroughed shoes,
And ill broken in;
Or in wild tempests
Tossed in a helmless ship;
Or trying to capture
Deer mid the thawing snow of
   the hills.

XCII.

Now speak I truly,
For I know what I speak of,
Deceitful to woman is the pro-
   mise of love:
When we speak fairest,
Then mean we foulest;
The purest heart may be beguiled.

XCIII.

He speaketh smoothly
Who would win the maiden;
He offers property,
And praises the beauty
Of the fair maiden;
He wins who is in earnest.

XCIV.

The love of another
Let no man
Find fault with.
Beautiful colours
Oft charm the wise,
While they snare not the fool.

XCV.

For that failing
Which is common to many
No man is blamed.
From the wise man to the fool,
'Mong all children of men,
Goes he, Love, the mighty one.

XCVI.

Thought alone knoweth
What the heart cherisheth,
It alone knows the mind.
No disease is worse
For the wise man
Than joy in nothing.

XCVII.

This I experienced
When I sate mid the rushes
Awaiting my love.
The good maiden
Was to me life and heart;
Mine is she no longer.

XCVIII.

The maid of Billing
White as snow found I,
In her bed sleeping.
Princely glory
Was to me nothing
If I lived not with her !

XCIX.

"To the court, Odin,
Come towards the eventide
If thou wilt woo me ;
All will be ruined
If we do not in private
Know how to manage."

C.

Thither I sped again ;
Happy I thought myself,
More so than I knew of,
For I believed
I had half won her favour
And the whole of her thoughts.

CI.

So again came I,
When the quarrelsome people
All were awake.
With candles burning
And piled-up firewood
Received she my visit.

CII.

A few morrows after,
When again I went thither,
All the house-folk were sleeping.
There found I a dog,
Of the fair maiden's
Bound on the bed.

CIII.

Few are so noble
But that their fancy
May undergo change.
Many a good girl
When she is well known
Is deceitful towards men.

CIV.

That I experienced
When the quick-witted maiden
I decoyed into danger.
She heaped reproach on me,
The merry maiden,
And I won her never.

CV.

Gay at home
And liberal, must
Be the man of wisdom.
Full of talk and pleasant memo-
ries
Will he be ofttimes,
With much cheerful converse.

CVI.

He is called Fimbulfambi
Who but few things can utter;
'Tis the way of the simple.
I was with the old giants,
Now am I returned;
There was I not silent,
With affluence of speech
I strove to do my best
In the hall of Suttung.

CVII.

Gunlöd gave me,
On a golden chair seated,
A draught of mead delicious;

But the return was evil
Which she from me experienced,
With all her faithfulness,
With all her deep love.

CVIII.

I let words of anger
By me be spoken,
And knawed the rock.
Above and below me
Went the paths of the giants;
Thus ventured I life.

CIX.

Dear-bought song
Have I much rejoiced in;
All succeeds to the will;
Because the Odrejrer
Now have ascended
To the old, holy earth.

CX.

Uncertain seems it

If I had escaped
From the courts of the giants
Had I not been blessed by
The dear love of Gunlöd,
She, whom I embraced.

CXI.

On the day following
Went the Rimthursar
To ask the gods council,
In the halls lofty;
Ask whether Bölverk were
Come mid the mighty gods,
Or if Suttung had slain him.

CXII.

A holy ring-oath
I mind me, gave Odin.
Now who can trust him.
Suttung is cheated;
His mead has been stolen
And Gunlöd is weeping.[1]

[1] These specimens of old Icelandic poetry are selected from "The Literature and Romance of Northern Europe," by William and Mary Howitt: 2 vols. 8vo., Colburn & Co., 1852.

III.

POEMS ON NORTHERN SUBJECTS.

LAY OF THE VIKINGS.

BY MRS. ANDREW JAMES SYMINGTON. [1]

In an unceasing, ebbless flow, around
The peaceful homes of Thulé, her best safety
Roll Arctic billows, rearing giant crests
In proud defiance—bulwarks impassable
Against the intruder's steps.   Fiercely and bold,
Even as a lioness doth guard her 'fenceless young,
Do they, the unconquerable surges, foam and champ,
And keep unslumbering vigils round the graves—
The restless, storm-rocked graves—of the Vikings
Their sons—those tameless spirits of the past—
Whose dirge their sighing parent hourly waileth
As erst they rode exultant on his bosom.
    Boldest and noblest of earth's kind were ye—
Conquerors of nations—fathers of a race
Of giant princes—ah! how fallen now!
    Meet were it that your honoured dust should slumber

[1] Written in reply to the following lines, by Delta, sent her by way of a challenge.

"To where the Arctic billow foams
Round Shetland's sad and silent homes,
There sighs the wind and wails the surge.
As 'twere of living things the dirge."

In these old heathen days, be it remembered, where all were sea-rovers there were good and bad among them.   For a fine description of the best type of the Viking and his code of honour, see Tegner's beautiful northern poem, "The Frithjof Saga."

In this your polar cradle; rocked by northern gales,
Lulled by the sighing surges whose strong hands
Have hung a cloudy curtain o'er your rest.
 Meet were it that the springtide rain should weep
O'er the degeneracy of your race—
The scattered glory of your Fatherland!
 Fitting were it that the dark thunder-cloud
Should be the swift-winged chariot upon which
Your spirits love to ride—your path meanwhile
Lit by the fitful rays of yonder cold
Mysterious, flickering night-lamp, *Borealis.*   .
Nought less sublime, less wildly grand than these
Would be in harmony with your proud spirits.
Would ye not laugh to scorn the spicy breezes
Of India's drowsy clime, or soft Italia's
Radiant skies?—and ah! methinks ye whisper,   ·
Were but the ocean charmed, that he should cease
His mournful lullaby around your pillow;
Or did old Winter's gales less rudely blow,
Ye then would rise in vapoury clouds, and leave
A land unworthy even to be your tomb.

———

VÍKÍNGA BRAGUR.[1]

Öflluga hraðar	Og öflugust vígi
Öldur streyma	Byggja um kyrrar
I'shafs hins nyrðra,	Byggðir Thúlu.

———

[1] The "Lay of the Vikings," translated into Icelandic verse by the Rev. Olaf Pálsson. It is in the free metre of the old sagas—the same as that which Thorlakson adopted in his translation of "Paradise Lost." The following is the translation of Delta's lines:

þar sem um Hjaltlands	Stynja þar stormar,
Heimkynni þögul	Stúra brimboðar,
Norðurhafs öldur	Lifandi veru
O'lmar freyða,	Líkar sorgröddum.

Hamramar æ
Þær hreykja kollum,
Ogöruggar varnir
Mót árásarmönnum
Búa, þær aldrei
Bila kunna.
Sem vakir ljónsinna
Varnarlausum
Ungum yfir
Með afarmóði,
Freyða svo öldur
Ósigrandi
Halda þær vörð
Um Víkinga leiði;
Því blunda í klettum
Brimi skelfdum
Harðúðgir niðjar
Frá horfnum dögum;
Fékk þeim ei hugur
I'brjósti bilað;
Harmar því móðer
Og hryggðar saungva
Aldrei fær slitið,
Er hún minnist
Þeirra, er áður
Ungir léku
Meginglaðir
A' móðurbrjósti.
  Leit ei nokkur
Af niðjum jarðar
Aðra tignari
Eður knárri
Yður, sem þjóðir
Unnuð sverðum,
Feður jötna,
Er fólki styrðu.
  Horrfinn er heiður,
En heiðraðar moldir
Náðu hvíld hæfri
Und norðurheimsskauti;

I'vöggu þeim velta
Vindar stríðir;
Vögguljóð kveða
Veinandi unnir,
Þær er með mundum
Meginstyrkvum
Lögðu skýblæur
A' leiði niðja.
  Var það veröúng,
Er varandi unnir
Yðar æ gráta
Ættar hnignun,
Og frama horfinn
Fósturjarðar.
  Það og vel hæfði,
Er þrumuskýin,
Vagnar þau urðu
Vængjum búnir,
Yðar sem aka
Andar glaðir;
En lýsa á vegi
Ljósgeislar kaldir
Leiptrandi Norður—
Ljósa skærra.
  Sízt fær lægra neitt
Eður svipminna
Yðar samboðið
Anda háum.
Munduð þér kýma
Megnum hlátri
Að ilmandi vindum,
Um er þjóta
Ofurdrúnga lopt
Indíafoldar,
Eður geislandi
Uppheims boga,
Yfir er breiðist
I'talska grund.
Er mér semheyri
Yður hvísla:

Ægir ef fengi,	Geysa svo vinda,
Umvafinn fjötrum,	Sem gjörir hann nú;
Sorgleg ei leugur	Munduð þer þá
Súngið kvæði	I'mekkjum sudda
Þau um hægindi	Hefja látast
Heyrast yðar,	Frá hauðri burtn,
Ogaldinn vetur	Yðra óhæfu
Ei ólma léti	Gröf að geyma.

THE VIKING'S RAVEN.[1]

BY MRS. ANDREW JAMES SYMINGTON.

Beside a weird-like Norway bay,
Where wild and angry billows play,
And seldom meet the night and day,
    A Raven sat.

He was the last of all his race
That lingered in that lonely place;
Age, grief, were stamped upon his face,
    Sad, desolate.

[1] The raven was regarded as sacred, and greatly venerated by the old Norse Vikings, who had always one or two of these birds in their ships. When setting out on marauding expeditions the raven was let loose and his flight followed by the bold voyagers, in the belief that he led them to war and victory. These birds it was supposed lived to a fabulous age. Odin's shield had a raven on it, and so had the *Landeyda* or battle-flag of Sigurd, which ever led to victory, although its bearer was doomed to die. Hiatland is the ancient name of Shetland. The Norse rovers thought it a disgrace to die in their beds in peace; and when they found their end approaching, clad in armour, had themselves carried on board their ships which were then set fire to and sent adrift, that the old heroes might die, as they had lived, on the ocean, and thence worthily rise to Valhalla.

Yet to that darkling norland sky
He raised an undimmed, fearless eye,
As though he proudly would defy
           And battle fate.

His mate long dead, his nestlings flown,
The moss had o'er his eyry grown;
And all the scenes his youth had known
           Were changed and old.

For he had heard the vikings all
Responding to the mystic call,
That summoned to great Odin's hall
           Those heroes bold.

He oft had skimmed the Polar seas;
And Harold's sail aye wooed the breeze,
To follow where the Raven flees
           On tireless wing.

But victory ceased on them to smile.—
On Hialtland's rugged, rock-bound isle
He saw them raise the funeral pile
           Of the Sea-King.

   .   .   .   .   .

Once his unerring pinions led
To where the shafts of battle sped;
But, when the conquered Northmen fled,
           He scorned to flee;

But watched where brave young Ingolf lies,
With drooping heart and fading eyes,
Pining for his native skies,
           A captive he.

A maiden of the sunny South
There loved and would have freed the youth,
But he was wed to Gulda Brûth.
    His norland bride.

And she, across the stormy main,
Had turned her weary eyes in vain;—
Her hero ne'er returned again:
    And so she died.

No Saga tells where rests the brave,
No mourner weeps by Ingolf's grave;
The Raven's sable pinions wave
    There all alone.

And then he spread his pinions wide
Upon the free north wind to ride,
With mien erect, and eye of pride;
    His task well done.

And nought around, howe'er so bright,
Could win his stay, or stop his flight
From where he saw the pole-star's light
    Shine o'er the north.

When, hark! a wild exulting cry
Falls on his ear; his piercing eye
A burning vessel can descry
    That flashes forth,

Like to the fitful spirit-gleam
Of the Aurora's restless beam;
But ah! he knows it is no dream,
    And droops his wing.

Beside the blazing spectral pyre—
A spark from Baldur's sacred fire
Lighteth to death a Norseman sire,—
    Brave old Thorsteing.

His arms are folded o'er his breast,
And on his noble brow doth rest
The shadow from his warrior crest
    That waves on,high.

His glances on the ocean fell;
Fondly he marked its rising swell—
That ocean he had loved so well—
    Then raised his eye.

And when he saw the faithful bird,
The soul of song within him stirred.

 Hast thou once more returned,
 Thou trusty friend, to me?
 What news hast thou of Ingolf,
 My son, the brave and free?
 Hath he in battle fallen,
 His good sword by his side?
 Or, captive, is he sighing
 To see once more his bride?

 Ah! no, his soul would scorn
 In captive chain to lie;
 I know he hath been borne
 To Valhalla's halls on high,
 And I'll meet him in the sky
    E're the morn.

Alas! with us will perish
  The Vikings' race and name,
That long made foemen tremble
  When Scalds rehearsed our fame.
And thou, dark bird of omen,
  Back to our country hie,
And tell her recreant children
  How Norsemen ought to die.
But to guard my mountain home
  My spirit yet will soar,
And on old ocean roam
  As in the days of yore.
Oft to visit yon loved shore
              I will come.

The song hath ceased, and Thorsteing brave
Is sleeping now in Odin's cave.

Athwart the sky the lightnings flash,
While down the Fiords the thunders crash,
And sullen waves in fury lash
              The fretted shore.

Where is that Raven, grim and lone?—
Uprooted is the old grey stone
Where late he sat, and he is gone
              To come no more.

DEATH OF THE OLD NORSE KING.

BY A. J. S.

Haste, clothe me, jarls, in my royal robe;
My keen biting sword gird ye.
Haste! for I go to the Fatherland,
Both king of earth and sea.
My blade so true, with a spirit-gleam—
Death lurks in its skinkling fire—
I grasp thee now as of olden time
In conflict hot and dire.

I've trampled foes; from their blanchéd sculls
Now drain off the dark-red wine;
Fall bravely all in the battle field,
Be crowned with wreaths divine!
My eyes wax dim, and my once jet locks
Now wave with a silvery white;
Feeble, my arm cannot wield the blade
I dote on with delight.

Grim Hela breathes a chilling shade,
I hear the Valkyrii sing;
Now to the halls of the brave I'll rise,
As fits an old Norse King.
Heimdallar's ship, with the incense wood,
Prepare as a pyre for me;
Blazing, I'll rise to the Odin halls,
At once in the air and sea!

They've lit slow fire in the incense ship;
The sun has just sunk in the wave;
Set are the sails, he is launched away,
This hero-king so brave!

The death chaunt floats in the deep blue skies,
All wild, in the darkling night;
Fearful there glares from the blazing ship
A wild red lurid light.

It shimmering gleams o'er the lone blue sea,
The flickers shoot wild and high—
Odin hath welcomed the brave old king
To his palace in the sky !
The bale-flames die, and a silence deep
Now floats on the darkness cold,
Where so fearless and free, on the deep blue sea,
Had died this Norse king bold !

1845.

― ―

DAUÐI GAMALS NORÐMANNA-KONUNGS.[1]

1.

Skundið þèr, jarlar !
Skjött mig bùið
Skrúðklœðum, beztu
Skarti jöfurs,
Og meginbitrum
Mœki girðið;
því heim vil eg halda
Til hùrsa föður,
A' láði bœði og lög
Lávarður kjörinn.
Tryggvan, gljáandi
Tek eg mœki—
Af honum leiptrar
O'lmur dauði—
Hann vil eg nù
I'höndum bera,

Sem áður í grimmum
Oddaleikum.

2.

Hefi eg fjendur
Fo'tum troðna;
Myrkrauðar drekka
Megið nù veigar
Skýgðum af hausa—
Skeljum þeirra.
Hnígið sem hetjur
I'hildarleiki,
Örlög þá kalla,
Æðstum heiðri
Krýndir af goðum
þeim á Gimli bùa.
Daprast mér sjón

---

[1] The "Death of the Old Norse King," translated into Icelandic verse by the Rev. Olaf Pálsson.

Ogdökkvir áður
Leika silfurlit
Lokkar á höfði;
Armur aflvana
Ei fær valdið
Mæki, þeim unað
Mestum veldur

3.

Hefur upp myrkva
Irá Helju kaldan;
Að berst eyrum
O'mur Valkyrju;
Hefur mig hugur
Til hetjusala;
Svo ber Norðmanna
Nýtum jöfri
Aldurhnignum
Æfi Gúka.
Heimdalls þer snekkju
Hraðir búið,
Og ylmandi látið
Eldskíð loga;
Vil eg þar nar
A' vita brenna;
En hugur mig ber
Til hallar O'ðins
Til upphimins jafnt
Og Unnar sala.

4.

Brennur skíðeldur
A'skipi kveiktur;
Mær hverfur sól

I'marar skauti;
Undin eru segl,
Ytt frá landi
Siglir þar hetjan,
Hilmir frægur.
Nötra ná hljód
I'niðmyrkvu lopti;
Bregður á býsnum
I'blindmyrkri nætur;
Leiptra geigvænir
Logar frá snekkju,
Og dökkrauðri miðla
Dauðaskýmu.

5.

Brunnar einskipa
Um bláan Ægi
Umvafin skeið
I'ógna blossum;
En O'ðinn fagnandi
Aldinn sjóla
Til himinsala
Hefir leiddan,
Dvína burt logar
Og djúpri lystur
Megin þögn yfir
Myrkva kaldan;
Þar í myskbláu
Mararskauti;
Hilmir Norðmanna,
Hetjan frægust,
Hugprúður, frjáls,
Réd Sielju gista.

IV.

INFORMATION FOR INTENDING TOURISTS:

A LETTER RECEIVED FROM THE REV. OLAF PÁLSSON IN ANSWER TO
QUERIES ABOUT TRAVELLING IN ICELAND.

Reykjavik, 20th Nov. 1861.

My Dear Friend,

According to your wish in your
kind note of 15th August this year, I will now try to
give some answers to the queries you have there put to
me, about several matters which it may be useful for
strangers who travel in Iceland to know.

I have since conferred with Zöga, who is assuredly the
very best guide in this place, and well versed in these
matters. The hints that I am able to give are as follows, and correspond to the order of the queries put.

1st. I have not such an extensive acquaintance with
the coasts of Iceland as to be able to describe all places of
shelter that might be found around the island; for doubtless they are many. But I am sure, that it will not be
advisable for any foreign vessel to approach the south
coast; for, from Cape Reykjanes to Berufiord, there is no
shelter at all along the whole south side of Iceland, except in the Westmanna Islands, which lie some ten miles
from the shore.

As a general rule, every merchant place, marked on
the map, will be found tolerably safe.

2d. For the Englishman who arrives at Reykjavik, or
for any traveller who has some knowledge of English, it
is not absolutely necessary to know other languages; for

T

guides who know that language can be had there, and these make tolerably good interpreters in the country.

This, however, will scarcely be the case in any other merchant place in Iceland.

3d. As to expenses of travelling; I can only remark that a guide is paid about 2 rix dollars[1] a day (4/6).

Every gentleman will be obliged to have two ponies each at 64 skillings per day (1/5). A jack horse is to be got at 48 skillings per day, and will not comfortably carry more than 100 to 120 lbs. weight. If this horse is provided with pack saddle and chests for preserving goods in, it will cost 64 skillings. If the travellers should wish to be away for a longer time from human habitations, it will be necessary for them to bring with them a tent, a sufficient quantity of victuals, &c. Thus it will be found that two gentlemen travelling cannot easily do with less than five pack horses, and then they will require to have two guides, one to take care of the horses and baggage, and the other to attend upon themselves when they wish to travel faster, or to visit places where the train of baggage horses cannot easily go with them.

From this I hope an idea can be formed of the average cost of such travelling for a week or so. For a more protracted journey through the island, it will certainly be preferable to buy the horses, and dispose of them again by auction on returning to Reykjavik. The average price of a pack horse will be 24 rix dollars, and for a riding pony 30 to 40 rix dollars. They will again

---

[1] A rix dollar is equal in value to 2/3 English. A skilling is a fraction more than a farthing.

sell at a half, or at least a third of the money, according to the length of the journey, their condition, and the season of the year. This calculation is made for a journey begun from Reykjavik, which in most respects will be found the most convenient place to start from.

4th. An india-rubber boat will very probably be serviceable, but it will seldom be needed; for on almost every one of the larger rivers there are plenty of ferries.

5th. The very best month for travelling in Iceland undoubtedly is July, and next to it August. A journey can be begun in the middle of June. At an earlier time there will not be sufficient grass for the horses. The journey can usually, without the risk of getting bad weather, be prolonged to the middle of September.

These, my dear sir, are all the hints I am able to give you. I am sure there are many other things which might be taken into consideration, but I have written this to my best ability, although in great haste, which may excuse the many faults I am sure will be found with my English. With my best wishes &c.

Yours very truly,

O. PÁLSSON.

Note.—The screw steamer *Arcturus* makes six trips during the season, carrying the mails from Copenhagen to Iceland, and calling at Grangemouth and the Faröe Islands. The first sailing north is generally about the beginning of March, and the last towards the end of October. Fares—First cabin £5; second do. £3 10s. Return—only available for the same voyage—first cabin £9; second do. £6. Further information may be obtained by applying to Mr. P. L. Henderson, 20 Dixon Street, Glasgow; Messrs. David Robertson & Co., Grangemouth; or Messrs. Koch & Henderson, Copenhagen.

V.

GLOSSARY.

The following Explanatory List of Geographical Terms will assist the memory, aid the pronunciation, and, it is believed, prove of interest and practical utility.[1]

á *or* aa, *river.*
bakki, *hill.*
beru, *bare.*
beru-fjördr, *bare frith.*
blá, *blue.*
bœr, *farm.*
bol, *or* bol-stadr, *main farm,* or *steading* (bu *or* boo, in Orkney).
brekka, *brink of a precipice.*
brú, *bridge.*
dalr, *valley.*
eingi, *or* hagi, *meadow,* or *field.*
ey (eyjar, genitive singular; eyja, genitive plural), *an island*
eyri, *sand, sand-bank* or *bar* (ere, in north of England)
fell, *same as* fjall.
ferjur, *ferries.*
fjall, (plural fjöll), *fell,* or *height;* as Blá-fjall, *blue fell,* or, in English, *Scawfell, &c.*
fjördr, *frith.*
fljöt, *a river* (*fleet*)
fors, *force,* or *waterfall.*
hals, *ridge,* or *col.*
hædir, *heights.*
heidi, *heath.*
hof, *or* hofdi, *head,* or *headland.*
holl, *hill.*
holt, *wood.*
hraun, *lava,*
hreppr, *a rape* (whence divisions of land, and "rapes" of Sussex).
hvamm, *a combe,* or *recess surrounded by hills;* as *Ilfra-combe.*
hvit, *white* (hence hvit-á, *white river.*)

jökull, *ice mountain.*
jökuls-á, is the name given to many rivers, and means only *ice river;* but it is usually associated with another name, such as Axa-firdi Jökuls-á, or *ice river of the Axa frith.*
kirk, *church.*
kverk, *chin* (hence Kverk-fjöll, *Chinfell*).
lid, *lithe,* provincial for *a sloping bank* (whence Reykja-lid, *the smoking bank*).
lœkr, *brook, stream.*
muli, *mull,* or *cliff;* thing-muli, *the heights,* or *cliffs, under which an assembly was held.*
myri, *morass.*
ness, *headland.*
nupr, *bluff,* or *inland cliff.*
orœfi, *wastes.*
rafn, *raven.*
reyk, *smoke.*
sandr, *sands.*
skard, *pass, defile.*
skógr, *underwood.*
stadr, *stede, stead,* or *sted;* as *Hampstead.*
strönd, *strand.*
sýsla, *or* sýssel, *district.*
thing, *meeting.*
vatn (plural, vötn), *lake.*
vellir, *plain.*
vik, vikr, *bay;* Grunda-vik, *green. bay;* Greenwich = Green-vik.

---

[1] Extracted from the postscript to Mr. William Longman's "Suggestions for the Exploration of Iceland"—an address delivered to the members of the Alpine Club, of which he is Vice-President.—Longman & Co., 1861.

VI.

OUR SCANDINAVIAN ANCESTORS.[1]

Few subjects possess greater interest for the British race than the Scandinavian North, with its iron-bound rampart of wave-lashed rocks, its deeply indented fiords, bold cliffs, rocky promontories, abrupt headlands, wild skerries, crags, rock-ledges, and caves, all alive with gulls, puffins and kittiwakes; and in short, the general and striking picturesqueness of its scenery, to say nothing of the higher human interest of its stirring history, and the rich treasures of its grand old literature.

The British race has been called Anglo-Saxon; made up however, as it is, of many elements—Ancient Briton, Roman, Anglo-Saxon, Dane, Norman, and Scandinavian—the latter predominates so largely over the others as to prove by evidence, external and internal, and not to be gainsaid, that the Scandinavians are our true progenitors.

The Germans are a separate branch of the same great Gothic family, industrious, but very unlike us in many respects. The degree of resemblance and affinity may be settled by styling them honest but unenterprising inland friends, whose ancestors and ours were first cousins upwards of a thousand years ago.

To the old Northmen—hailing from the sea-board of Norway, Sweden, and Denmark—may be traced the germs of all that is most characteristic of the modern

[1] This chapter, written in December 1859, has already appeared in the pages of a periodical.—A. J. S.

Briton, whether personal, social, or national. The con-
figuration of the land, and the numerous arms of the sea
with which the north-west of Europe is indented, necessi-
tated boats and seamanship. From these coasts, the
Northmen—whether bent on piratical plundering expeditions, or peacefully seeking refuge from tyrannical
oppression at home—sallied forth in their frail barks or
skiffs, which could live in the wildest sea, visiting and
settling in'many lands. We here mention, in geographical
order, Normandy, England, Scotland, Orkney, Shetland,
Faröe, and Iceland. Wherever they have been, they have
left indelible traces behind them, these ever getting more
numerous and distinct as we go northwards.

Anglen, from which the word England is derived, still
forms part of Holstein a province in Denmark; and the
preponderance of the direct Scandinavian element in the
language itself has been shewn by Dean Trench, who
states, that of a hundred English words, sixty come from
the Scandinavian, thirty from the Latin, five from the
Greek, and five from other sources.

In Scotland many more Norse words, which sound
quite foreign to an English ear, yet linger amongst the
common people; while, as in England, the original Celtic
inhabitants were driven to the west before the Northmen,
who landed for the most part on the east. In certain
districts of the Orkneys a corrupt dialect of Norse was
spoken till recently, and the Scandinavian type of features is there often to be met with.

The Norse language is still understood and frequently
spoken in Shetland, where the stalwart, manly forms of
the fishermen, the characteristic prevalence of blue eyes
and light flaxen hair, the universal observance of the

Norse Yule, and many other old-world customs, together with the oriental and almost affecting regard paid to the sacred rites of hospitality, on the part of the islanders, all plainly tell their origin.

The language of the Faröe islanders is a dialect of the Norse, approaching Danish, and peculiar to themselves. It is called Faröese. The peaceful inhabitants not only resemble, but are Northmen.

In Iceland we have pure Norse, as imported from Norway in the ninth century, the lone northern sea having guarded it, and many other interesting features, from those modifications to which the Norwegian, Danish, and Swedish have been subjected by neighbouring Teutonic or German influences. This language, the parent, or at least the oldest and purest form of the various Scandinavian dialects with which we are acquainted, has been at different times named Dönsktunga, Norræna, or Norse, but latterly it has been simply called Icelandic, because peculiar to that island.

The language, history, and literature of our ancestors having been thus preserved in the north, we are thereby enabled to revisit the past, read it in the light of the present, and make both subservient for good in the future.

Herodotus mentions that tin was procured from Britain. Strabo informs us that the Phœnicians traded to our island, receiving tin and skins in exchange for earthenware, salt, and vessels of brass; but our first authentic particulars regarding the ancient Britons are derived from Julius Cæsar, whose landing on the southern portion of our island, and hard-won battles, were but transient and doubtful successes. The original inhabitants were Celts from France and Spain; but, as we learn from him, these had long before been driven into the interior and western portion of the island by Belgians, who crossed the sea, made good their footing, settled on the east and south-eastern shores of England, and were now known as Britons. With these Cæsar had to do. The intrepid bravery of the well-trained and regularly disciplined British warriors commanded respect, and left his soldiers but little to boast of. The Roman legions never felt safe unless within their entrenchments, and, even there, were sometimes surprised. Strange to realise such dire conflicts raging at the foot of the Surrey hills, probably in the neighbourhood of Penge, Sydenham, and Norwood, where the Crystal Palace now peacefully stands. Even in these dark Druid days, the Britons, although clothed in skins, wearing long hair, and stained blue with woad, were no mere painted savages as they have sometimes been represented, but were in possession of regularly-constituted forms of government. They had naval, military, agricultural and commercial resources to depend upon, and were acquainted with many of the important arts of life. The Briton was simple in his manners, frugal in his habits, and loved freedom above all things. Had the brave Caswallon headed the men of Kent, in their attack upon the Roman maritime camp, Cæsar and his hosts would never, in all likelihood, have succeeded in reaching their ships, but would have found graves on our shores. His admirable commentaries would not have seen the light of day, and the whole current of Roman, nay, of the world's history might have been changed.

Our British institutions and national characteristics were not adopted from any quarter, completely moulded and finished, as it were, but everywhere exhibit the vitality of growth and progress, slow but sure. Each new element or useful suggestion, from whatever source derived, has been tested and modified before being allowed to take root and form part of the constitution. The germs have been developed in our own soil.

Thus, to the Romans, we can trace our municipal institutions—subjection to a central authority controlling the rights of individuals. To the Scandinavians, we can as distinctly trace that principle of personal liberty which resists absolute control, and sets limits—such as Magna Charta—to the undue exercise of authority in governors.

These two opposite tendencies, when united, like the centripedal and centrifugal forces, keep society revolving peacefully and securely in its orbit around the sun of truth. When severed, tyranny, on the one hand, or democratic license, on the other—both alike removed from freedom—must result, sooner or later, in instability, confusion, and anarchy. France affords us an example of the one, and America of the other. London is not Britain in the sense that Paris is France; while Washington has degenerated into a mere cockpit for North and South.

From the feudal system of the Normans, notwithstanding its abuses, we have derived the safe tenure and transmission of land, with protection and security for all kinds of property. British law has been the growth of a thousand years, and has been held in so much respect that even our revolutions have been legally conducted, and presided over by the staid majesty of justice. Were more evidences wanting to show that the Scandinavian element is actually the backbone of the British race—

contributing its superiority, physical and moral, its indomitable strength and energy of character—we would simply mention a few traits of resemblance which incontestably prove that the "child is father to the man."

The old Scandinavian possessed an innate love of truth; much earnestness; respect and honour for woman; love of personal freedom; reverence, up to the light that was in him, for sacred things; great self-reliance, combined with energy of will to dare and do; perseverance in overcoming obstacles, whether by sea or land; much self-denial, and great powers of endurance under given circumstances. These qualities, however, existed along with a pagan thirst for war and contempt of death, which was courted on the battle-field that the warrior might rise thence to Valhalla.

To illustrate the love of freedom, even in thought, which characterises the race, it can be shewn that, while the Celtic nations fell an easy prey to the degrading yoke of Romish superstition, spreading its deadly miasma from the south, the Scandinavian nations, even when for a time acknowledging its sway, were never bound hand and foot by it, but had minds of their own, and sooner or later broke their fetters. In the truth-loving Scandinavian, Jesuitical Rome has naturally ever met with its most determined antagonist; for

" True and tender is the North."

In the dark days of the Stuarts, witness the noble struggles of the Covenanters and the Puritans for civil and religious liberty.

Notwithstanding mixtures and amalgamations of blood, as a general rule the distinctive tendencies of race survive, and, good or bad, as the case may be, reappear in new and unexpected forms. Even habit becomes a second nature, the traces of which, centuries with their changes cannot altogether obliterate.

On the other side of the Atlantic, the Puritan Fathers, their descendants, and men like them, have been the salt of the north; while many of the planters of the south, tainted with cavalier blood, continue to foster slavery—"that sum of all villanies"—and glory in being man-stealers, man-sellers, and murderers, although cursed of God, and execrated by all right thinking men. John Brown of Harper's Ferry, who was the other day judicially murdered, we would select as an honoured type of the noble, manly, brave, truth-loving, God-fearing Scandinavian—*The Times* and *Athenæum* notwithstanding.[1] His heroism in behalf of the poor despised slave had true moral grandeur in it—it was sublime. America cannot match it. Washington was great—John Brown was greater. Washington resisted the imposition of unjust taxes on himself and his equals, but was a slaveholder; John Brown unselfishly devoted his energies—nay, life itself—to obtain freedom for the oppressed, and to save his country from just impending judgments. The one was a patriot; the other was a patriot and philanthropist. The patriotism of Washington was limited by colour; that of Brown was thorough, and recognised the sacred rights of man. He was hanged for trying to accomplish that which his murderers ought to have done

---

[1] These journals, while admitting, in a general though apologetic way, that great evils exist in connection with slavery, yet, somehow, on every occasion, systematically and persistently uphold pro-slavery measures and interests.

—nay, deserved to be hanged for not doing—hanged for that which they shall yet do, if not first overtaken and whelmed in just and condign vengeance; for the cry of blood ascends. He was no less a martyr to the cause of freedom than John Brown of Priesthill, who was ruthlessly shot by the bloody Claverhouse. These two noble martyrs, in virtue alike of their name and cause, shall stand together on the page of future history, when their cruel murderers and the abettors of them have long gone to their own place. For such deeds there shall yet be tears of blood. The wrongs of Italy are not to be named in comparison with those of the slave. Let those who boast of a single drop of Scandinavian blood in their veins no longer withhold just rights from the oppressed —rights which, if not yielded at this the eleventh hour, shall be righteously, though fearfully, wrested from the oppressors, when the hour of retribution comes.[1]

Perhaps the two most striking outward resemblances between Britons and Scandinavians may be found in their maritime skill, and in their powers of planting colonies, and governing themselves by free institutions, representative parliaments, and trial by jury.

The Norse rover—bred to the sea, matchless in skill,

---

[1] Fuller information and subsequent events in America have justified and amply confirmed this estimate of Brown, formed at the time. Having had access to documents, published and unpublished, and being in a position to judge, we would confidently refer the reader to a volume of 452 pp. 8vo., since published by Smith, Elder & Co.—"The Life and Letters of Captain John Brown, edited by Richard D. Webbe"—as presenting a fair statement of the facts of the case. From Brown's deeds and words, therein recorded, it will be clearly seen, how calm, noble and dignified was the bearing of the man whom short-sighted trimmers, on both sides the Atlantic, have attempted to brand as a fanatic.

daring, loving adventure and discovery, and with any amount of pluck—is the true type of the British tar. In light crafts, the Northmen could run into shallow creeks, cross the North Sea, or boldly push off to face the storms of the open Atlantic. These old Vikings were seasoned "salts" from their very childhood—"creatures native and imbued unto the element;" neither in peace nor war, on land nor sea, did they fear anything but fear.

> " Tameless spirits of the past !
> Boldest and noblest of earth's kind were ye—
> Conquerors of nations—fathers of a race
> Of giant princes." [1]

In them we see the forerunners of the buccaneers, and the ancestors of those naval heroes, voyagers, and discoverers—those Drakes and Dampiers, Nelsons and Dundonalds, Cooks and Franklins, who have won for Britain the proud title of sovereign of the seas—a title which she is still ready to uphold against all comers.

In Shetland, we still find the same skilled seamanship, and the same light open boat, like a Norwegian yawl; indeed, planks for building skiffs are generally imported from Norway, all prepared and ready to put together. There the peace-loving fishermen, in pursuit of their perilous calling, sometimes venture sixty miles off to sea, losing sight of all land, except perhaps the highest peak of their island-homes left dimly peering just above the horizon-line. Sometimes they are actually driven, by stress of weather, within sight of the coast of Norway, and yet the loss of a skiff in the open sea, however high the waves run, is a thing quite unknown to the skilled

[1] See "Lay of the Vikings," p. 278.

Shetlander. The buoyancy of the skiff (from this word
we have ship and skipper) is something wonderful. Its
high bow and stern enables it to ride and rise over the
waves like a sea-duck, although its chance of living seems
almost as little, and as perilous, as that of the dancing
shallop or mussel-shell we see whelmed in the ripple.
Its preservation, to the onlooker from the deck of a large
vessel, often seems miraculous. It is the practice, in
encountering the stormy blasts of the North Sea, to
lower the lug-sail on the approach of every billow, so as
to ride its crest with bare mast, and to raise it again as
the skiff descends into the more sheltered trough of the
wave. By such constant manœuvering, safety is secured
and progress made. When boats are lost—and such tragedies frequently occur, sometimes leaving poor lonely
widows bereft, at one fell swoop, of husband, father,
and brothers, for the crews are too often made up of
relatives—it is generally when they are caught and
mastered by strong currents running between the islands,
which neither oar nor sail can stem. Such losses are
always on the coasts—never at sea.

Of the Scandinavian powers of colonising:—There is
ample evidence of their having settled in Shetland, Orkney, and on our coasts, long before those great outgoings
of which we have authentic historical records. To several
of these latter we shall briefly advert, viz., the English,
Russian, Icelandic, American, and Norman.

We may first mention that, in remote ages, this race
swept across Europe from the neighbourhood of the region
now called Circassia, lying between the Black Sea and
the Caspian, to the shores of the Baltic, settling on the
north-west coast of Europe. Their traditions, and num-

erous eastern customs—allied to the Persians and the inhabitants of the plains of Asia Minor in old Homeric days—which they brought along with them, all go to confirm their eastern origin. Nor did they rest here, but, thirsting for adventure in these grim warrior ages, sailed forth as pirates or settlers, sometimes both, and, as can be shewn, made their power and influence felt in every country of Europe, from Lapland to the Mediter_ ranean.

They invaded England in A.D. 429, and founded the kingdoms of South, West, and East Seaxe, East Anglia, Mercia, Deira, and Bernicea; thus overrunning and fixing themselves in the land, from Devonshire to North of the Humber. From the mixture of these Angles, or Saxons, as they were termed by the Britons, with the previous Belgian settlers and original inhabitants, we have the Anglo-Saxon race. The Jutes who settled in Kent were from Jutland. In A.D. 787, the Danes ravaged the coast, beginning with Dorsetshire; and, continuing to swarm across the sea, soon spread themselves over the whole country. They had nearly mastered it all, when Alfred ascended the throne in 871. At length, in A.D. 1017, Canute, after much hard fighting, did master it, and England had Danish kings from that period till the Saxon line was restored in 1042.

In the year A.D. 862, the Scandinavian Northmen established the Russian empire, and played a very important part in the management of its affairs, even after the subsequent infusion of the Sclavonic element. In the "Mémoires de la Société Royale des Antiquaries du Nord," published at Copenhagen, we find that, of the fifty names of those composing Ingor's embassy to the

Greek Emperor at Constantinople in the year A.D. 994, only three were Sclavic, and the rest Northmen—names that occur in the Sagas, such as Ivar, Vigfast, Eylif, Grim, Ulf, Frode, Asbrand, &c. The Greeks called them Russians, but Frankish writers simply Northmen.

In the year A.D. 863, Naddodr, a Norwegian, discovered Iceland,[1] which, however, had been previously visited and resided in at intervals for at least upwards of seventy years before that time, by fishermen, ecclesiastics, and hermits, called Westmen, from Ireland, Iona and other islands of the Hebrides. Of these visits Naddodr found numerous traces.

In A.D. 874, Ingolf with followers, many of whom were related to the first families in Norway, fleeing from the tyranny of Harold Harfagra, began the colonisation of Iceland, which was completed during a space of sixty years. They established a flourshing republic, appointed magistrates, and held their Althing, or national assembly, at Thingvalla.

Many of the Northmen who at various times had settled on our shores, accompanied by their acquired relatives, also set sail and joined their brethren; thus making use of Britain as a stepping stone between Scandinavia and Iceland. Many traces of these early links yet remain. We heard of a family in the island that can trace its descent, in a direct line, from a royal ancestor of Queen Victoria.

---

[1] The antiquarian book to which we have already referred, erroneously attributes the discovery to Garder, a Dane of Swedish origin. Our authority is Gísli Brynjúlfsson, the Icelandic poet, now resident in Copenhagen, to whose kindness we are also indebted for the copy of this work which we possess.

Thus, in this distant volcanic island of the Northern Sea, the old Danish language was preserved unchanged for centuries; while, in the various eddas, were embodied those folk-songs and folk-myths, and, in the sagas, those historical tales and legends of an age at once heroic and romantic, together with that folk-lore which still forms the staple of all our old favourite nursery tales, as brought with them from Europe and the East by the first settlers.[1] All these, as well as the productions of the Icelanders themselves, are of great historical and literary value. They have been carefully edited and published, at Copenhagen, by eminent Icelandic, Danish, and other antiquarians. We would refer to the writings of Müller, Magnusen, Rafn, Rask, Eyricksson, Torfæus, and others. Laing has translated "The Heimskringla," the great historical Saga of Snorro Sturleson, into English.[2] Various other translations and accounts of these singularly interesting eddas, sagas, and ballads, handed down by the scalds and Sagamen, are to be met with; but by far the best analysis, with translated specimens, is that contained in Howitt's "Literature and Romance of Northern Europe."[3] We would call attention, in passing, to that Edda, consisting of the original series of tragic poems from which the German "Niebelungen-lied" has been derived. Considered as a series of fragments, it is a marvellous production, and, to our

[1] For these last, we would refer to Thorpe's "Yuletide Stories," Dasent's "Popular Tales from the Norse," our own Nursery Lore, and to preceding Stories and Tales in this appendix.

[2] Mr. Dasent has since published an admirable translation of "Njal's Saga," which presents a vivid picture of life in Iceland at the end of the tenth century.

[3] See the preceding specimens of old Icelandic poetry.

U

thinking, absolutely unparalleled in ancient or modern literature, for power, simplicity, and heroic grandeur.

Christianity was established in Iceland in the year 1000. Fifty-seven years later, Isleif, Bishop of Skalholt, first introduced the art of writing the Roman alphabet, thus enabling them to fix oral lessons of history and song; for, the Runic characters previously in use were chiefly employed for monuments and memorial inscriptions, and were carved on wood staves, on stone or metal. On analysis, these rude letters will be found to be crude forms and abridgments of the Greek or Roman alphabet. We have identified them all, with the exception of a few letters, and are quite satisfied on this point, so simple and obvious is it, although we have not previously had our attention directed to the fact.

Snorro Sturleson was perhaps one of the most learned and remarkable men that Iceland has produced.

In 1264, through fear and fraud, the island submitted to the rule of Haco, king of Norway:—he who died at Kirkwall, after his forces were routed by the Scots at the battle of Largs. In 1387, along with Norway, it became subject to Denmark. In 1529, a printing press was established; and in 1550 the Lutheran reformation was introduced into the island—which form of worship is still retained.

True to the instinct of race, the early settlers in Iceland did not remain inactive, but looked westward, and found scope for their hereditary maritime skill in the discovery and colonising of Greenland. They also discovered Helluland (Newfoundland), Markland (Nova Scotia), and Vineland (New England). They were also acquainted with American land, which they called

Hvitramannaland, (the land of the white men), thought
to have been North and South Carolina, Georgia, and
Florida. We have read authentic records of these
various voyages, extending from A.D. 877 to A.D. 1347.
The names of the principal navigators are Gunnbiorn,
Eric the Red, Biarne, Leif, Thorwald, &c. But the
most distinguished of these American discoverers is
Thorfinn Karlsefne, an Icelander, "whose genealogy,"
says Rafn, "is carried back, in the old northern annals,
to Danish, Swedish, Norwegian, Scottish, and Irish ancestors, some of them of royal blood." With singular
interest we also read that, "in A.D. 1266, some priests at
Gardar, in Greenland, set on foot a voyage of discovery
to the arctic regions of America. An astronomical observation proves that this took place through Lancaster
Sound and Barrow's Strait to the latitude of Wellington's
Channel."

When Columbus visited Iceland in A.D. 1467, he may
have obtained confirmation of his theories as to the
existence of a great continent in the west; for, these
authentic records prove the discovery and colonisation of
America, by the Northmen from Iceland, upwards of five
hundred years before he re-discovered it.

The Norman outgoing is the last to which we shall
here allude. In A.D. 876 the Northmen, under Rollo,
wrested Normandy from the Franks; and from thence,
in A.D. 1065, William, sprung from the same stock,
landed at Hastings, vanquished Harold, and to this day
is known as the Conqueror of England. It was a contest
of Northmen with Northmen, where diamond cut diamond.

Instead of a chapter, this subject, we feel, would require a volume. At the outset we asserted that northern subjects possessed singular interest for the British race. In a very cursory manner we have endeavoured to prove it, by shewing that to Scandinavia, as its cradle, we must look for the germs of that spirit of enterprise which has peopled America, raised an Indian empire, and colonised Australia, and which has bound together, as one, dominions on which the sun never sets; all, too, either speaking, or fast acquiring, a noble language, which bids fair one day to become universal.

The various germs, tendencies, and traits of Scandinavian character, knit together and amalgamated in the British race, go to form the essential elements of greatness and success, and, where sanctified and directed into right channels, are noble materials to work upon.

It is Britain's pride to be at once the mistress of the seas, the home of freedom, and the sanctuary of the oppressed. May it also be her high honour, by wisely improving outward privileges, and yet further developing her inborn capabilities, pre-eminently to become the torch-bearer of pure Christianity—with its ever-accompanying freedom and civilisation—to the whole world!

INDEX.

www.ingramcontent.com/pod-product-compliance
Lightning Source LLC
Chambersburg PA
CBHW060527030726
47498CB00004B/1107